5.

ACROSS

1. Relief-pitchers' area
8. Southern battlefield site
15. Lack of energy
16. Small opening
17. Glowing
18. ——— France
19. More, in music
20. Truly
21. Pronoun
22. Miquelon
23. Little terrors
25. Ski area
27. Philippine tree
28. Colonist's Indian friend
30. Nigerian town
31. Bat man
32. Diner menu listing
34. Royal raiment
36. Bound
38. Candia people
41. Cardiff citizens
45. Cautious
46. He's ——— it
48. Go over briefly
50. Own
51. Describing some shad
53. Vergil word
54. Nepal peak
55. Pro.
56. Islet
58. Against: Abbr.
59. Motto's cousins
61. Au courant
63. Scarlett's friend
64. Boss
65. Wages
66. Sties

DOWN

1. Brooch
2. Pointed, as at random
3. Paved the way
4. French pronoun
5. Beseech
6. ——— Tages (one day): Ger.
7. Christmas, in Italy
8. Measuring instrument
9. Take the stump
10. Flies' hazards
11. U.S. writer
12. Geometrical figure
13. Nice or nervous
14. Hard
24. Family member
26. South Russian
27. Fleming
29. Soft material
31. Drink
33. Song syllable
35. Pet sound
37. Thrown, in a way
38. Necklace
39. Pasta dish
40. Before
42. Grazing area
43. Dickens character
44. Memorable U.S. actor
45. Abysses
47. Skip out
49. Documents
51. W. Pacific island group
52. ——— Lama
55. Temple, old style
57. Goose honk
60. Space
62. Diagram

6.

ACROSS

1. Secretary
5. Skeins
10. Fellow
14. Entr'———
15. Constellation
16. Angel feature
17. The Deacon's masterpiece
18. Discuss
20. Short-tempered one
22. Gluttonize
23. Eye: Suffix
24. Pen name
25. Middy
28. Item for a gang weapon
32. Leered
33. Vetch
34. An, in Germany
35. Dover's state: Abbr.
36. Tag specially
39. Lilting
40. Science course: Abbr.
42. Kind of sign
43. Take ——— (accept a challenge)
45. Some servicemen
47. Fifths, on a car
48. Ave atque ———
49. Incentive
50. Snow White word
53. Unsophisticated
57. Support
59. There is: Fr.
60. Waltz city
61. Word with horse and comic
62. Noun suffix
63. De ——— (you're welcome): Sp.
64. Sang praises: Colloq.
65. Attains

DOWN

1. Track event
2. Reverberation
3. Copy, for short
4. Basketball court area
5. Empty talk
6. Plowed land
7. Zero
8. G. & S. immortal
9. Whimpering one
10. Girl in the line
11. New father's words
12. Greek goddess
13. Sweet wine
19. Prefix for gram
21. Poetic form
25. Fountain drinks
26. Spacecraft booster
27. Lacking wisdom
28. One of the Sporades
29. Afghanistan neighbor
30. Finnish lake
31. Kings, in Spain
33. Expedition
37. Forebear
38. Done for: Slang
41. Russian noble
44. Name for Clementine
46. Drinks
47. Sumptuous meal
49. ——— bleu!
50. Grovel
51. Largest of seven
52. Coarse cloth
54. Rob't ———
55. Method: Abbr.
56. Impertinence
58. Silver state: Abbr.

7.

ACROSS

1. W.W. II vehicle
5. Burns and others
10. Kind of tool
14. Late cartoonist
15. Extremely
16. Outer: Pref.
17. Offers
18. Morning song
19. Abstain
20. Shout
22. Lengthwise
24. Swiss mathematician
26. Deserve
27. Governs badly
30. Rented
34. Old French coin
35. Lithuanian port
37. —— nous
38. Take it easy
40. Combats
42. River in Kenya
43. Enroll
45. Once-snazzy footwear
47. Mae West role
48. Attempts
50. Garages' predecessors
52. Spanish lady
54. Famous name in comedy
55. Subdues
59. Made a record
62. Prefix for motive
63. One at ——
65. La Douce
66. Hebrew letter
67. Certain birds
68. L.A. team
69. Unheeding
70. Perfume
71. Girl's name

DOWN

1. Boxing maneuvers
2. Famous explorer
3. Outcomes
4. Pretender
5. Beat
6. Palm leaf
7. Diminutive suffix
8. Threefold
9. Shoe
10. Deep and full
11. Suffix for heart or head
12. Bewilder
13. Pool
21. Astringent
23. Ash, for one
25. Famous twin
27. Free-for-all
28. Images
29. Leaks
31. Russian city of W.W. II
32. Pyle
33. Transactions
36. Andes inhabitant
39. Starts an inning
41. Most peaceful
44. Indian peasant
46. W. W. II battle city
49. Furtive ones
51. Journey of escape
53. Dido
55. Covered
56. Calcutta had one
57. Suffix in zoology
58. Location
60. Novel heroine
61. L. I. commuter word
64. Brothers

8.

ACROSS

1. Offspring: Abbr.
5. Fragrances
10. Pretense
14. Bonneville Flats state
15. Strong fiber
16. Totem
17. By hand: Prefix
18. Dismal, in verse
19. —— go bragh
20. Banana
22. Key
24. Net
25. Hastings and Orleans
26. Fiddlers' audience
30. Make use of
31. Says in another way
36. Glacial snow
37. Swiss river
38. Cousin of 51 Across
39. Auctioneer's tone
42. Fabric
43. Winter carnival V.I.P.
46. Braid again
50. Gould's railroad
51. Gulch
52. In power
56. Amphibian
57. "—— With Me"
59. Arrow poison
60. Italian family
61. Kind of orange
62. River of Africa
63. Understands
64. Coasters
65. Guys' friends

DOWN

1. Jettison
2. And others: Abbr.
3. Yemen capital
4. City on the Yangtze
5. Decree
6. Fearless
7. Sign
8. Inlet
9. Soap operas
10. Kind of wheat
11. Hourly
12. Straighten
13. Heals
21. Follow
23. Printing term
25. Smuts was one
26. Bumpkins
27. Roman 57
28. Drat!
29. Steep rocks
32. Alarm clock's job
33. Noted French actor
34. Scot's city: Abbr.
35. Join the choir
37. Dill
40. Delay
41. Reds, Browns and Indians
42. Mouthful, as of rum
44. Required
45. Bay windows
46. Charges
47. Uneven
48. Talk idly
49. 49ers' quests
52. Split
53. Amazon dolphin
54. Little girl
55. Right turns, horsewise
58. French dance

The New York Times

GIANT CROSSWORD PUZZLE BOOK

VOLUMES 1-4

❖

250 Daily-Size Puzzles

❖

Selected & Edited by
WILL WENG

WINGS BOOKS
NEW YORK · AVENEL, NEW JERSEY

Solutions to the puzzles are found at the back of each volume.

This 1992 edition is published by Wings Books,
distributed by Outlet Book Company,
a Random House Company,
40 Engelhard Avenue, Avenel, New Jersey 07001,
by arrangement with Times Books,
a division of Random House, Inc.

Random House
New York · Toronto · London · Sydney · Auckland

Printed and bound in the United States of America

ISBN 0-517-08463-5

8 7 6 5

VOLUME 1

Whether it's a peak in Thessaly or an inhabitant of Lower Slobbovia, some people just can't resist the urge to find out what it is. Here are 20,000 chances—give or take a few—to add to your store of interesting, if not always useful, knowledge. These crosswords are taken from the daily puzzle pages of *The New York Times*.

WILL WENG

1.

ACROSS

1. Jalopy's call
5. Opening words for Caesar
10. Bad marks on a report card
14. Willing's companion
15. TV's George
16. Ingenue, for one
17. Dog that eats beans?
19. Way out
20. Menuhin's teacher
21. Milady's ritual
23. Rain cover, for short
25. Heavy stake
26. Cream pastry
30. Variety of fig
33. Market place
34. Hood
36. Oriental
37. Famous Auntie
38. Kind
39. Marks on beans
40. After printemps
41. Portends
42. Senses
43. Sequence
45. Gem shape
47. "—— of robins . . ."
49. Men's gathering
50. Tools
53. Oona's father
57. Rose's mate
58. Dog that eats honeydew?
60. Shah's land
61. Heath genus
62. Word with shoppe
63. Bombast
64. Drive away
65. Annie Oakley

DOWN

1. Innocent one
2. Black
3. Differently
4. Where to buy a dog
5. Pay no mind
6. Male swan
7. Border
8. Cyclades isle
9. Mark for omitted words
10. Without stint
11. Partly sly dog
12. Pass lightly
13. Honor
18. Central Florida city
22. Portray
24. Having tiny openings
26. Appoints
27. Small type
28. Dog that eats apples?
29. Piece for nine
31. A bid to win no tricks
32. Breathless
35. Public carriers
38. Filmy
39. Fly low
41. Parties
42. French money
44. Notch
46. Lacking musical key
48. Poetic verb
50. Chair stuffing
51. Start of a magic-spell word
52. Err
54. City in S.E. Kansas
55. Degrees
56. Soap ingredients
59. King's superior

2.

ACROSS

1. Pantheon
5. Large drink
10. African town
14. Aid's companion
15. Czar's dictate
16. Tropical staple
17. Misrepresenter
18. Bewildered
19. W.W. II powers
20. Twined
22. Praise
24. Bivouac
26. Twinge
27. Bracer
31. Wagner opera
35. Spanish article
36. Record
38. French numeral
39. Mink and seal
41. Instructor
43. The bench
44. Abnormality
46. Flycatcher
48. New: Ger.
49. Sycophant
51. Asks
53. Entreaty
55. Fees
56. Rash ones
60. Provoking
64. To him: Fr.
65. Rodeo man
67. Brainstorm
68. Hindmost
69. Intrepid
70. Defoe character
71. Over
72. Votes for
73. Mexican pot

DOWN

1. Relatives of qts.
2. Newspaper item
3. Expensive
4. Beat
5. Finding
6. Tula's river
7. Destroy
8. Exhaust
9. Crabapple's cousin
10. Consternates
11. Hack
12. State: Abbr.
13. Rx datum
21. Moniker
23. Step ——
25. Contrived
27. Short-winded
28. Habituate
29. Apprehensions
30. Ustinov
32. Certain words
33. Asiatic civet cat
34. Where Alexander defeated Darius
37. Sculled
40. Glasswort
42. Entails
45. Garden green
47. Your: Ger.
50. At hand
52. Native of Alaska
54. Worship
56. Troublesome
57. Spread
58. Eastern title
59. Resorts
61. Revered one
62. Dickens character
63. Festive
66. Poet's time of day

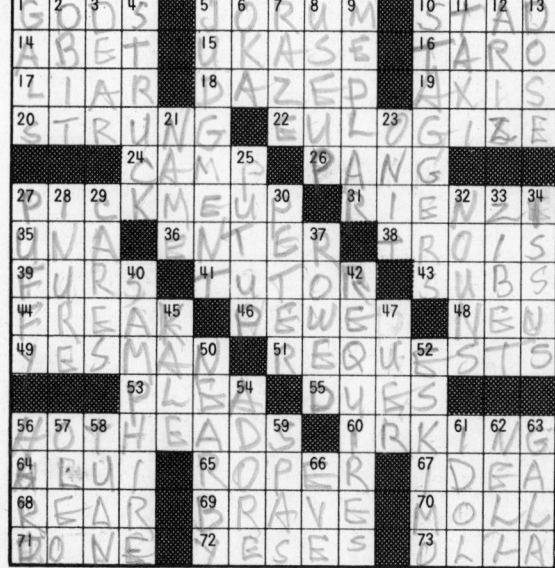

3.

ACROSS

1. Exclamation
4. Vapor
9. Latin abbr.
13. Part of speech
15. Cuddly bear
16. Cyrano's worry
17. Of an age
18. Misstepped
19. Type of oak
20. Night club
22. Discounts
24. Nonsense!
25. Pagodas
26. Delicate flowers
29. Horseplayer
33. Actress Christian
34. Roofed passage by a house
37. Dated
38. Vaunt
39. Japanese statesman
40. Count your —
43. Culet
45. Related items
46. Carpenter's joints
47. Be an angel, on Broadway
49. Marsh bird
50. Civil War site
53. Frauds
57. Turkish regiment
58. Small bits
60. Samoan port
61. Mountain lake
62. Coil
63. Laze
64. Difficulty
65. Deride
66. —— King Cole

DOWN

1. With: Fr.
2. Greek Juno
3. Urchin
4. Long-handled scoops: Naut.
5. Civil wrongs
6. Spike of corn
7. Warning
8. Wagered
9. Hurriedly
10. Footwear
11. Key
12. Party men: Abbr.
14. Trumpeted
21. Pro ——
23. Singer Joan
26. Small lumps
27. French city
28. Below
30. Once again
31. Horse opera
32. Indian peasants
34. Marché or ton
35. Tease
36. Letter
38. Cookies, in Soho
41. Child
42. Scorch
43. Steadfast
44. Drum
46. A cat is one
48. Familiar
49. Hero of a Western
50. Goes to the plate
51. —— Bator
52. Venezuelan state
54. Once —— a time
55. Arizona river
56. Corn
59. Bond

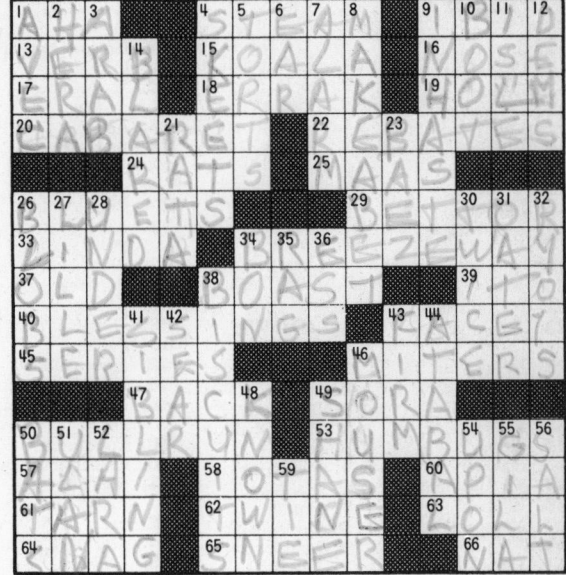

4.

ACROSS

1. Tightens: Naut.
6. Foot: Prefix
10. Tenting area
14. Fix over
15. Foreboding
16. Olive genus
17. Opening words, for short
18. Movie writer
20. His god was Mazda
22. Pesky insects
23. Words on "Arrivals" board
24. State wrongly
25. Gentle ——
27. Evian
28. Kick
29. Wings
31. Cygnus
33. College subject
37. Border on
38. Relative of the ibis
39. A kind of year
40. See 23 Across
41. Felled
42. Cabbage variety
43. Bring up
45. E. Indian tree
48. Spanish hero
49. Without success
52. Optimally
54. Indian coins
55. Sideline
58. Memorable
60. Monotone
61. Indigo
62. Skin: Suffix
63. Chop up
64. Sojourn
65. Solidifies
66. Comforted

DOWN

1. Form into tufts
2. Western city
3. Modern hero
4. Argentine name
5. Weasels
6. Man of zip codes
7. Entertainer
8. Red or roe
9. River to the Danube
10. Fall field sight
11. Cover-up name
12. Perle
13. Scapegoat: Slang.
19. Discount word
21. Use a straw
24. Fra, for one
25. Idol
26. Historic island
28. Makes one-night stands
30. Immutably
32. Yipes!
34. Counter tendencies
35. Ankles
36. Hurried
38. One-hoss ——
44. Otherwise
46. Basic fact
47. "—— to the altar, Walter"
49. Spanish measures
50. Regarding
51. Kind of ink
52. Turn away
53. Threadlike line
55. To ——
56. Formerly
57. Exigency
59. Football scores

9.

ACROSS

1. Grass
5. With "on" and 32 Across, honest
10. Sleepwear, for short
13. Weevil's goal
14. Cardiff people
15. Covering
16. Sunup
18. Expectation
19. Range of vision
20. Strained, as peas
22. Arabic letter
23. —— d' hotel
25. Official of India
28. Mastered
31. Muscovites
32. See 5 Across
33. Pasture sound
34. Receives
35. Vestige
36. Neon, for one
37. Noun ending
38. Bake eggs
39. Porous rock
40. Divination by fire
42. Becomes dim
43. Santa's vehicle
44. Brynner
45. Oratorio composer
47. Draws from
51. Jai ——
52. Compromise
55. Companion of Paul
56. Unavailing
57. "—— boy!"
58. Word of disapproval
59. Office furniture
60. Etymon

DOWN

1. French cleric
2. Australian parrot
3. Decamp
4. Certain Eskimos
5. —— a kind (pair)
6. Weight
7. Yore, of yore
8. G.I. initials
9. Build
10. Often said
11. Make fun of
12. Expedited
15. Reporter's question
17. Eastern rulers
21. Whoop ——
23. Butterfly
24. Hue ——
25. Ferret out
26. Without exception
27. Moccasin, for one
28. Solicitous
29. Golfing feat
30. Men from Aarhus
35. Cambodia's neighbor
36. Gardens near Lahore
38. "Peter Pan" pirate
39. Finishing kick
41. Last week's song, to a teen-ager
44. Go-aheads
45. Moiety
46. His: Fr.
47. Sundown
48. Forbid
49. Inner: Prefix
50. Suffix for thermo
53. Forest denizen
54. Au ——

10.

ACROSS

1. Various: Abbr.
5. Hindu deity
9. Fountain drink
13. "Do —— others" ...
14. Dye
15. Indian physicist
16. Pollux
17. Philosopher of Elea
18. Raise
19. Often-gaudy fabric
21. Everything
23. Roof sights
25. Branch angle
26. Vapor
28. Rendezvous
32. Bishop's throne
35. Landlord's concern
36. Cretan mountain
37. Honshu city
39. Arab garment
40. City in Iran
43. Have fun
46. Substitute
47. Endure
48. Knock down
50. Groups of eight
54. Handle badly
58. —— at the switch
59. Farewell
60. Animal suffix
62. Personal: Prefix
63. Fire
64. British queen: Abbr.
65. Enthusiasm
66. —— wear
67. Art style
68. Superlative suffixes

DOWN

1. Southern constellation
2. Paris —— spring
3. Step
4. Breed of chicken
5. Flashy doings
6. Chemical suffix
7. Denver building
8. Greeting on Oahu
9. Girl's name
10. Part of an ephah
11. Deficiency
12. Insects
15. Fix a lamp
20. London gallery
22. Lavish production
24. Briton's shirt
27. Posts
29. Fixed: Abbr.
30. Banned
31. Blow
32. Mention
33. Shebat's follower
34. Items picked up by hosts
38. Josip Broz
41. Roof supports
42. Again: Lat.
44. Fragments
45. Admire highly
49. Loafed
51. Mosquito genus
52. Follower of a belief
53. Pips on cards
54. Word of respect
55. Loaf
56. City in China
57. Indian weight
61. Resembling: Suffix

11.

ACROSS

1. Wild guess
5. Proper Bostonian name
10. Mountain
13. Gray wolf
14. Subside
15. ——— canto
16. Arab land
17. Argentine dictator
18. Temporary star
19. "A" student's reward
21. Make soundproof
23. Sun orbiter
25. Trapshooting
26. Place for sports gear
30. Hire
32. Fatigued
33. Equine of a kind
34. Deceive
38. Heston film
41. Trolled
42. Race of a sort
43. Left, at sea
44. Relative of chum
46. Thirty: Fr.
47. Attack
50. Invest with
52. Eccentrics
54. Benevolence
59. Resounded
60. City in New York
62. Can. province: Abbr.
63. Function
64. Stendhal's name
65. Munich's river
66. Old Turkish title
67. Impudent
68. Frying-pan item

DOWN

1. Dross
2. Foofaraw
3. Genesis figure
4. London shopper's street
5. Catcher
6. Off a ship's middle
7. Symbol of fun
8. Sioux
9. Watch over
10. Dwelling
11. Embankment
12. Place firmly
18. Best-seller of the '60s (with "The")
20. Vista
22. Letter
24. Trial runs
26. Times around the track
27. Earthen jar
28. Campbells, for one
29. He climbed the Empire State
31. Kind of blonde
33. Great throng
35. Atop
36. Jaunty
37. Punta del ———
39. Wee one
40. A type of seal
45. Squid's fluid
46. Dempsey's successor
47. Cancel, as a space launch
48. Clear the blackboard
49. Dred Scott case jurist
51. Computer controls
53. Weeps
55. Brad or spad
56. Girl's name
57. Play the lead
58. Chalcedony
61. Pasture

12.

ACROSS

1. Humbug
5. Power source
10. Party disciplinarian
14. Seine tributary
15. Range of Utah
16. Screen
17. Student's concern
18. Dimmed
19. Winnie ——— Pu
20. Free
22. Baby transit
24. Bankruptcy
26. Before zwei
27. Le Roi Soleil
31. Alit
35. "——— moi, le deluge"
36. Claro, for one
38. New Zealand parrot
39. V.I.P.'s
40. Halloween get-up
41. Improbable
42. Pronoun
43. Suppress
44. Pumpkin and squash
45. Deliverance
47. Detroit Tiger star
49. Publicizes
51. Kennel sound
52. Unused
56. Dawdled
60. Eastern V.I.P.
61. Big bargain: Colloq.
63. Level
64. Not touch with ——— foot pole
65. French house feature
66. Tilted
67. With 8 Down, cozy meeting
68. Teamed up
69. Not settled

DOWN

1. Sense
2. De ———
3. Smell ———
4. Computer parts
5. Word adjunct
6. Spanish aunt
7. Closes
8. See 67 Across
9. Vocal piece
10. During, of old
11. Feature of Rome
12. Not in use
13. Viscount
21. Uproar
23. ——— about
25. Statue spot
27. Item on a repair bill
28. Allow as how
29. Presses
30. Shakespearian role
32. Giraffe's cousin
33. Wrongdoer
34. Spurious
37. Erosion product
40. Dairy cow
41. Wire
43. Chaw
44. One of the Bears
46. Tooth
48. Vetoed
50. Brawl
52. Neighbor's child
53. Appraise
54. French writer
55. Ineffectual
57. Cat: Sp.
58. Pinza
59. Gov't. branch
62. Vital statistic

13.

ACROSS

1. Marshal's badge
5. "—— the torpedoes..."
9. White House family
14. Soda flavor
15. Kirghiz range
16. The Hunter
17. Part of a rallying cry
19. "Good-bye" composer
20. Balmoral Castle's river
21. Night watches
23. Hunt bargains
24. Manner of expression
26. West Pointers
28. Sigmund Romberg song
31. Dickens boy
34. Neighbor of Neth.
37. Four-in-hand
38. Of no difference
40. Served
42. On the loose
43. Resentment
44. Money sent by wire: Abbr.
45. Veto word
46. Upshot
47. Small-time
50. Store-counter sign
52. Movie accolade
56. Code word for "A"
58. —— not (probably)
61. Poem
62. Repast
64. Companion of 17 Across
66. Hold dear
67. Convex moldings
68. Great Barrier island
69. A partisan
70. River of myth
71. Sinewy

DOWN

1. Oodles
2. Real estate sign
3. Byway
4. W.W. II fliers
5. Sorghum of India
6. Sleep like ——
7. Clerical arm scarf
8. Decorated metal work
9. Little one
10. Came up
11. Fib
12. "Wizard of Oz" dog
13. Swatch
18. Hot from the ——
22. Washington athlete
25. Reasoning
27. Angelus
29. Perpetual
30. Befriend
32. "Picnic" author
33. Sports event
34. Divulge
35. Welsh name
36. Sleep
39. Bowling place
41. Blondes' promoter
42. I love: Lat.
44. Tie
48. Writer George and others
49. Mediocre
51. Oyster product
53. Raccoonlike animal
54. Name in psychiatry
55. Track event
56. Word of regret
57. Games: Lat.
59. Uncanny
60. In —— (troubled)
63. Pronoun
65. Squabble

14.

ACROSS

1. Bilks
7. Columns
13. Diner's choice
14. Unusual
16. Fabray
17. Post-Bronze period
18. Commonplace: Abbr.
19. Noncoms.
21. —— Remo
22. Spanish jar
24. Inclined, British style
25. Another: Sp.
26. Noblemen
28. Thus: Latin
29. Actress Garson
30. Methods
32. Benes
34. —— moment
35. German article
36. Blurry
39. College in Upstate N.Y.
43. Devilfish
44. French season
46. Transfer design
47. Stake
48. Finnish islands
50. Spanish hall
51. Map Abbr.
52. Ran swiftly
54. 2d century date
55. Before
58. Portuguese, for one
60. Stretchable
61. Gasoline buyer's concern
62. Transferred legally
63. Indolent

DOWN

1. —— horse
2. Deals with
3. Netherlands city
4. Tricky actions
5. Complete
6. Cassandra
7. School subject
8. American novelist
9. Nigerian people
10. Fiver
11. Dinette appliance
12. Made palatable
13. Pries
15. Man from Malaga
20. Cheerful: Fr.
23. Entertainer
25. Fruit
27. Wagner heroine
29. Hansa
31. Miss West
33. —— volente
36. Covered
37. Hospital staff man
38. Held up
39. Part of a peseta
40. Locust trees
41. Feudal tax
42. Arthurian lady
43. French Revolutionist
45. Pitch
48. Confuse
49. C.P.A.'s entry
53. Food shop, for short
56. Direction
57. Assist
59. Old car

15.

ACROSS

1. Whit
5. Pasteboard
9. Social group
14. Tiff
15. Oft-quoted Persian
16. Hollywood memento
17. English philosopher
18. Sea-story writer
19. Type of rock
20. Intuition
23. Feature of "Arabian Nights"
24. Painting medium
25. Chemical substance
27. Dishevel
30. Shout of greeting
31. Concur
32. Shoe part
33. Where Provo is
37. ——majesty
38. Bird
39. Type of rubber
40. Raw-boned
41. Ill-fated date
42. Calumny
43. Exhaust
45. Handbook
46. Throb
49. Tibetan beasts
50. Chemical suffix
51. Speak cattily
56. Diving duck
58. Half-and-half ingredient
59. Algerian port
60. Cup: Fr.
61. Aleutian island
62. Flier
63. First woman M.P.
64. Tide
65. Otherwise

DOWN

1. Theories
2. English painter
3. Powdery substance
4. Undecided
5. Pamper
6. Gather
7. Hindu title
8. Hot-rod contests
9. Pertaining to ribs
10. Rowan tree
11. Produce (with "up")
12. Eagle feature
13. At attention
21. Abukir's river
22. Traubel
26. Vanish
27. Like a pro cager
28. Molding
29. Bear
30. Port
32. Attentive escort
34. Interdiction
35. Zone
36. Nordhoff co-author
38. Gaucho item
42. Deep-red pigment
44. Front-door fixture
45. Retailer's concern
46. Italian dish
47. Last Mohican
48. Minimal
49. W.W. II conference site
52. Locale
53. Seed part
54. Word of disgust
55. Halfback's vulnerable spot
57. Servicemen's friend

16.

ACROSS

1. Pintails
6. Shoe part
11. Bookseller of a kind
14. More oppressive
16. Memorable actor
17. Novelist Thirkell
18. Humpty Dumpty
19. Having a thrilling sensation
21. Bird's beak
22. Hayden of Arizona
24. Menu favorite
25. Narrative
26. Source of heat
28. Transport systems: Abbr.
29. Short spell
30. Gaucho gear
32. Asian country
33. Garments
35. Political goal
36. Peeled
37. African language
38. Feels concern
39. Pronoun
40. Store (away)
44. Unique thing
45. Tempus ——
47. Normandy town
48. Name meaning grace
49. Key played with a finger
51. Headgear
52. Keen-scented canine
54. Grandpa's pride
56. Shirking responsibility
57. More furtive
58. Well-known college
59. Auto trips

DOWN

1. "The —— eve..."
2. In spite of, old style
3. House part
4. Girl's name
5. South African statesman
6. Schoolroom need
7. Sprinter's pathway
8. Work unit
9. German statesman
10. Message
11. Glasses, for short
12. "——Dance"
13. Forty-——
15. Moroccan capital
20. Form of fuel
23. Important worker
25. Young shoots
27. Breakwaters
29. Loosely woven wools used for shoddy
31. Went first
32. Understanding
33. Wrenches
34. Ancient Italian city
35. New Jersey river
37. Sets about
38. Take it easy
39. Cling to
41. Arrive at
42. Satisfies
43. Big hit
45. Forth, for one
46. Makes docile
49. Surface flaw
50. Vault
53. Asian
55. Engage in a sport

17.

ACROSS

1. Frilly neckpiece
6. Chimps
10. Sharpen
14. Latin friends
15. Minor or Major
16. Greek letter
17. Infuse
18. Fallen angel
20. Be lazy
21. Hebrew letter
22. Casabas
23. Role in "Othello"
25. Like some college halls
27. Last stop, financially
30. Spanish verb
34. Particularly: Abbr.
35. Stanch
37. Cabinet post: Abbr.
38. "O Sole ——"
39. Bohea
40. Topple
42. "——man of . . ."
43. Benelux member: Abbr.
45. Seed for rolls
47. Hero of many a movie
48. Space
49. Frees
51. Lariat
54. Fortune
55. Spacecraft name
58. Beam
60. Pile
63. Birds named for their song
65. Veld animal
66. Hodgepodge
67. Stew flavoring
68. With full force
69. Cozy home
70. Coins of Peru
71. Film great

DOWN

1. Lock up
2. Ordnance: Slang.
3. Bookseller
4. Visual
5. Kind of score
6. Seine tributary
7. Hypothesis
8. Direction: Abbr.
9. Ragout
10. Brandished
11. Rod-rider
12. Vingt-——
13. Bills
19. Hudson's Tappan ——
21. Archie et al.
24. Ganges sight
26. Pure
27. Island off Tanganyika
28. Willow
29. Asp.
31. Grilled delicacy
32. Greek valley sacred to a god
33. Quite —— (quite a distance): Colloq.
36. Opportune
41. ——de soie
44. Clodhopper: Var.
46. Skindiving aid
50. Outline
52. Wholly
53. Smears
55. ——marché
56. Cracow man
57. Sashes
59. Inquires
61. Seed coat
62. Facet
64. Recent: Prefix
65. Sharp turn

18.

ACROSS

1. Italian city
5. Auto parts
10. Mexican tidbit
14. Rainbow
15. West Indian sorcery
16. Military acronym
17. Asian land
18. Where Patchogue is
20. Matched
22. ——Bergeres
23. A French Louis
24. Retards
25. Bare
27. Common adverb
28. Luau course
29. Squared accounts
31. Beehive
35. Certain bags
37. ——Abner.
38. Honshu volcano
39. Jewelry item
40. Airport for Washington
42. Pitcher feature
43. Iron
45. Layers
47. Interlace
49. Tailor's concern
50. Amos —— Stagg
51. Astern
55. Miss Liberty's neighbor
57. First name of noted basso
58. Nichols' hero
59. Tidal bore
60. Eisteddfod item
61. Mix-up
62. Sere
63. Sportswear

DOWN

1. Heap
2. Where Mosul is
3. Morningside College's site
4. Set on
5. Meet head-on
6. Reed
7. Go, poetically
8. Dally
9. Moved
10. Stature
11. Look for
12. Ice-cream ——
13. Automotive pioneer
19. Whisky drink
21. Unreliable ones
24. Pitchman's decoy
25. Capable
26. Time of day
27. Cries
30. Luxurious
32. City in Michigan
33. Throw off
34. Family member
36. Outgo
38. Flower
40. Lured
41. Tried
44. Demolish
46. Most inexperienced
47. West Pointer
48. Lemur of India
50. In——(trouble)
51. Swiss peak
52. Raison d' ——
53. Encircle
54. Follows closely
56. Coach

19.

ACROSS

1. Assurance
7. Talk freely
14. Men, grammatically
15. Savage
17. Salad ingredient
18. Speedy animal
19. Nautical rope
20. Against
22. Of age: Latin abbr.
23. Large barrels or casks: Abbr.
24. Stages
26. Wildly enthusiastic: Slang
29. Lands a fish
32. Outstanding thing: Slang
33. Island near Corsica
34. Dress alterations
38. Soviet river
39. Actor's big day
41. Go into bankruptcy
42. Term of address
44. Withered
45. Word with "trial offer"
46. Diplomat of 1853 purchase
48. Enrich
49. Bright
52. Bail
54. ——-les-Bains
55. Famous theater name
58. A kind of drop
61. Unusual
63. Paderewski
65. False show, British style
66. Old cask
67. Hammers
68. Bore young, as a sheep

DOWN

1. Date: Abbr.
2. Oneupmanship word
3. Guitar's ancestor
4. —— pro nobis
5. Lighter of a sort
6. Color
7. Analyze verse
8. Pulsate
9. Makes an appearance
10. Type of barometer
11. Metric distance: Abbr.
12. Sea marauder
13. Kind of tiger
16. "——man do it"
21. Ineffectual
23. Transportation charge
25. Part of a bridle
26. Depressed
27. Emanation
28. Pleased
30. Declined
31. Victor's reward
35. —— avis
36. Row
37. Vehicle
40. Persistence
43. Like prime beef
47. Textile process
49. Creator of the schmoo
50. French yesterdays
51. Outdo
53. Orphan calf
56. Product of Alençon
57. Son of Zeus
58. Mild oath
59. "—— homo"
60. Do a garden task
62. Western Indian
64. Teacher's org.

20.

ACROSS

1. Champion of a cause
8. Biblical mountain
14. Chill excessively
15. Defensive wall
17. Daydream
18. Platinum alloy
19. Overused
20. Cinderella's destination
21. Container
22. With solicitude
25. Twinge
26. Moslem V.I.P.
27. Viva voce
28. Like a brewing ingredient
29. One's real wealth
32. Vapid writing
33. Originate
34. Arden or Sherwood
37. Kyushu park
38. Prudent
40. Babble
43. Fail
44. —— green
45. Hurt sound
46. Prize seeker
49. Illuminated
50. Outburst
51. City in Afghanistan
52. Believer in a doctrine
54. Servitude
56. Auto gear
57. Speak haltingly
58. Make soundproof
59. Restraining cords

DOWN

1. Eric ——, British actor
2. Found a mean
3. Float in air
4. Mountain ridge
5. More serious
6. Here: Fr.
7. Born
8. Dismay
9. Tennis exchange
10. Asian sea
11. Coiffure gadget
12. At a summit
13. Renter
16. Flavorful
20. Empty talk
23. Red ——, jazz musician
24. Commedia dell'
25. Document
28. —— Antony
30. Anger
31. French river
32. Sheriff's men
34. Louis's weapon
35. Part
36. Member of the go-go set
38. Break bread
39. Rags
40. Pivotal
41. Done in
42. On the go
43. Liquefied
46. Breakage: Fr.
47. Yell
48. Tithe
50. Encircle
53. ——culpa
54. Sound to catch attention
55. French summer

21.

ACROSS

1. A game of sorts
6. Flavor
10. Look over
14. Asian city
15. Indonesian islands
16. Quote
17. Oust
18. Words to a Gypsy sweetheart
20. Muses
22. A relative
23. Fibs
24. Musters strength
25. Cater to
28. Islet
29. Loose, as a boat
30. Precede in time
35. New Zealand native
36. Objective
37. Not citified
38. With warmth
40. Ratify
41. Liquid meas.
42. Light dessert
43. Pleased
47. Observed
48. Taste
49. One out of line
54. Whittier wrote about one
56. Avoid
57. Deserve
58. Wings
59. Networks
60. Meets
61. Millay pseudonym
62. Scoff

DOWN

1. Noah's son
2. Own
3. Oklahoma city
4. Places, in law
5. Pinkies
6. Took a bite of
7. French city
8. French pronoun
9. Muffin
10. Locale
11. Greek sorceress
12. Pacific sight
13. Hawaiian geese
19. Clumsy one
21. Common vulgarism
24. Order to a dog
25. Hebrew month
26. Walked
27. Akron output
28. Or's relative
29. Doctor's group
30. Before one or body
31. Boiled pudding
32. Seed cover
33. Weed
34. Tree
36. House wing
39. Urchin
40. District
42. Called
43. Sigmoids
44. Veranda
45. Left, at sea
46. Communities
47. Wander
49. Recital piece
50. Valley
51. Old instrument
52. —— Adams
53. Erect
55. Bill

22.

ACROSS

1. Form
6. A kind of talk
10. Players
14. Canadian peak
15. Root
16. Winglike
17. Cooling agents
18. Type of test
19. Cleave
20. September song
23. Breakfast meal
24. Puts in appearance
25. Reddish brown
28. Increase
29. Space
30. Abba
33. Uppish ones
38. A kind of year
39. Smarted
41. Siouan
42. Beginning
44. Consumer
45. Container
46. Records
48. Hits the silk
50. Bar of a kind
54. Iron and carbon
56. Reader's guide
61. Spread
62. Position
63. Put aside
64. Profits
65. French verb
66. Spirit lamps
67. Being: Latin
68. Loom part
69. Pours

DOWN

1. Opening
2. High: Ger.
3. Askew
4. Short item
5. Guarantee
6. Pub drink
7. Causes trouble
8. Algerian port
9. Sampled
10. Weight
11. Vibrant
12. Bank customer
13. Hair
21. Flooring
22. Book items
25. Spanish room
26. City on the Oka
27. Gather
28. Girl's name
31. Cooling measures, for short
32. Out of, in Munich
34. Short work
35. Auricular
36. Craft
37. Concert pieces: Abbr.
40. Olive or pea
43. Helm position
47. Literary hack
49. People on the move
50. U.S. architect
51. Stakes
52. Supports
53. Terminate
54. A kind of crow
55. Lugged
57. Celebration
58. Zero
59. London street sight
60. Meeting: Abbr.

23.

ACROSS

1. Drug
8. Paper sizes
15. Solve
16. Consistent
17. Enliven
18. Diving equipment
19. Sparks
20. Faddish item
22. Diamond lady
23. Branch of math
25. Flourishing
26. European
27. Palate part
29. Poets' word
30. Willowy
31. Old tune title
33. Critic of a sort
34. N.L. team
35. Marsh
36. Game
39. Shook
43. Wavy, in heraldry
44. ——generis
45. Deteriorate
46. Noun suffixes
47. Dilutes
49. Prod
50. Certain radios: Abbr.
51. Zagreb is its capital
53. "——on parle français"
54. Actor
56. Rather
58. Ahead: Fr.
59. Women's golf titlist, 1967
60. Councils
61. Chose

DOWN

1. A theory in physics
2. Fluster
3. Platinum-like element
4. Industrialist's org.
5. John's relative
6. Colonist's greeting to an Indian
7. Inspires
8. Have —— (be apprehensive)
9. Completeness
10. Unsubstantial
11. Take on gas: Abbr.
12. Grooms
13. Bird: Prefix
14. Ore processor
21. Ivy League men
24. —— in (takes pride)
26. Dawdles
28. Spur on a peak
30. Allowance
32. Psychoanalyst's concerns
33. Russian composer
35. Statistician's term
36. Voids
37. Disentangle
38. Certain Ukrainian
39. Because: Latin
40. Most viscous
41. Instruct
42. Laughed at
44. Fires
47. Threefold
48. Relating to a head part
51. Suffix for Dixie or auto
52. Engineer's group: Abbr.
55. Board created in 1933
57. Rap: Fr.

24.

ACROSS

1. Mexican snack
5. Units of progress
10. Collude with
14. Completed
15. Refuge
16. Chinese wormwood
17. Minor-league club
18. In reserve
19. River of Belgium
20. Emporium employe
23. Bankroll
24. Tennis stratagem
25. Hungarian violinist
27. Western forest sights
32. Kennel sound
33. Elected: Fr.
34. Lighter part
36. Purposive
39. ——in one's bonnet
41. Comedian of silent films
43. Spanish youngster
44. Handle
46. Contrite
48. Timetable abbr.
49. Sisters
51. French meal
53. English courts
56. Tree
57. Baseball gear
58. Military aircraft
64. Nerve-cell process
66. Without joy
67. Many
68. Municipality
69. Thin as ——
70. The Middies
71. Nine: Prefix
72. Where Innsbruck is
73. Cat's-paw

DOWN

1. Soho swell
2. Grandparental
3. Atlantic game fish
4. Decorative brass
5. Poster
6. Source of the Blue Nile
7. Maleficence
8. Sharp digs
9. Doc's friend
10. Girl of song
11. Like a famous biographer
12. Clerical permission to leave
13. Late: It.
21. Overhead item
22. Disturbance
26. Verdon
27. Large waves
28. River of Germany
29. South African city
30. Is distressed
31. Hairnet
35. Spare, in Soho
37. Concerning
38. Certain journalist: Abbr.
40. Small case
42. R.L.S. character
45. Spanish weight
47. Bark
50. ——large (frees)
52. Vowel sign
53. Slacken
54. Lowlander
55. Owl-eyed
59. Hebrew month
60. Thalia's sister
61. Furthermore
62. Words of warning
63. Catchall abbr.
65. Compass reading

25.

ACROSS

1. Famed showman
6. Maid, in India
10. "Grand Old ——"
14. Chicago airport
15. Wool: Lat.
16. Old instrument
17. Relative of sorts
18. Machinist: Abbr.
19. Name in journalism
20. Soldier's chest
22. Demonstration
23. Luxury
24. High principles
26. European
30. City in Illinois
32. Rice dish
33. Genuses of the maidenhair fern
37. Malay town
38. Golf club
39. —— first you . . .
40. Weed
42. Troll
43. Correct
44. Playground item
45. Word on a movie trailer
48. Lake, in Italy
50. Genesis figure
51. Parts of newspaper plants
57. Indigo
58. Cries
59. A relative, familiarly
60. Type: Abbr.
61. Small land area: Var.
62. Enroll
63. British sand hill
64. French marshal and others
65. Untidy

DOWN

1. Small hat
2. Words of dismay
3. Circle
4. Smell ——
5. A change for the better
6. Guinness and Templeton
7. See 1 Across
8. Angel: Fr.
9. Song for 1 Across
10. Italian
11. Lammermoor name
12. Massachusetts town
13. Exploits
21. Indigo
25. Hubbub
26. Miner's nail
27. Italian coin
28. Luise Rainer role
29. Start of career of 1 Across
31. Celebrity
33. Neat as ——
34. Flying saucers
35. Family member
36. Goulash
38. Stays full time, as a servant
41. Large bird
42. See 1 Across
44. Certain doctors: Abbr.
45. Cloth design
46. French income
47. French spa
49. Helpers: Abbr.
52. Part
53. French river
54. Cereal
55. French women: Abbr.
56. Full of life

26.

ACROSS

1. Yonder, out yonder
5. Trades
10. Heavy cloth
14. Atmosphere
15. Who's ——?
16. Material for publication
17. Pompous one
18. Kind of jacket
20. —— attention
22. Sailed
23. Staff men
25. Herb
26. Carroll beasts
29. Closing words
34. Small craft
35. Green quartz
36. Aloha item
37. Sports place
38. —— polloi
39. Look ahead
40. Girl's name
41. Fall
43. Stop
44. Headlong
46. Swindled: Colloq.
47. Fuel
48. Reprove
50. Thwart
53. Turned
57. Relief for an ailment
59. Lopez song
60. Church part
61. Fishing gear
62. Decorate
63. Marina part
64. Literary first name
65. Sinecure

DOWN

1. Parts of dancing shoes
2. Impair
3. Song
4. Final destruction, in myth
5. Suffixes for home or road
6. Supreme Court Justice
7. Roman bronze
8. Executive: Abbr.
9. Spanish women
10. Orchestrates
11. U.S. inventor
12. Copied
13. Circle: Prefix
19. High: Fr.
21. Dutch sight
24. Saunters
26. Discard
27. Ingenuous
28. Yearly record, old style
30. Call
31. See 64 Across
32. Renter's concern
33. Did a coat job
35. Bandman Harris
39. Pieces of jewelry
41. Black or Arrow
42. Fur-lined mantle
43. Baltimore player
45. Lumberman
46. Barrel maker
49. Eye: It.
50. Indian
51. Yorkshire river
52. Looked at
54. Ripped
55. Essayist
56. Moist
57. Uniform part
58. Manipulate, as bids

27.

ACROSS

1. Tiny amount
5. Central
10. Golden shiner
14. Calendar abbreviation
15. Place of entertainment
17. Exacerbates
18. Highly chagrined
19. Scottish alder
20. French name
21. Persian Gulf port
22. Ornament
24. Farming concern
26. Swiss abode
27. Property
31. Egyptian abode of the dead
32. Pencil mark
34. Permit
35. Fists: Slang
37. Swiss river
38. —— Lama
40. Season on the Loire
41. Concerned
44. Yielded
45. Geometric figure
47. Idolizes
49. Exclamation
50. Shoe
51. Assuage
54. Hamper
55. St. Pierre, e.g.
57. Estrangement
60. Unique thing
61. Man from Mankato
62. Diminished by
63. Iron molds
64. Hit hard: Slang
65. Being

DOWN

1. Global area
2. Hoosier city
3. Type of trading
4. Rockies: Abbr.
5. Natural resources
6. Begins
7. Hand over
8. Constellation
9. —— Cruces
10. Blue color
11. Outcries
12. Customer
13. Greek letter
16. Garbed
20. Salty relish
23. Color
24. Cut
25. Hardwood tree
26. —— blue
27. Actress Jeanne
28. Hollywood name
29. Without tempering influence
30. Farm structures
33. Starchy roots
36. Type of triangle
39. Eager
42. Oriental notable
43. French river
46. Birds
48. Follow closely
50. Puff up
51. Indian hominy
52. Et ——
53. Food fish
54. Townsmen
56. Gaelic
58. Serpent
59. "—— Water fowl"
60. Cadiz cheer

28.

ACROSS

1. Electric units, for short
5. Protective group: Abbr.
9. Civil War general
14. Uncover
15. Shut in: Fr.
16. Went together
17. Informal wear
19. Mine pit
20. Penn ——
21. Joins
23. Man's name
24. Feature of some trousers
27. Ships' decks
28. Spica or Rigel
29. Caribbean
30. Machetes
31. Tête-à- ——
33. Kitchen tool
36. Tyrants
40. Military assault
42. Actor Guitry
43. Lawyer: Abbr.
46. Sour
47. Furrowed
48. Dry run
51. Regale
52. Conjuration
53. Enlisted men
55. Baffle
57. Make unfit
59. Beatle name
60. Part of speech
61. Put up stakes
62. Satisfies
63. Part song
64. U. N. member

DOWN

1. Girl's name
2. Famous Mrs.
3. Dress fabric
4. Understand
5. Parts of operas
6. Level land
7. Challenge
8. Complied
9. Drs.
10. Fire ——
11. —— fingertips
12. Dethrone
13. Ancient city of Asia Minor
18. Fashion wear
22. Declare
25. Cheers
26. Compelling forces
27. Outmoded: Abbr
32. Footwear
34. Nonsense poet, and others
35. In harmony
37. Tile pattern
38. Enter ——
39. Pitiful
41. Type of alcohol
43. Snakes
44. Jottings, usually
45. Occupant
47. Contemporary of Molière
49. Sweet flag
50. Invest (with)
54. Prophet
56. Aurora
58. Sarong

29.

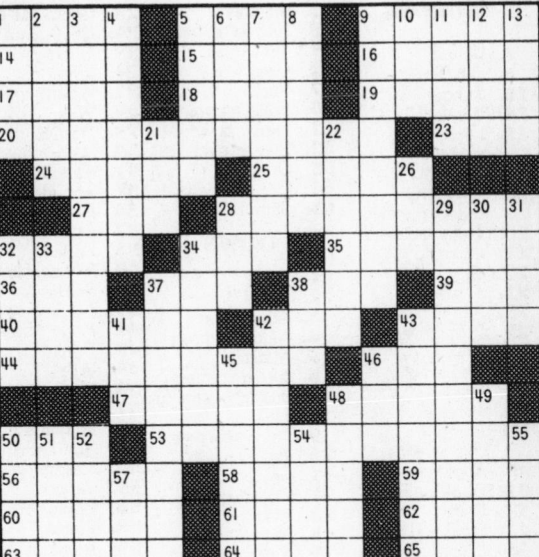

ACROSS

1. Gag line
5. Kind of worm
9. West Indies magic
14. Rose's spouse
15. ——— risk
16. Crimean city
17. String
18. Cards
19. Push aside
20. With 28, 36, 44 and 53 Across, a Presidential quote
23. Refuge
24. Waif
25. Mortise's companion
27. Former Broadway name
28. See 20 Across
32. Phone
34. Usually 72, in golf
35. Land holdings
36. See 20 Across
37. Shout
38. ——— Alamos
39. Swiss river
40. ———-oo
42. Musical notes
43. Whale
44. See 20 Across
46. Chinese leader
47. ——— pink
48. Italian city
50. School subj.
53. See 20 Across
56. Hebrew precept
58. Italy's Aldo ———
59. Give ———
60. Container
61. Cellar: Abbr.
62. Black: It.
63. Author of quote
64. Meeting: Abbr.
65. Part of Q.E.D.

DOWN

1. Composer
2. Clarinets' cousins
3. Down-elevator's goal
4. Word for U.S. Government
5. Meat juices
6. Time Inc. man
7. Type of general
8. Ring of metal
9. Court cries
10. Dance: Fr.
11. Tuscan island
12. Noun suffix
13. Predatory bird
21. Gamma or beta
22. Emcees' chores
26. N. Y. Knicks' league
28. Wages
29. Oil testing device
30. Copy, for short
31. Ancient city
32. Weight units: Abbr.
33. ". . . scratch it with———"
34. Immediately
37. Draws together
38. ———low (hide)
41. 506
42. On———(exactly)
43. Rifle
45. Flicks pages
46. Month
48. Church people: Abbr.
49. Ad———
50. Engrave
51. Ibsen character
52. Hoary
54. Rail centers: Abbr.
55. Blast
57. Partook of

30.

ACROSS

1. Prohibition
5. Kind of dream
9. Goat: Sp.
14. State
15. Map listings
16. To the point: Lat.
17. Neckwear of sorts
19. Antoinette, for one
20. Field
21. Word for a fille
22. Nurse, in Australia
23. Southern caverns
25. Wardrobe
26. Chalice
28. Fine-grained rock
29. Bored
31. Good: Fr.
34. As well
35. Pique
36. Star in Lyra
37. American humorist
38. Name on an insurance policy
42. Street sign
43. Sets store by
44. Peanuts, for one
47. City on the Willamette
48. Caparisons
49. Pit
50. Mouth: Prefix
53. Real estate sign
54. Things to be pulled
56. Portly
57. ———many words
58. Seminar product
59. Aeries
60. One of the Hebrides
61. Dutch painter

DOWN

1. Jejune
2. Plains Indian
3. Guantanamo
4. Popular article
5. Churchman
6. Capri's neighbor
7. Foot: Suffix
8. Letter
9. Horse-drawn vehicle
10. ———Fideles
11. B'nai ———
12. French name
13. N. and S.
18. Headgear
22. Bulgar
24. Business abbreviation
25. Dominant
26. Menotti
27. Exclusive
28. Broadcast
30. Curtain material
31. Smart set
32. Mythical creature
33. Some votes
36. Contemptible
38. Sisters of note
39. Greek god
40. Classic of 1819
41. Biblical leader
42. Idle
44. Part of a Williams title
45. Mexican home
46. Functions
47. Mama's boy
49. Fur
51. Spool
52. Britisher's comment
54. Midwest state: Abbr.
55. Auto need

31.

ACROSS

1. Mountain
5. Old card
10. Range
14. Whaler
15. Like a certain animal
16. Italian river
17. Presidential speech opener
20. Traffic violators
21. Ohio city
22. Galena
23. Swells
25. Berths
29. Drops given by oculists
33. Man's name
34. Life——
35. Turmeric
36. Bambi's companions
40. Apple-giver
41. Dispels
42. C-men
43. Fools and trifles
45. Like a grove
47. Matures
48. Railroad of a kind
49. 1836 locale
52. Great many
57. Puck
60. Waste allowance
61. French byway
62. Russian river
63. Only
64. U.S. historian
65. Stirred up

DOWN

1. Louts
2. Fields
3. Transaction
4. Kind of seaman
5. Minarets
6. Moliere's miser
7. Just misses the cup
8. Unit
9. Numerical prefix
10. Bigot
11. vocal
12. English queen
13. Hart
18. Repute
19. To an extent
23. Celtics and others
24. Olive genus
25. Hungry
26. Irritate
27. Wharf supports
28. Wing
29. Dashes
30. Went astray
31. Cattails
32. Impudent
34. Rabbit tails
37. State
38. Lasted
39. Sky sight for some
44. Silk fabric
45. Ate, in a way
46. Leer
48. Drink
49. Wiles
50. Monk parrot
51. Actor Walter
52. French author
53. She: Latin
54. Cassini
55. Taboo
56. Booty
58. Prattle
59. Arena cheer

32.

ACROSS

1. Word with man or mat
5. Mineral
9. Pampas weapon
13. Wings: Lat.
14. Court figure
15. Latin abbr.
16. With 57, 36, 48 and 44 Across, a famous phrase
18. Discovery
19. Some buildings
20. Arm of the Arctic
22. Twofold
24. Torme
25. Eleanor's cousin
28. Paragon
33. Play to the gallery
34. Ridge on a coin
35. —— pro nobis
36. See 16 Across
37. Carplike fish
38. English statesman
39. Labor group
40. Mythical king
41. Kentucky college
42. Guard
44. See 16 Across
45. Ending with block or stock
46. Luxor's river, Latin style
48. See 16 Across
52. City in West Germany
56. Clue
57. See 16 Across
59. Kelp
60. Excite
61. Prefix for meter or tude
62. Agent
63. Terrier
64. English school

DOWN

1. Blackbirds
2. Chemical suffix
3. Attestation
4. Delaware beach
5. Southwest city
6. Onassis
7. Wrestling term
8. Pitchers
9. Happen to
10. First name in stage lore
11. Highway feature
12. Former opera star
14. De la Roche title
17. Silk fabric
21. Old Spanish coin
23. Nebraska city
25. 1930 Nobel author
26. "South Pacific" role
27. —— a bet
29. Certain payments
30. Shearer
31. Russian co-op
32. Brazilian port
34. "Citizen ——"
37. Alcoves
38. Dramatis
40. Area of France
41. Obligated
43. Mongol
44. Signal
47. "—— to get up . . ."
48. African country
49. Hawaiian port
50. Heavenly being: Fr.
51. Vitellus
53. Electrical unit
54. Inner: Prefix
55. Check
58. Direction

33.

ACROSS

1. Norse god
5. Certain southerner
10. Starch
14. Name for an island
15. Marketplace
16. Reward, old style
17. Guinness
18. Word for some city areas
20. Difficulties
22. Poker move
23. Devotion
24. Calling
25. Desserts
28. Barnum word
30. Tolerates
32. Sculls
33. Mrs. Sprat's choice
36. A god
37. Beldame
39. Bring to light
40. Aries
41. Put down
42. Part of a tea setting
44. Decanter
46. Trace
47. Shopping area
50. Oust
52. Contract
53. Constant companions
57. Novelist's dream
59. Kind of dancer
60. Employer
61. Set aside
62. List unit
63. Prefix for zoa
64. Communities
65. A tide

DOWN

1. Goneril's father
2. Heraldic border
3. Ukraine city
4. Master at Cambridge
5. Root
6. Akin
7. He's lauded in song
8. U.S. author
9. Mets' league
10. Sullies
11. Penthouse for birds
12. Honkers
13. Stranger
19. Volcanic earth
21. Venture
24. Ops's daughter
25. Structural shape
26. Weapons: Lat.
27. Space
29. Operated
31. False alarm
33. Save ——
34. Vicinity
35. Semester
38. Inlet
39. News item
41. Stows
43. Dyeing apparatus
44. Dictator
45. Nonresident hospital aide
47. Music-room item
48. Pee Wee
49. Looks over: Colloq.
51. French clerics
53. Tall: Sp.
54. Get the ——
55. Sponge spicule
56. Short for an oaf
58. New York time

34.

ACROSS

1. Grape jelly
5. Nerve
10. Kind of dog
14. Rounded hill
15. Do a kitchen chore
16. Certain quarry
17. "How sweet ——"
18. Stoutness
20. Chickens
22. U.S. observatory
23. Yonkers offering
24. Dress feature
25. Effervesce
27. Pulitzer winner, 1943
31. Letter
32. Misdid
34. Seven: Prefix
35. Huntsman's quarry
37. Cooking fats
39. New World area: Abbr.
40. Alternative words
42. Forestalls
44. Cheer
45. Fawn on
47. Indexed
49. Je ne —— quoi
50. Gloat
51. Sweetening the pot
54. Inactivated
59. Showy plant
60. Specify
61. Racetrack pest
61. —— a limb
62. Word on U.S. coins
63. Thereabouts
64. Approximates
65. Sponsorship

DOWN

1. Turn the pages
2. Opposed
3. Direct
4. Soak up
5. Wraiths
6. Western animals
7. Roman city
8. Modem: Prefix
9. Citizen of Nairobi
10. Utters gleefully
11. Arab's garment
12. Caen's river
13. Drizzles
19. Common fish
21. Characterization
24. Had an effect
25. Brush broom
26. Far out
27. Take care of
28. Designating
29. With "know," a smarty
30. Alias Ouida
33. Suffers disuse
36. Enters
38. Highland purses
41. Malayan titles
43. Old dagger
46. Roller, for one
48. Grass
50. Previous
51. Capable
52. Destitute
53. Name of many Popes
54. —— boy!
55. Holder for small items
56. Certain voters: Abbr.
58. Abbreviation used on calendars

35.

ACROSS

1. Bargains, familiarly
5. Was off guard
10. Color
14. Ocean fish
15. Bird's abode
16. Essayist
17. Take a walk
20. Western country
21. Showy flower
22. Sea god
23. Apparel item
25. Took off
29. Type of seat
33. Remaining
34. Asian
35. Conjunctions
36. Get into hot water
41. Ivy Leaguer
42. Of grandparents
43. Jackknife
44. Soothing
46. Type of mining
48. Historic waterway
49. Region of India
50. Irish city
53. Seasonings
58. Grieve
61. Antiquing device
62. Wasteland tracts
63. Renowned novel
64. Marsh bird
65. Flounder
66. Call it ——

DOWN

1. Empty talk
2. Doing
3. Narrative
4. Structure
5. Kind of cow
6. Operetta composer
7. Greek god
8. Golfer's target
9. Golfer's aid
10. Leases to another
11. Grocery item
12. "Keep Off," for one
13. Kind of mark
18. Bulrush
19. Vent stopper
23. Chinese: Prefix
24. Ruin
25. Saps
26. Immature seed
27. Not fragrant
28. Back
29. Plunder
30. Type style
31. Hunt
32. Acid salt
37. Member of Iroquois union
38. Offensive
39. Except
40. Mountain of Crete
45. Woolen cloth
46. Soap ingredient
47. Late comedian
49. Leavers
50. Waves
51. Italian lake
52. Chariot route
53. Word of contempt
54. Vessel
55. Map line
56. New Guinea town
57. Check
59. German river
60. Peruvian coin

36.

ACROSS

1. Latvian
5. Edged
10. Town near Amsterdam
14. Government agency
15. Earnest
16. Gallic name
17. Western park
18. Winglike
19. Part of a litter
20. Part of 4 Down
22. Breaks off
24. Ones: Scot
25. Kind of farmer
26. Display
29. "The —— Sixpence"
32. Genoese admiral
33. Magazine: Fr.
34. Swerve
36. Hip bones
37. Gloves, in a way
38. Spoiler
39. Man's nickname
40. Stay near
41. Agreements
42. More meaty
44. Slate
45. Certain times
46. A friar
47. Housewife's concern
50. Beaten
54. Cheer
55. Number
57. Slick
58. Voice
59. French river
60. Berg
61. Part of a decade
62. Arabian state
63. Caring

DOWN

1. Activity
2. Map area
3. Famous one
4. African nation
5. Navy man
6. Asian pines
7. Gelling agent
8. Emeritus: Abbr.
9. Overnice
10. Corrigenda
11. God: Lat.
12. Girl's name
13. Baseball team
21. Indian
23. Bird
25. City in Kent
26. Cut (with out)
27. Rodents
28. Rainbow: Prefix
29. Measure
30. Town on Hudson
31. Alighieri
33. Carries on
35. U.S. novelist
37. On a low key
38. Retreats
40. Busy place
41. Type size
43. Reader in a church
44. Dish
46. Common adverb
47. Petition
48. Part
49. Greek letter
50. Decorate
51. Hawaiian city
52. Biblical judge
53. Processed, in a way
56. Implement

37.

ACROSS

1. Star in Virgo
6. Animal
11. Spatial wave senders
13. Other senders from space
15. Lie
16. Black Sea country
17. Poem
18. Radio wires
20. Rank: Abbr.
21. Metalwares
23. Carnegie
24. Seine tributary
25. Tools
26. Ort
27. Opinions
29. A league
32. Wrap in cloth
33. Meaning: Colloq.
34. Latin abbreviation
36. Per ——
38. Miles
42. Impossible
44. Flat: Abbr.
45. Zany
47. Widespread
48. Leather
50. Sierra ——
51. State: Abbr.
52. Character in "Lear"
54. Profane, in Hawaii
55. Long Island city
57. Asian animals
59. Dress sizes
60. "——, match" (tennis call)
61. Certain murals
62. Seasons

DOWN

1. Time of day
2. Knee part
3. Middle East land: Abbr.
4. Plywood shapers
5. Vissi d'——
6. Spiky rose plant
7. Trees
8. Grieg character
9. More arenose
10. Adriatic port
11. Share
12. Chiaroscuros
13. Container
14. Herbs
19. Information
22. A lover of beauty
24. ". . . just —— to give . . ."
26. —— appétit
28. Habitat plant
30. Metric foot
31. Child's game
35. Blaster's need
36. Newspapers
37. Spanish king's son
39. Fiction
40. Pronto
41. Balzac et al.
42. Hamper
43. Lycées
46. Minimum
49. Duck genus
50. Camel's cousin
52. Deity: Ger.
53. —— much as
56. Norse god
58. Set

38.

ACROSS

1. Famed Idahoan
6. Effort: Colloq.
10. Ceremonial word
14. Iowa community
15. Shakespeare character
16. Roman courts
17. Stand-in of a sort
19. Future racer
20. Well-known nickname
21. Highland hillside
22. Small lump
24. Familiar
25. —— cry
26. Hetty
28. Reflected
32. Former Broadway star
33. Harden
34. Quality
35. Man's name
36. French passage
37. Cudgel
38. Separate
39. Author of "Mildred Pierce"
40. Barters
41. Reflex action
43. Biblical verb
44. Function
45. Visionary
46. Shaken
49. Italian city
50. Davis's domain
53. Western Indian
54. —— Day
57. Stage direction
58. Muffle
59. Veranda
60. Duck
61. Anti
62. Wagnerian role

DOWN

1. A dessert
2. Poet
3. U.S. physicist
4. One
5. Tarnished idol
6. Popular instrument
7. London gallery
8. Time
9. Elsa's story
10. Theater area
11. Sap
12. Of a time
13. Eastern campus
18. U.N. member
23. Middle East initials
24. Old-fashioned
25. American poet
26. Name in bridge
27. Lyons' river
28. Russian U.N. name
29. Rustic
30. Come out
31. Flatfish
32. Worry, old style
33. Noise
36. Place linked to Judas
40. Cries loudly
42. G.I. nickname
43. Name linked to Rama
45. Gray
46. Fair
47. Indian
48. Refrain words
49. Prefix for meter
50. Pilot
51. Sultan of ——
52. Locale of the Himalayas
55. Drag
56. New Guinea port

39.

ACROSS

1. Feign
5. Asian land
9. Grape refuse
13. Scabbard point
14. Use a stylus
15. Biblical name
16. Partner of lost
17. Countertenor
18. Fading star
19. Partner of ram
20. Forever: Lat.
23. Bay in east Atlantic
25. Narcotics
26. Angry
28. Drug plant
29. —— Miguel
30. Skin
34. Disparages
36. Aides to M.D.'s
38. Sunfish
40. Precipitous
42. Addition to Carmel or Juan
44. Malaysian vessel
45. Rock-'n'-roll room
48. Object
52. Short-tailed monkey
53. National shrine
55. Airline abbreviation
57. Tip
58. Chemical prefix
59. Sound combination
61. Series of questions
62. Old Lithuanian coins
63. Excess of solar over lunar year
64. Individuals
65. Go through a sieve
66. Soviet press agency

DOWN

1. Posters
2. Settle
3. Copy
4. Physician, familiarly
5. 1968, for one
6. Salt tree
7. European tax
8. Marketed
9. Devilfish
10. Nearby
11. Musical show
12. Quahogs
13. Small: Suffix
21. Seizes: Colloq.
22. Duck
24. Cubic measure
26. Notes of the scale
27. Invigorating
31. Ring enclosures
32. Pacific islands
33. Musician's concern
35. Jewish festival
37. Accumulated
39. Own, in Scotland
41. Seed-bearers
43. Sports: Abbr.
46. Come between
47. Head covering
48. Noted Greek
49. Mature
50. Corpulent
51. Themes
54. Snack
56. Play the part of
60. —— tree

40.

ACROSS

1. Star in Cygnus
6. Scovels
10. Tableland
14. Noisy
15. About 3.7 quarts
16. Areas in the Seine
17. Kind of auk
18. Stoics' leader
19. Stoolie, in Southampton
20. Rascals
22. Shade
23. Plant pore
24. Dealt with
25. Cygnet's sire
28. Quoits peg
29. I.O.U.
30. Open
32. Erose
37. Greek cape on Aegean Sea
38. —— vadis
39. Papal veil
40. Power failures
42. Gall
43. Cattle, old style
44. Michigan locks, for short
46. Usual bill footer
47. United
50. Foam
52. Active
53. Lunch order
57. In disagreement
58. Netherlands coin
59. Moth genus
60. Honey buzzard
61. Waugh
62. Moves cautiously
63. Trillion: Prefix
64. Chicken bone
65. Dejected ones

DOWN

1. Hoover and Roosevelt
2. Cordage fiber
3. Girl's name
4. Nobles
5. Exciting
6. African area
7. Alpha's opposite
8. Pig and fountain
9. Broadway sign
10. Some poodles
11. Antelope
12. Worsted
13. Wall St. word
21. Court
22. One skilled in math
24. Article
25. Search
26. Stadium
27. Lugosi
29. Cantankerous one
31. Dead ——
33. Existence of sorts
34. Shortening
35. Edison's middle name
36. Calamus
41. Pronoun
45. "—— Town"
47. Modify
48. Independent one
49. Measure
50. Snoops
51. Ancient Sumerian city
53. Scala offerings
54. U.S. playwright
55. Swanky or stout
56. Lip
58. Grackle

'41.

ACROSS

1. Show stamina
7. George W. confessed to him
10. Voucher
14. Collar, in a way
15. "—— seen everything now"
16. Sharpen
17. George's deed, in a way
19. Gardner
20. Hard look
21. Netherlands port
23. Fine fur
25. Victimizes (with "on")
26. Printers' frames
28. Shop
29. Do housework
30. Inferior
33. Col.'s superior
36. Standing advice for George
39. W.W. II agency
40. Complete
41. Secure, as a line
42. "—— Rheingold"
43. Shrewd
45. Endured
48. Strikes
50. Operates, as a drawer
52. One at ——
56. Indigo
57. Helpful dosage for Feb. 22
59. Hindu divinity
60. Western group
61. Use a spray
62. River of Germany
63. French season
64. Meetings

DOWN

1. Words of derision
2. Common Latin verb
3. Ionian Sea gulf
4. Backslider
5. Theater workers
6. Army man: Brit. abbr.
7. Burgundy city
8. Cast ——
9. National figure
10. Color for Feb. 22
11. Massed group
12. Ornamental setting
13. Pours
18. Divide an angle
22. Pattern to be traced
24. Fruit-store treats
26. Bird's cry
27. "—— soit . . ."
28. Command
29. Half a musical title
31. Alpine gear
32. Strong tension, poetically
33. Capricorn
34. Let up
35. A degree
37. Studies
38. Like some days
42. It went a long way for George
44. Movie trailer
45. Card
46. Did a piano job
47. Cocktail additive
48. Jack
49. French river
51. Western Indian
53. Cleopatra's maid
54. Nonthoroughbred
55. Dutch uncles
58. Medicine or old

'42.

ACROSS

1. In style
5. Slant
10. Word for a horse
14. Blood: Prefix
15. Ancient Indian king
16. Island in the Hebrides
17. Sins
19. Tobacco portion
20. Retarded
21. Cooks in a way
23. Being
24. Peace ——
25. Part of a toast
28. Shopping places
30. For: Sp.
33. Talkative
35. Dissolute one
36. Chemical suffix
37. Parisian friend
38. Nymph
40. Type size
41. Bulgarian coin
42. School official: Abbr.
43. Winter gear
45. Dutch commune
46. Fish
48. Certain drinks
49. Sharp sound
50. Cozy spot
52. Game
55. Arrow poisons
58. Relative
59. Type of competition
62. French novelist
63. Apple varieties
64. Poon tree
65. Army destinations
66. Uneven
67. This: Sp.

DOWN

1. Greek letter
2. Fowl
3. Not an orig.
4. Flirt
5. Teases
6. Prize
7. Useless
8. Piece out
9. Lethargy
10. Excite curiosity
11. Boor
12. Pacific fish
13. Wanders about
18. Like some diamonds
22. Vaulted recess
24. Native craft
25. Cartographer's concern
26. Arabian name
27. Artless
29. Common contraction
30. Tommy's ally in W. W. I.
31. Coveted prize
32. Harvests
34. Pudding
39. Inlets
40. Thrust forward
42. Greek letters
44. Indian state
47. Hardens
49. Emotions
51. Take out
52. Iliad
53. Bon mot
54. Ruin
55. Italian coin: Abbr.
56. Greek goddess
57. —— away
60. Common correlative
61. Voodoo deity

43.

ACROSS

1. Tech areas
5. Air-race feature
10. N.F.L. team
14. Got off
15. Rhone tributary
16. Biblical character
17. Lake Lucerne's backdrop
18. Big
20. Wet blanket
22. Tidbit
23. Puff up
24. Flood, in a way
25. ——— to say
27. ——— eight
31. Vehicle
32. Illusory
33. Wall: Fr.
34. Babylonian god
35. Laps
36. Plural suffix
37. Noun suffix
38. Disconcerts
39. Shut up like ———
41. Talk in a certain way
43. Blue glasses
44. City on Lake Michigan
45. Son of Cain
46. Tacit
49. Small pit
52. Sky sight
55. Depart
56. Protected
57. Take ———
58. See 52 Across
59. Sens' colleagues
60. Like some highways
61. Appraisals: Abbr.

DOWN

1. Bird
2. Others, in Rome
3. Pros' milieu
4. ——— come
5. Men on the bridge
6. Belgian violinist
7. God
8. Assn.
9. Superfluous
10. Declaim
11. ——— example
12. Grain product
13. Chop ———
19. Chef's concern
21. Adherent of Indian faith
24. Breathing organs
25. Clemens
26. Early guild
27. Gay
28. Not prime time
29. ——— the plate
30. Beats: Colloq.
32. Unclear
35. Truman slogan
38. Lambaste
39. Cupid
40. Latin American political boss
42. Marbles
43. Caught in a way
45. Duck
46. Adjective ending
47. Giza's river
48. Gait
50. Tilt
51. Greek letters
53. Garment
54. German article

44.

ACROSS

1. Stupid
6. Give orders
10. Asian prefix
14. Remnant in Rouen
15. Mine: Fr.
16. Fasten
17. Used
18. Shop of sorts
20. Baseball listings
22. Masking and friction
23. Starchy plant
24. Half a Hollywood name
25. Fowl
26. Kind of bank account: Abbr.
28. Pastry shell
32. Globe: Abbr.
35. Church officer
38. Caspian tributary
39. Babe Ruth specialties
42. Arena figure
43. Emblems
44. Youth group: Abbr.
45. Substitute
47. Sweep
49. Huge amount
50. Navy officers: Abbr.
52. Lamb
56. "——— cockhorse"
59. Custer's claim to fame
61. Scottish golf course
63. Windbreaker
64. French poet's output
65. Yes
66. Cheer finale
67. Head part
68. Sprightly
69. A certain noise

DOWN

1. Top
2. Lasso on the llanos
3. "Fair as ———..."
4. Working girls
5. Shopper's word
6. Wedding notice
7. Finale
8. Farm animals
9. Noun suffix
10. Port on the Bosporus
11. Tide
12. Hamlet or dog
13. Auto pioneer
19. Flower bearer
21. Paper Ivan reads
25. Rear
27. Increase
28. Style
29. Street urchin
30. Songs
31. Maxwell
32. Army men: Abbr.
33. First: Prefix
34. River in Mongolia
36. Weigh ———
37. Spiteful woman
40. Balderdash
41. David's songs: Abbr.
46. Obsolete
48. Keep in mind
50. More wintry
51. Money, for one
53. Stately music
54. Stamp pad
55. Take ———
56. Invitation letters
57. Willow
58. Move fast
59. ——— majesty
60. Boston and others: Abbr.
62. Sleeper

45.

ACROSS

1. Rounded: Prefix
6. Skits
10. Household members
14. Void
15. Decorative wear
16. Secular
17. Presidential nickname
18. Early Colbert role
20. French river
21. "Après——..."
22. Prayer
23. Stage villain
25. Wager
27. Lovelace's friend and others
30. Shred
34. One: Scot.
35. Moves furtively
37. W. W. II battleground
38. Hebrew letter
39. Wire: Abbr.
40. Suffix for bleacher
42. Part of a cheer
43. Part of a monogram: Abbr.
45. Rodent
47. Presidential nickname
48. Hiding place
49. Don and others
51. Loosened
54. Hebrew letter
55. Deep absorption
58. German article
60. Goad
63. Operatic role
65. Supernatural being
66. Brisk, in music: Abbr.
67. Sailor's call
68. Greek isle
69. Part of a horseman's gear
70. Chaps
71. West Pointer

DOWN

1. Position
2. Of air pressure: Abbr.
3. Current play
4. Win over
5. King: Sp.
6. Prefix in botany
7. Shakespearian slave
8. Lao——
9. Fire
10. Legal grievances
11. Uses up
12. Novice
13. Glance over
19. P.G.A. player
21. Mohammedan
24. Pith
26. Arctic dweller
27. Carp
28. Climbing vine
29. Fodder
31. Wharton character
32. Legal excuse
33. Inveigles (with "in")
36. Potbellies
41. Latin abbreviation
44. City on the Delaware
46. Questioned in a way
50. Of a body system
52. Card
53. Of an ecological group
55. Skiers' lift
56. Sway
57. King of the Huns
59. Some votes
61. Shapeless mass
62. Other
64. State: Abbr.
65. Kitchen abbreviation

46.

ACROSS

1. Rebuff
5. Basic part
9. Printing term
13. ——my-thumb
14. Buzzing
15. Fulcrum pin
16. Designedly
18. Fanon
19. Waver
20. Barbara Frietchie and others
22. Dire
24. ——-tikki-tavi
25. Country house, in Russia
27. Patches
30. Porridge
33. Days of yore
35. River to English Channel
36. Droops
37. Be in accord with
38. Be in motion
39. Grape: Lat.
40. Magnate
41. Historic island
42. Friend of Odysseus
44. Glacial ice
46. Meted out
48. Carrier stops
51. Mixes
54. In direct succession
56. By and by
57. Prepared beforehand
59. Food acid
60. Bond
61. Cutting part
62. Gains
63. Auld lang ——
64. Indigos

DOWN

1. Ruined: Colloq.
2. Three trios
3. ——Peninsula
4. Caprices
5. Goatlike
6. Exclamation
7. Marsh grass
8. Eastern chieftain
9. Butcherbird
10. Precisely
11. French pronoun
12. Letters
15. Amassed
17. Highborn
21. Bring to perfection
23. Musical group
26. Voices
28. Familiar sign
29. Desertlike
30. Frowning
31. Travel
32. Doing
34. Feasted
37. Passengers
38. Supported
40. Spanish dance
41. Fur
43. Emblems
45. Describe
47. Smee and smew
49. Man's nickname
50. Army man, familiarly
51. Cinders
52. Part of a harness
53. Unimportant
55. Caustics
58. Short or long

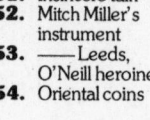

47.

ACROSS

1. Thoroughbred
10. Takes on
15. Evasion
16. Bouquet
17. Strips
18. Round bands
19. Scottish answer
20. Dam
21. Parts of an epic
22. Extra to a Highlander
24. French name
26. —— wild oat
27. Suffixes for bone
29. Asian evergreen
31. Wetland
32. Paganini's birthplace
34. Prefix for gate or dome
35. Three: Prefix
36. Mordant
38. Concocted
40. Enlistment places: Abbr.
41. Slack
43. Listens to
44. Johnny ——
45. Common French verb
46. Shape
47. Apropos of
49. A record, old style
51. Hit in a way
54. Cooks
56. Cuckoos
58. Excessively
59. Do a political chore
60. Lure
62. Chilean export
63. Most corpulent
64. Boats: Abbr.
65. Mast support

DOWN

1. Italian philosopher
2. Of the moon
3. Privately
4. By ——
5. Beer or ale
6. Also-rans
7. True being
8. Oppressive
9. Dental degree
10. Laughter
11. Handcuffs
12. Quintessence
13. Enabled
14. Ancient Persians
21. Barton
23. Zither's ancestor
25. —— river
28. Postpone
30. Bantu tongue
32. Military posts
33. Unconventional
34. Kind of squash
37. Particles
39. Document: Abbr.
42. Long
46. Flighty ones
48. Estaminet patron
50. Cavity: Prefix
52. Game animal
53. French door
55. Celestial lines: Abbr.
57. East Indian trees
60. Headache dosage: Abbr.
61. Native of a sort: Abbr.

48.

ACROSS

1. Nonprofessional
5. Kind of steamer
10. Evoke
14. Quality
15. Nest
16. Spread
17. Monkey
18. At
19. Pro ——
20. Yearly report
23. Processes in a way
24. Way: Abbr.
25. Dissolves
28. South African port
33. Then: Fr.
34. Breadwinners
35. Eggs
36. —— go
37. Fiend
38. Front
39. Scottish uncle
40. Worried
41. Refrigerate
42. Jolly
44. Offensively bold
45. Clumsy fellow
46. South African
47. Be formal
55. Twinge
56. Feminine name
57. Nichols character
58. —— ben Adhem
59. Kind of tube
60. State: Abbr.
61. Adjust
62. Europeans
63. Some votes

DOWN

1. Divination by ——
2. Entrance
3. Speck
4. Cowpoke's herd
5. Parts of locks
6. Shortens sails
7. Smell ——
8. —— mash
9. Darling children's teacher
10. Musical instrument
11. Turkish regiment
12. Apollo's mother
13. Banking deal
21. Spikes
22. Indians
25. Western capital
26. Brand of fig
27. Good citizen
28. Nautical float
29. Footless animal
30. Early gold lace
31. Angora and alpaca
32. Afresh
34. Incas' home
37. Spring flower
38. Hospital section
40. African lake
41. Indian
43. Oxford part
44. Shipworms
46. U.S. poet
47. Quarrel
48. Forbidden
49. After a while
50. Mets or Braves
51. Insincere talk
52. Mitch Miller's instrument
53. —— Leeds, O'Neill heroine
54. Oriental coins

'49.

ACROSS

1. Misbehave
6. Pet
11. British money: Abbr.
14. Sophisticated
15. Island, in Italy
16. Scoreboard trio
17. Example of lagniappe
19. —— tree
20. Watched
21. St. ——, France's West Point
22. Swerved
24. Craft of sorts
26. Unserviceable
27. Start of a game
31. Obligations
32. ——dare
33. Reluctant
35. Common French verb
38. Invigorating
40. Title of respect: Abbr.
41. Erect
42. Impress clearly
43. Snub
45. Communication initials
46. German philosopher
48. Passes
50. Louis XV's favorite
52. Neighbor of Ida
53. Poem
54. ——Paulo
56. Scoria
60. Increase
61. British composer
64. Wind direction
65. Littoral
66. Prepare new defenses
67. Measures: Abbr.
68. Attempt
69. Off-target

DOWN

1. French clergyman
2. The Great Pacificator
3. Receipts, familiarly
4. Depleted
5. Through
6. Redd up
7. Hebrew lyre
8. Dickens
9. Delightful
10. American Leaguer
11. Foul-weather gear
12. Bends the elbow
13. Stimuli
18. Gibe
23. Church man
25. A Saratoga purchase
26. Notable
27. Olympian
28. Army group
29. Containers of a sort
30. Ad lib
34. Fireproofing: Abbr.
36. Competition
37. Geologic times
39. All of ——
41. Remote
43. Altar screen
44. Bright light
47. Where the Alpheus flows
49. Shot
50. U.S. admiral
51. ——coming
54. Fencer's cry
55. Bohemian
57. Seaweed
58. Latin-American measure
59. Multitude
62. Common verb
63. Noun endings

50.

ACROSS

1. Lead
5. Shade of blue
10. October stone
14. Tops
15. Elevator sign
16. Fix
17. Score
18. Knitting stitch
19. Rock
20. Begin with energy
22. September stone
24. Greek letters
26. ——exempli
27. Flower for April
31. Doodad
35. U.S. author
36. Tennyson hero
38. Mountain: Prefix
39. Units in a code
40. Doers: Suffix
41. ——fide
42. Bravo
43. Opera name
44. Valentine objectives
45. Of the chin
47. February stone
49. In the center
51. Bell song
52. Flower for July
56. Load
60. Pointed arch
61. Quixote's foes
63. Princess in myth
64. Tolerate
65. Writer for Friday
66. English composer
67. Advantage
68. Ferments
69. Stingy

DOWN

1. Story
2. Spree
3. College subj.
4. Scheherazade and others
5. Kind of truck
6. Collection of quotes
7. ——the wrong way
8. Eastern faith
9. Leaks
10. Lady's-slipper
11. Fairy
12. Jewish month
13. Box
21. Down: Prefix
23. Drawing
25. Memberships
27. Sinful place
28. In good health
29. Used
30. Palm tree
32. Silly
33. Sea eagles
34. Skoal
37. High action
40. Single-hoofed animals
41. Native of an island vacation spot
43. Some people's headgear
44. Enliven
46. Participants in a wager
48. Uses a pencil top
50. Bedquilt of down
52. Wolf
53. Like good wine
54. Interpret
55. Prevalent
57. Golf word
58. Arm bone
59. Be the villain
62. Beneath contempt

51.

ACROSS

1. Leveling wedges
6. Is beholden to.
10. Branches
14. Spiral: Prefix
15. Gaming pieces
16. Trig
17. Fragrance
18. Underline
20. Mean
22. Math ratios
23. Locality: Suffix
24. Apollo's mother
25. Man's nickname
26. Title
27. Build up
32. Must
35. Acronym for short take-off craft
36. Babylonian god
37. Trifling
41. Goddess: Lat.
42. Metal clasping piece
43. Church part
44. Reckon
47. Little ——
48. Man's nickname
49. Hindu goddess
51. Dec. 31, for one
54. Of birds
57. Hybrid fruit
59. Censor
62. Mythical girl suicide
63. Regal name
64. Dismiss: Slang
65. Linen or cotton cloth
66. Black stuff
67. Periods of time
68. Norse sagas

DOWN

1. Ghost
2. —— to you
3. Translation of amo
4. Girl of song
5. Leek
6. Poet
7. Of course
8. Postwar U.S. agency
9. Choice: Abbr.
10. —— regime
11. Halter
12. Confusion
13. Jeanne and Bernadette
19. Russian log hut
21. Comparative ending
25. up to
26. I stand: Lat.
28. Disperse
29. Sacred bird
30. Fervor
31. French pronoun
32. Cloak
33. Once: Scot.
34. Shoo!
35. Shipped
38. Office copy, for short
39. Find one's way
40. Spanish aunt
45. "Pease porridge ——"
46. Teen hairdo
47. Fish-eating bird
50. Stops
51. Spanish hero
52. Behold: Fr.
53. Curves
54. Bow shapes
55. Tricycle, for short
56. Thought: Prefix
58. Electric force
60. Direction
61. Cote sound

52.

ACROSS

1. Hawaiian beach feature
5. Riders
10. Relative of Cheddar
14. Of the mouth
15. Hollywood man
16. Baltic port
17. Often-quoted newsmakers
20. Choruses
21. Chatters
22. City in Sicily
23. Eagerness
24. Farm group
27. Seethes underneath
31. Weapon
32. Dotted ——
33. Achieved
34. Bonne ——
35. Confines
36. Pelee overflow
37. Call of sorts
38. Climbs
39. Yields
40. Furtive
42. Prodigal
43. Not taped
44. Bern's river
45. Like Smokey
48. Calexico's county
52. A revolt of sorts
54. Scrutinize
55. Sidestep
56. Encircled
57. Gets the hot rod ready
58. Presumes
59. Midi summers

DOWN

1. Bon ——
2. Vase: Fr.
3. Rabble
4. City on the Arno
5. Lean times
6. Rendezvous rocket
7. N. L. team
8. Annapolis abbr.
9. Kind of order to a broker
10. Chore
11. Word book: Abbr.
12. Pulitzer winner, 1958
13. Gather
18. Cowpoke's territory
19. Soviet chain
23. Gives out
24. Spy
25. Spanish name
26. Aromatic plant
27. Danced in a way
28. Islands off Sicily
29. Wanders
30. Hide
32. Serge affliction
35. Splintered
36. Lifting power
38. Trappers' ware
39. Insert mark
41. Outsiders
42. Runs out
44. Ammonia compound
45. Familiar initials
46. Strong current
47. Czech
48. Danube tributary
49. Monogram: Abbr.
50. Palestine port
51. Rents
53. A Gabor

53.

ACROSS

1. Hippie's relative
8. Russian space vehicle
15. Frenchman's name
16. Worldly
17. Not pleasant
18. Back
19. Baseball great
20. German city
22. Axe
23. Gob
25. Sea call
27. Scoring base
31. German state
35. Inflate in value
36. Applies soil to
37. First year on calendar
38. Atlantic nation
40. Umpire's decision
41. Attitude
43. Contest in a way
45. End: Prefix
46. Entertainer of a kind
47. Robust
49. Rail pension unit: Abbr.
50. Obstreperous one
53. French port
55. Harte
59. Prior
61. Young birds
63. Permission
64. Clergyman's cap
65. Showed disdain
66. Appropriate

DOWN

1. "Oz" author
2. Sicilian town
3. Counsel: Abbr.
4. Appliance
5. Yugoslavia city
6. Weave
7. Small land areas
8. Load cargo
9. State: Abbr.
10. Indian bean
11. Racehorse
12. Black, in Siena
13. —— many words
14. Centerboard
21. See 8 Across
24. Fruit
26. More furtive
27. Elevate
28. Rounded
29. Bronze Star
30. Used
32. Ermine
33. Author of "On the Beach"
34. Chemical compound
36. Consider
39. Clear the ——
42. Cuddler
44. Double-talker
46. Trimmed, in a way
48. Bloated
50. Acoustical units
51. Shower
52. Using a bow: Music
54. Suets: Lat.
56. Sent back: Abbr.
57. Diminutive suffix
58. Nicholas
60. Banking abbreviation
62. Amount: Abbr.

54.

ACROSS

1. Chatters
5. Guatemala people
9. Deep drink
14. El Bahr
15. Bucolic sounds
16. Family member
17. Jewish month
18. Bar offerings
20. Port of Brazil
22. Whitetail
23. Mil. unit
24. Early Norse bards
26. Computer need
28. Inactive state
29. Slingshot ammo
33. Traffic situation
35. Out of the way
38. Part of R.F.D.
39. Etats ——
41. Roman goddess
42. Pyramid area
43. Passé
45. Frets
48. Miniscule
49. Extras
51. Mark of honor
53. Temperate
55. Least risky
57. Acknowledge
60. Barkley
62. Puffed
64. Tires
67. City south of Moscow
68. Veranda
69. Stead
70. Man's name
71. Inexorable
72. Small spring
73. Phoenicia's capital

DOWN

1. Growl
2. Staffmen
3. Racetrack worker
4. Magazine feature
5. Blocks
6. French pronoun
7. Soviet moonship
8. Invited
9. Football period
10. German conjunction
11. Rich in silica
12. Shun
13. Ending for song or gab
19. ——year
21. Circus employe
25. Protracts
27. Touch
30. Preoccupied state
31. Gown material
32. River of Germany
33. Relative of karate
34. Med. course
36. Musical symbol
37. Office V.I.P.'s
40. Feign
44. Movie
46. Recaps
47. Chesterfield
50. Part of a basket
52. Tackled
54. Does business
56. Tissue-like
57. Birds
58. Reporter's question
59. Mets or Reds
61. Ballet position
63. Title
65. Road surface
66. F.F.V. name

55.

ACROSS

1. Chest
5. Fevers: Abbr.
10. Wilson's predecessor
14. Droplet
15. Heep
16. Seth's father
17. One-time vamp
18. Ham's field
19. Restrain
20. Firm
22. What——
23. Family member
24. Hesitant sounds
25. River to the Moselle
27. Early Washington name
33. ——in need of
34. Turkish president
35. One of the maters
36. Winglike parts
37. Enrich
38. Store areas: Abbr.
39. Actress Rita
40. Type of verse meter
41. Mule parts
42. Economist
44. Bills
45. Pea or hazel
46. Madrid woman: Abbr.
47. Inventor of diving bell
49. Famous Peter Pan
56. Ule, for one
57. Comedian Fred
58. Lily plant
59. Hub
60. Canonical hours
61. Parcel out
62. Whistle-wetters
63. Russian stockade
64. O'Casey

DOWN

1. Biblical title
2. Interpret
3. Beloved in Italy
4. A drink
5. Spins
6. Quod——...
7. South of France
8. French bread
9. Pump
10. Knightly tunic
11. A certain node
12. Fairy: It.
13. Agents
21. Ethereal
24. Parisian water
25. Caesar, for one
26. Twosome
27. Muslim spirit
28. They say, in St. Lo
29. Booze
30. Wind direction
31. Widows' coins
32. Impertinence
33. Forsyte, for one
37. Business initials for a certain time
38. TV comic
40. Doer: Suffix
41. Rail
43. Eden and others
46. Grasp
47. Sicilians' Mongibello
48. Russian sea
49. Jungle neckpiece
50. Thanks——
51. Arm bone
52. Davy Jones' home
53. Hard——
54. Baseball's Manny
55. Spied

56.

ACROSS

1. Sergeant——
7. Spurt
10. Certain resources
14. Sideboard item
15. Middle East initials
16. Slangy reply
17. Captain——
19. Theater sign
20. Brewer's need
21. Butane, for one
22. College course, for short
23. Noncoms
24. Chateau——
25. Provisioner
29. Comeback
33. Began
34. Lieutenant——
35. One of seagoing trio
36. Grain
37. Contempt
38. General——
40. "Tristram Shandy" author
41. Dessert
42. Pauses of a sort
43. Layer
44. Ship's wheel
45. Worship
48. Arrive
49. Instrument
53. Pretty: Fr.
54. Corporal——
56. Iowa city
57. Tribe in Nigeria
58. Convert into particles
59. Color
60. Surfacing
61. Tolerates

DOWN

1. Mighty mite
2. Porous rock
3. Seed covering
4. Budget item
5. Pre-——
6. Extinguished
7. Early invaders of Britain
8. Peer
9. Beset
10. Marshal——
11. Old movie palace
12. Large-scale
13. Son of Adam
18. Sugar: Prefix
22. Trouser style
23. "We, the people ...", e.g.
24. Math chore: Abbr.
25. Panama gum trees
26. Following blindly
27. Future, for one
28. Private——
29. Bosh
30. Horsey sound
31. Return: It.
32. Sea birds
34. Spritely
36. Danube tributary
39. Turkish title
40. Soft cotton twill
42. Partly: Prefix
44. ——guard
45. Open
46. Major——
47. Bravos
48. Early plane-hijackers goal
49. All: Prefix
50. Star in Eridanus
51. French numeral
52. French summers
54. Stone
55. Quoits peg

57.

ACROSS

1. Skipper: Abbr.
5. Name in French history
10. Urban nuisance
14. Angler's need
15. Rotund
16. Acquired (with "by")
17. Greek god
18. World-weary
19. King
20. Dessert
22. Part of a news dispatch
24. Scotsman's so
25. Baker's need
26. Police pavement-pounder
30. Twin, in a way
34. Booth
35. Stadium sounds
37. Legal paper
38. Metric measure
39. Cuts, in surgery
41. Army officers: Abbr.
42. A Beatle
44. Unfailing
45. Kind of club
46. Will item
48. Dreamer
50. Free-for-all
52. American Indian
53. Ammunition
56. Safe
59. One of an eager trio
60. Muse of poetry
62. Pakistan's neighbor
63. Kind of generation
64. Castor began derivative
65. Caustic stuff
66. Sea areas
67. Location
68. Hats: Slang

DOWN

1. Sound of approval
2. Emanation
3. Broadway fixture
4. Having a will
5. —— Dick
6. Latin case: Abbr.
7. Bawls out
8. Musical tempo direction
9. Waver
10. A triangle
11. African land
12. Muscat and ——
13. Biologist's concern
21. Money back: Abbr.
23. Wrongs
26. Spread outward
27. Lemur
28. Assayer's concern
29. Kiln
31. Former opera soprano
32. Western park
33. Replace
36. Run before the wind
39. Accustomed manners
40. Palmer's need
43. Rubber rings
45. Pertaining to ice floes
47. Surgeon's needs
49. "Peer Gynt" character
51. Japanese portal
53. Coffee cake
54. Over, to Germans
55. Symbol of silence
56. "—— and Lovers"
57. Foray
58. Results
61. Teutonic sky god

58.

ACROSS

1. Sea
6. Latin grammar word
10. Roof part
14. Flavorful seed
15. Signalled, in a way
17. Words of wisdom
18. Putting in order
19. Pegasus
20. Australian tree-dweller
21. Former U.N. name
22. First-rate
24. Sea queens
26. Name for a Parisienne
28. —— as the hills
30. Municipal officer: Abbr.
31. Goat willow
33. Hebrew letter
37. Area of France
39. Common contraction
40. African tree
41. Senator from Indiana
42. Greek letters
44. Distillery item
45. Egyptian city
47. Medicine chest item
49. Father of genetics
52. Woody or Mel
53. In the manner of
54. Runyon
57. Rye fungus
60. A Plantagenet
62. Puerto ——
63. Like some violets
64. Dried up
65. Colors
66. Hindu
67. Clans

DOWN

1. Bounders
2. Step ——
3. Part of the Asian landscape
4. Abaft
5. Certain wires
6. Alert
7. Spanish painter
8. Indian city
9. Butterfly
10. Breakfast item
11. Spry
12. Arrive, in France
13. Borders
16. "For want of —— "
23. Rural songsters
25. Western state: Abbr.
26. Door post
27. Kazan
28. Standish stand-in
29. For a ——
32. City in Ohio
34. Trophy
35. Enthusiasm
36. Lot
38. "—— a little nut tree . . ."
43. Vintage sherries
46. Body style
48. Mock
49. Lowland
50. Root
51. Iridescent substance
52. Near to, old style
55. Renaissance date
56. Farm sound
58. Oven
59. Explosives
61. Pronoun

59.

ACROSS

1. Hesitates
5. Spar
9. Intoxicating
14. Stage direction
15. ——out
16. A Ford
17. Uris's "——18"
18. Unaspirated consonant
19. Proportional charges
20. Broadway show
23. Capitol Hill frequenter
24. Manitoba Indian
25. Pallid
26. What Italian's ella means
27. Gay blade
31. Perfect
34. Operatic segment
36. Free from
37. Phrase from show of 53 Across
40. Samuel's teacher
41. Trite: Colloq.
42. Type of blouse
43. Dismissed
45. Tit for ——
46. Fall behind
47. Leave undone
49. Resplendent
53. "Laugh-In" stars
56. Pivotal
57. Nonsense character
58. Orchestra man: Abbr.
59. Aside
60. Raison d' ——
61. Celestial being: Fr.
62. "Peter Pan" lass
63. Fix
64. Started a hole

DOWN

1. Bhang and abaca
2. Banish
3. Edison's Ohio birthplace
4. Avoid
5. "Il Penseroso" poet
6. Close to, poetically
7. Canzone
8. Perfidious business
9. Ruhr city
10. Pencil part
11. Architectural pier
12. Per ——
13. An answer
21. Type style
22. One of the Horae
26. Fragrance
28. Jejune
29. Sort
30. Nervous
31. Burl
32. Cross out
33. Shamrock land
34. Trick
35. Eritrean city
38. Out
39. Ocelot or serval
44. Heading for
46. Massed
48. Oscar winner
49. Embellish
50. Expiate
51. Suffusing shade
52. Called a halt
53. Cheap cigar
54. Pearl Buck heroine
55. Remark
56. Handle rudely

60.

ACROSS

1. Fenced
6. Trampled
10. Sound of impact
14. Like greatly, informally
15. Golden or general
16. Moki Indian
17. Beans
18. Mine passage
19. Wild goat
20. Type of type
21. A bird's reply
23. Nice and Aspen
25. Sister of Ares
26. Small container
28. Inviter to a parlor
32. Set out
37. Staircase, in Sicily
38. Part of the eye
39. Bleak
41. Actor Ladd
42. Betrothal notice
44. Slender
46. Got away from
48. Augur
49. Kind of estate
51. Most heedless
56. Hub for Congressmen
60. Old school necessity
61. Bird of prey
62. Kon-
63. Old card
64. Nonworking
65. Of an age
66. Former dancer Castle
67. State of being: Suffix
68. Escritoire
69. Gives up

DOWN

1. Like a stake
2. Italian river
3. City of Peru
4. A Muse
5. Merit
6. Deals
7. Unpolished
8. Kind of drab
9. Causes second thoughts
10. Word for Milne's works
11. Rods rider
12. Mimic
13. Mexican Indian
22. Clothing mishaps
24. Cans
27. Items measured in Calaveras County
29. Modern painter
30. Impetuosity
31. Chimed
32. Kind of root
33. A White House room
34. Item in a cafe window
35. May apples
36. Dairy product
40. Leg part
43. Go after
45. Severe
47. Flitted
50. French river
52. Signal
53. Describing an otary
54. Word with sand or cobble
55. French heads
56. Jabber
57. Stow cargo
58. Birds
59. Cheeses made by Trappists

61.

ACROSS

1. Unfamiliar
4. ——crossroads
9. Workplace
13. Urchin
15. Argentine name
16. Corrida star
17. European leader
18. Makeup: Colloq.
19. Single
20. Series time
22. Blackbird
24. Cafeteria gear
25. Draw off
26. Disclose
29. Electioneers
33. Bearing
34. Arrange in a certain way
37. Residence, in Soho
38. Dessert items
39. French beverage
40. Suburban implement
43. Long-necked guitar
45. Sight——
46. Light wraps
47. Sweeten the pot
49. Basra's country
50. Small heron
53. Habitué
57. Together, in music
58. In difficulty
60. Leningrad's river
61. Foists, with "off"
62. European
63. Forbidding
64. Shoe or slipper
65. TV, in Soho
66. Cheer for 16 Across

DOWN

1. Western pact
2. Famed explorer
3. Electrical unit
4. Attraction
5. Lachrymose
6. Numerical prefix
7. Chinese warehouses
8. Commits
9. Conceited: Colloq.
10. Aviary sound
11. By word
12. Spar
14. Arcturus's constellation
21. Soft cheese
23. Proceedings
26. Apia's island
27. "—— is an island"
28. Considers
30. "Can Do," for one
31. Sound of irritation
32. Seventh sons
34. Yak away
35. Luau accompaniment
36. Dry: Prefix
38. Shrink
41. Least cluttered
42. Word on the wall
43. ——State, in Burma
44. Wearying
46. Compact
48. ——nous
49. Goal
50. Golf stroke
51. Revered one
52. Brass member
54. Thermometer reading
55. Malefic
56. Christen
59. Money of Lima

62.

ACROSS

1. Range finder
6. Fictional sleuth
10. Cavernous openings
14. Hebrew precept
15. Irish isles
16. English painter
17. Gladden
18. Like housewife's work
20. Quill
21. Pick out
23. Tributary stream
24. Honeyed word
26. Peruvian coins
27. Infuriate
29. ——two
33. ——for one's money
34. Single-colored textiles
36. Rubber tree
37. Kind of tire
39. Resinous substance
40. Mesa dwellers
42. German pronoun
43. Friendly
46. Venison
47. Onetime site of Yale
49. Medals
51. Supports
52. Heads the cast
53. Urbane
56. Son of Noah
57. Partner of flow
60. Leastwise
62. Baptista's home
64. Friendly talk
65. Historic waterway
66. Set in a way
67. Sharps and flats
68. Machine of a sort
69. Punkie

DOWN

1. Procedure
2. Hercules's captive
3. Luxembourg, for one
4. Fedora
5. Spore cases
6. Brave
7. Russian city
8. Hebrew letter
9. Undivided
10. Unassuming
11. Like peas in——
12. Oporto export
13. Prophet
19. Hot-dog additive
22. Coffeemakers
25. Poet Millay
26. Star in Virgo
27. Home-run star
28. Betel palm
29. Not busy
30. Supplanted
31. Epic poem
32. Homes for fledglings
35. Medleys
38. Equivalence
41. Sharif
44. Up-to-daters
45. Slow
48. Part of L.B.J.
50. Money for Hiawatha
52. Newspaper, familiarly
53. Kind of floating ice
54. Sioux
55. Indolent
56. Normandy town
58. Cork for a cask
59. Invited
61. Complain
63. Nepal peak

63.

ACROSS

1. Sound
5. Planet
10. Wad of tobacco
14. Came down
15. Old Greek district
16. Homely
17. Awkward spot
18. Fast draws
20. Exclamation
21. Golf shot
22. Weeds, for short
23. Baby garments
25. Dagger
26. Elevator buttons
27. Solitary
31. Eastern judges
34. Feature of a U.S. building
35. Guinness
36. Meandered
37. Provided
38. House features
40. Sidestep
41. Export shipping
42. Glasgow negative
43. Of a glacial period
44. Oil well feature
48. Confine
50. But: Fr.
51. Greek letter
52. Stimulating
54. Lock-up
55. Migrate
56. Western farm
57. Ferber
58. Lectures: Abbr.
59. Bond and others
60. Gatherings of sorts

DOWN

1. Sunken fences
2. Greeting in Oahu
3. Popular shrub
4. Hot time in Nice
5. Irritates
6. Clods
7. Constituent
8. Fixation
9. Describing some shady walks
10. Liquid of sorts
11. Language: Prefix
12. Seine features
13. Bad: Prefix
19. Warning cries
21. Little animals
24. Some bridge holdings
25. Birds in the news
27. Item in a librairie
28. Music halls
29. Heal
30. Italian family
31. Hacks
32. Wings
33. Prefix for logue
34. Peas, beans, etc.
36. Kitchen appliances
39. Tea or milk
40. Corn on the cob
42. Whinnies
44. Reel
45. Turkish decree
46. Ridge
47. Nuts
48. Positive
49. Row
50. Prefix with skirt
52. Measures: Abbr.
53. Fabric surface
54. Stuart

64.

ACROSS

1. House, in Mexico
5. Neighbor of Ark.
9. Roof style
14. Wartime Secretary of State
15. Nothing for Pierre
16. Rainbow: Prefix
17. Seed covering
18. Suffixes meaning doers
19. Dogpatch character
20. Talk too soon
23. ——tizzy
24. Gather discards
25. Fish
27. Within: Prefix
28. Casserole
31. Free: Sp.
34. Extra
36. Name for a pet
37. Lined up, in poetry
38. Revises
39. Music group
40. Draped garment
41. Metal piece
42. River of Burns poem
43. Superficial
45. Blood vessel: Prefix
47. Loafer
48. Bridge item
52. Cereal
54. A certain voter
56. Lopez
58. Bond
59. Spanish peso
60. Playfully
61. Eagle
62. Boy's name
63. Turkish Moslem student
64. On its last ——
65. Virginia, for instance

DOWN

1. Gossips
2. Containing gold
3. ——cog
4. Ended
5. Adjust to
6. Part with, as money
7. River of oblivion
8. Handle: Lat.
9. Crown
10. Heavenly body
11. Girls' fashion
12. British statesman
13. Dumb ——
21. Hawaiian goose
22. Approaches
26. Baseball player
28. Going over the same route
29. Prefix for matic
30. Brightest point
31. Maid
32. Asian nation
33. Afflict with ennui
35. Veneto or Corso
38. A Kennedy
42. Taj Mahal site
44. Wright, Jr. or Sr.
46. Aristocrats
48. Intimidate
49. Feather
50. High dwelling
51. Diverting
52. U.S. inventor
53. Italian river
55. Steelworker's leader
57. Pistachio

65.

ACROSS

1. Peer Gynt's creator
6. U.S. tennis star
10. Fastening device
14. Relative of NATO
15. Contest
16. Concerning
17. Dostoevsky title (with "The")
18. Battle of 1775
20. French salt
21. Examination
23. Pain
24. Morsel
26. Flaubert heroine
28. Stimulus
30. Butterfly
31. Perch
32. One of the Little Women
33. Buenos ——
37. Lawyer: Abbr.
38. Dividing line
41. Basketball league: Abbr.
42. Okinawan port
44. Repulsive
45. Wore
47. Punctilious ones
49. Honshu metropolis
50. Viscous
52. Glossy varnish
53. At full speed, old style
54. Match parts, in a game
55. Sheep
58. Fellini film (with "La")
61. Blackbird
63. Prefix with morph or plasm
64. Sacred
65. Quaff
66. Card game
67. Scoots
68. Irish poet

DOWN

1. Cow-headed goddess
2. "Venerable" historian
3. Heavy canvas
4. W. W. II initials
5. Almost
6. Extemporize
7. Focal point in Mideast
8. Bewitch
9. Samuel's teacher
10. Rider
11. Old Times Sq. hotel
12. Hard
13. Jigger's relative
19. Blue
22. Masked man: Abbr.
25. Literary initials
26. Silly: Colloq.
27. Emperor 1900 years ago
28. Football's Tarkenton
29. Tittle
30. Zoo attraction
32. Carriage
34. Suharto's country
35. —— and his dog
36. Mideast capital
39. Sally
40. Musical piece
43. Fruit
46. Eastern title
48. Part of an old alphabet
49. Man's nickname
50. Atelier wear
51. 1945 conference site
52. Casual wear
53. Cool drinks
54. Period
56. Left
57. Fraternal group
59. Namely, Lat. abbr.
60. Here, in Paris
62. Noun suffix

66.

ACROSS

1. Variety of pear
5. More discerning
10. Casa division
14. Eye part
15. Suppress
16. Biblical name
17. Dozes
18. Violin maker
19. Goddess of Victory
20. Substance in wheat flour
22. Region in Central Asia
24. Philippine island
26. Serve at tea
27. Sounds off
30. Close
34. German exclamation
35. Glossy
37. Gaze
38. Bifurcation
40. City in China
42. Scope
43. Whip
45. Cowboy
47. Home: Abbr.
48. Cowardly: Colloq.
50. Strengthening
52. Sculling equipment
54. Poisonous snake
55. Part
59. Counsel
62. Hideaway
63. Ointments
65. Holiday times
66. Lamp
67. Speak hoarsely
68. —— to high heaven
69. Je ——
70. Former columnist Hopper
71. Inquires

DOWN

1. Stopper
2. Face shape
3. Gloomy
4. —— Gandolfo
5. In a meager manner
6. Prepare for action
7. One of the Marianas
8. Prevent
9. African game, for short
10. Resident in 10 Across
11. West Indian shrub
12. Norse god
13. On the briny
21. Nestling
23. Courage: Slang.
25. Arabian ruler
27. A Dean
28. Place for French teacher
29. Mexican gentleman
31. Tales
32. Color
33. Kind of cake
36. Tropical tree
39. Metric weight
41. State associated with Lincoln
44. Dark soil
46. Way
49. Tool
51. Mexican muralist
53. Kind of drum
55. Escaped
56. Deserve: Colloq.
57. Primitive Japanese
58. Stepped
60. Search
61. Some Alaskans: Abbr.
64. Family member

67.

ACROSS

1. Blue-nose
5. Note in a date book: Abbr.
9. Sassy
13. Nader subject
14. Paris time
15. Outburst
16. European
17. Essential
19. Transmit, in a way
21. Pressing
22. Bullish time
23. Thousand: Prefix
24. Lodestone
27. A kind of literature
31. Signboard symbol
32. Lost freshness
33. Rocket fuel
34. Movable property
35. Indulge
36. Ferrer
37. Elected ones
38. Part of the street scene
39. Flicker
40. Turns over
42. Take away
43. Weather word
44. ——fide
45. Wading bird
48. Decorative ties
52. Consumer complaint
54. Imitate
55. Where the Yalu flows
56. Place for an étoile
57. Pother
58. Farm animals
59. Small dogs
60. Simplify

DOWN

1. Beyond
2. Control
3. Type of type: Abbr.
4. Rockefeller
5. Baseball play
6. Aplomb
7. Languish
8. Three, in Italy
9. Large bottle
10. Highway feature
11. Golf bag item
12. Confined
15. Rolled up
18. Tremble
20. Outlook
23. Renown
24. Enchanting
25. Where the action is
26. Comprehension
27. Richmond's river
28. "The Man ——"
29. Finishes second
30. Put forth
32. Friction match
35. Joyous sound
36. Eastern people
38. White: It.
39. Nictitate
41. Participates
42. Carpenter's pins
44. Duffer's score
45. Laugh-getter
46. Declare openly
47. Part of parrot's bill
48. Con——, in music
49. Numerical prefix
50. Pronoun
51. Afflicted
53. Stage turn

68.

ACROSS

1. Vacation spot
5. Truck parts
9. Even if, for short
14. Blue shade
15. Sioux
16. Perfume ingredient
17. Plum brandy
19. Met's cousin in Italy
20. Card game
21. Cossack chief
22. Bows
23. Dance
24. Neckwear
27. Cowslip
30. Israeli port
31. Cheerless
33. Thin strip
34. Fixed: Abbr.
35. Tricorn
36. Pier group: Abbr.
37. Preserved
39. Soft speech sounds
41. Difficulty
42. Certain actresses
44. ——foie. . .
46. Sunday fare
47. Irish village
48. "Not even ——"
50. Minimal
54. Intimidate
55. Asian
56. Dumbbell
57. ——part
58. Albion's neighbor
59. Supported (with)
60. Besides
61. Word of warning

DOWN

1. Groom
2. Upolu port
3. Chagall
4. Appease
5. Twisted an arm
6. Mainstay
7. Roll of cloth
8. Witness
9. Canterbury's Saint ——
10. Scripture readers
11. Canvas net
12. Spanish greeting
13. Oriental heroine
18. Port of Italy
21. Animal coat
23. Fireplace
24. Suns
25. Musical group
26. Outsert
27. Certain songs
28. Waldorf
29. Floor: Fr.
32. Mitchell hero
38. Defeat
39. ——majesty
40. Like commuters, sometimes
41. Like some glass
43. Wore
45. Constellation
47. French relative
48. Increases
49. Hawaiian island
50. Austrian physicist
51. Black, in Rome
52. Hindu month
53. Seasonal period
55. Tabby

69.

ACROSS

1. Humble
6. After pi
9. Devour
14. Not so bright
15. Long time
16. Metric measure
17. It has tips for good dining
19. Cuban dance
20. Pronoun
21. Jewish month
22. Part
23. Fair amount
26. Accident
28. Make tracks
29. Indian tribe
32. Pilaster
33. Sight of Salt Lake City
37. Berate
39. Macadamia
40. Moving line
41. Priestly
44. Chalcopyrites
45. Invite
46. Goddess of dawn
47. Early ascetic
49. Entreated
52. Hockey player
55. Aspire to
56. Legendary Chinese emperor
59. Helmet
60. Little G. & S. girl
62. A kind of rule
63. Brew
64. Lariat
65. Ganges sights
66. Reply
67. Yuccalike plant

DOWN

1. Timber trees of Brazil
2. Shindig
3. Mountain climber's gear
4. Sargasso ——
5. Printing mistakes
6. Splendid
7. Muslim beauty
8. Cricket sides
9. Quite edible
10. United
11. Watch over
12. Importune
13. Anjou
18. Make fit
22. Cooking direction
24. Chicago airport
25. Greek letter
26. —— regiment of troops
27. Early Peruvians
29. Timid one
30. Strange
31. Perfume
34. Win by ——
35. Word of exception
36. Rebelled
38. Recluses
42. Info
43. Jumped
48. Pilots
49. —— France
50. Greenland base
51. Surf sounds
52. Sound of surprise
53. Paris airport
54. Muslim ruler
57. Limousine
58. Gem
60. Horse color
61. Spanish river

70.

ACROSS

1. Taste
7. Old fellow
13. Outstanding
15. A. L. team
17. Like a feather
18. Vicious circle
19. Pindaric poem
20. Steel mill group
22. Hosiery shade
23. More expensive
25. Held onto
26. Breed of fowl
28. Knight in a fight
32. British novelist
33. Cooperative
37. Prepared for a rainy day
39. Portentous
40. East Coast bay
42. Carthaginians' last stand
43. Spends
44. French writer: 1823-92
45. Sloping way
48. Testers
50. Hole-in-one
51. Apes
54. A dog, for short
57. Old weapon
59. Quondam
61. Cloying words
62. Felt hats
63. Lower
64. They make the grade

DOWN

1. Pumpkin or squash
2. Surrounded by
3. Typical Musial hit
4. Harding or Sheridan
5. Jasmine dealer
6. Script direction
7. Author Vidal
8. Tree of Morocco
9. Suits
10. Favoring
11. Make exultant
12. A kind of tire
14. Message-sending machines
16. Mailed
21. Group of three: Abbr.
24. Slackens
25. Old German coin
26. Opposite of fem
27. Indian nurse
29. Snug, as a roof
30. Correct
31. Humpty Dumpty
33. Bit player in Hollywood
34. Happen
35. Van Druten's "—— Camera"
36. Highland group
38. Prosecutors: Abbr.
41. Item from Flint
44. Shade of green
45. Transported
46. Squirrel's tidbit
47. Donnybrook
49. —— tube
51. Master of counterpoint
52. Wheel shaft
53. Lager
55. Poet
56. Jumble
58. Use up
60. Kiddie

ACROSS

1. Barney of ring fame
5. Thrash
10. Perform
14. Latin conjugation word
15. Weight
16. De ——
17. Retreat
20. Sign on a zoo house
21. Waterway
22. Letter, British style
23. Marina sight
25. Censured
29. Famed ballet company
32. Erudition
33. Bristles
34. Bend in a ship's plank
36. Makes a comeback
40. Oolong
41. Malay boats
42. Coagulate
43. Agrees to
45. First Stuart king
47. Some fliers
48. Ingot
49. —— frutti
52. Legends, photowise
57. Start of an alibi
60. Forest animal
61. Anything that tempers
62. Key symbols
63. Actual being
64. To a tee
65. Uriah

DOWN

1. Incline
2. Bradley
3. Literary pseudonym
4. Restrain
5. Paid the bill
6. Baited
7. Aardvark meal
8. I, in Leipzig
9. Light-Horse Harry
10. Pedestal base
11. Hiatus
12. Wheel support
13. Day before: Abbr.
18. Daunt
19. Gallery sounds
23. Nocturnal insects
24. Wings
25. Fruit decay
26. I —— parade
27. Spaces
28. Chess pieces
29. Greek letters
30. "—— Mio"
31. Japanese boxes
33. Places, as a cue ball
35. Abominable Snowman
37. Coin
38. Vase: Fr.
39. Metric units: Abbr.
44. Literary form
45. Jesting talk
46. Wiles
48. Confusion
49. Neap or rip
50. Shoshoni
51. Very: Fr.
52. Sac
53. Yen
54. Woodwind
55. Art subject
56. Phase
58. Latin goddess
59. Plan

ACROSS

1. Shapeless drop
5. In style
9. Equal
13. —— sunshine
15. Kind of weed
16. Malayan knife
17. Huron and Mohawk
20. Pince- ——
21. Chance
22. Twenty, at Monte Carlo
23. Swamplands
24. Retreats
25. Title for a woman
28. Essential part
29. Taste
32. Critical
33. To boot
34. Fountain item
35. Garden pests
38. City on the Oka
39. Fired
40. Herbage
41. Flushed
42. —— of worms
43. Storied ship
44. Tear at
45. Power unit
46. Korean metropolis
48. Rumanian city
49. Eau-de- ——
52. Salad garnish
55. Campus group
56. Kicked in a way
57. Append
58. God, in old Rome
59. Pitching statistics
60. Braces

DOWN

1. Cereal
2. Dress material
3. Court cry
4. City division: Abbr.
5. Categorize
6. Highway sound
7. Here: Fr.
8. Talk
9. Pelts
10. One of a Kipling trio
11. Popular garnish
12. Feminine ending
14. Name for relief pitchers
18. Movie, in Madrid
19. Wine's tagalong
23. Calamitous
24. Question
25. Army man
26. Not —— in the world
27. Tricked
28. Opponent of Pericles
29. Large gannet
30. That is: Lat.
31. Suburb of Paris
33. Word of disgust
34. Structural piece
36. Intensify
37. Self-centered one
42. His: Fr.
43. Groundwork
44. Outlays
45. Hospital divisions
46. Guaranteed
47. Son of Isaac
48. Impression
49. Outlook
50. Preposition
51. Personalities
52. Postal initials
53. Correlative
54. Perch

73.

(This one has a gimmick to look out for.)

ACROSS

1. Paid attendance
5. Pal
9. Guinness or Templeton
13. Mediterranean port
14. Western city
15. "This —— be love . . ."
17. Northern European
18. "—— been working on . . ."
19. Wabash or Ohio
20. Delightful
22. Dour
23. "Please —— eat the . . ."
24. Part of a Louvre name
26. Location
27. According to
29. South European currency
31. Dramatist Connelly
34. Having similar features
40. Dirksen, et al.
42. Mama's night order
43. Connoisseur of claret, port, etc.
45. Promises
46. ——'clock
47. U.S. humorist
49. Mediterranean sailboat
53. Chew on
55. Jeanne ——
59. Philippic
61. School term
63. South American fruit
64. "—— a long, long way . . ."
65. European capital
66. First name of a Jewish society
67. Not horizontal: Abbr.
68. Saltate
69. Cash holder
70. Neighborhood
71. Time periods

DOWN

1. Leave the straight and narrow
2. Plowed land
3. A claw
4. Play interlude
5. Farm structure
6. —— never be the same
7. Reveals
8. Man's nickname
9. Prefix for height
10. Covert homes
11. Literary postscript
12. "L'état ——. . ."
16. Ash
21. Ocean: Abbr.
22. Turkish sea
25. Long confinement
28. Put in order
30. German composer
31. Trim the lawn
32. Uris's hero
33. Took off
35. German port
36. "—— Sweet Song"
37. Nigerian people
38. Fresh
39. Wares: Abbr.
41. Indian
44. Browning device
48. Gettysburg initials
49. Casca's blow
50. "—— we got fun"
51. Teheran resident
52. Waterway
54. "—— all pals together . . ."
56. Bemused
57. Kind of race
58. Farmer's concern
60. Irish legislature
62. River to Lake Ilmen
64. Marsh elder

74.

ACROSS

1. Volcanic rock
6. Secular
10. River of Poland
14. A vocal style: Abbr.
15. Pelion's companion
16. Noble: Ger.
17. City in Turkey
18. Wedding music of sorts
20. British system, for one
22. Historic French river
23. Kind of pickle
24. Western plains bird
26. Name for Henry V
28. Backs down
31. Pub item
32. Figures of speech
33. Danube tributary
37. Ball club
39. Hole ——
40. God: Fr.
41. Dundee man
42. Railroad spur
44. "—— a drop to drink"
45. Paperhanger's receptacle
47. Objective
48. Man in the ring
51. Home for a jinni
53. Bring together
54. Victoria's Prime Minister
58. Store employe
61. Actor's part
62. Cuchulainn's wife
63. Sheep genus
64. Canal Zone city
65. Gielgud and others
66. Newcastle's river
67. Small anvil

DOWN

1. Mine vehicle
2. Renovate
3. Not hold ——
4. Biblical mountain
5. Hollywood hopeful
6. Lomond or Katrine
7. Ghastly
8. O. T. book: Abbr.
9. Sedan
10. Inspected, as troops
11. Make —— for it
12. Canton of the Jungfrau
13. Outsider
19. "Othello" character
21. French Franciscan nun
24. Picturesque
25. Ordnance depots
26. Radio buffs
27. Writer Waugh
29. Word on a marquee
30. English pottery
34. Old Irish shilling
35. A kind of sign
36. Voiceless, in phonetics
38. Historic church
43. Greet warily, dog style
46. Olympian god
48. Hoaxes
49. As a friend: Fr.
50. Office worker
52. Historic ship
54. Albania's longest river
55. German girl's name
56. Zodiac sign and others
57. "There —— any more"
59. Achieved
60. Campus vine

ACROSS

1. English school
5. Nagging one
10. Rights and lefts
14. Bean
15. Trifle with
16. Incite
17. River of Bolivia
18. What to do with four aces
19. Christmas trio
20. Onassis
22. Nut
23. Mountain ramble
24. Bruiting
26. Stumblebum
29. Made the first play
30. Brusque
31. Hang loosely
33. A kind of ad
37. Preposition
38. Cloud nine
40. Roused
41. Curb
43. Variety of ink
44. Stopper
45. ——'em
47. Book ——
48. Dangerous mine gas
51. Fall forecast
53. Propelled in a way
54. Dryad
59. Actor Beerbohm
60. Headdress
61. Untypical
62. Greek letters
63. Ledger entry
64. Catch-all abbreviation
65. Gold vein
66. Rhythm, British style
67. Ground corn

DOWN

1. Italian island
2. Shoelace, for one
3. All: Prefix
4. Former film actor
5. Crawl or trudgen
6. Vehement
7. Wading bird
8. Perfumes
9. Little
10. Early American settlement
11. Counting devices
12. Originated
13. Pain sharply
21. Floor material
22. Muslim divines
25. Common possessive
26. Fragrance
27. English composer
28. Pianist Waller
32. Food with a milk base
33. Fasten
34. Protuberance
35. Allied
36. Symbol of heaviness
38. Farm structure
39. Moreover
42. Way
43. Sacred image
45. Maker of points
46. An acid salt
48. Stopover spot
49. An —— the ground
50. Tire part
52. Ancient instruments
55. Kiln
56. First name in spying
57. Hyde Park sight
58. Lend a hand
60. Cap

ACROSS

1. Influence
5. Angers
9. Island nation
14. Piece of gossip
15. Fissure
16. Polish province
17. Right angles
18. Court proceedings
19. Month
20. Recent: Prefix
21. Capable (with "to")
22. Port of Brazil
23. Try sorely
25. Canvas canopy
27. Auditing word
28. Dashed against
31. Turkish coins
33. Chicago name
34. Small piece
35. Small paper book: Abbr.
38. Horror movie figure
40. King Kong
42. Teacher's ——
43. Roof ornaments
45. Bookmark of sorts
46. Western clay
47. Hellen, to Hellenes
48. Austrian composer
51. Loosely woven silk
53. Morsel
54. Pale
56. Certain signs
58. Self
61. Early age
62. Japanese race
63. A violation, in sports
64. Tears
65. Twist, as wool
66. Precept
67. Neighborhoods
68. Mrs. Dick Tracy
69. Seat of Nobel Institute

DOWN

1. British gun
2. Raised surface
3. Share
4. An answer
5. Baghdad's republic
6. Snip over again
7. Involves
8. Losing velocity
9. Maid of Orleans
10. Shocks
11. —— Alegre, Brazil
12. Otherwise
13. Dickens girl and others
21. Acted strongly
24. Pile: Fr.
26. Electron tube
28. Frolic
29. Succulent plant
30. Color worker's vat
32. Suitable
35. Fruitful
36. Recess activity
37. Injury
39. Dinner item
41. Stravinsky
44. Nautical measure
46. Program
48. Gateway to Russia in W.W. II
49. Chemical compound
50. Geneva's river
52. Cartes
55. Cape
57. Lumps
59. Delude
60. Spread
63. Partner of to

77.

ACROSS

1. Biblical book
5. Uncouth ones
10. Machine part
14. Mountain pass
15. Asian land
16. Assam silkworm
17. Detain
20. U.S. violinist
21. Alcoves
22. Hazard
25. Game animal
26. Angelico
28. Caucho trees
30. Football kick
34. Atmosphere: Prefix
35. Location
36. Hand over
37. Willy-nilly
42. —— eye
43. Biblical pronoun
44. Free from
45. Strip
48. Nautical man
49. Hesitant sounds
50. Irish hill
52. —— fuse
54. Showing response
58. Of destiny
61. Like Pearl White's friends
64. Meadow mouse
65. Lab liquid
66. Uniform
67. Farm animals
68. Upright
69. Support

DOWN

1. Middlemen: Abbr.
2. Gossip
3. Enter
4. Cubic meter
5. Container
6. Ottawa's prov.
7. Reputation
8. Style of potatoes
9. Barbecue items
10. Fattens, in a way
11. Greek god
12. Sidekick
13. X and beta
18. Influx
19. Small spring
23. Hipbones
24. Permits
26. Defied
27. Plunder, old style
29. Denominations
31. Restoring
32. "Robin——"
33. Provides, as aid
38. Grasps
39. Melville captain
40. Fee
41. Interrupt
46. Tropical fruit
47. —— bragh
51. Of birds
53. A kind of polo
54. Cleave
55. Plenty, to Omar
56. Tamarisk salt tree
57. Behold!
59. City in Iowa
60. Spring period
62. Relatives
63. Roulette bet

78.

ACROSS

1. One man, many women
6. Assist
10. Dwell on
14. Pass over
15. Major or Minor
16. Field
17. Fast
18. Quality of a honky-tonk piano
20. Part of Sermon on the Mount
22. French painter
23. Volume
24. Inducing sleep
25. Ill humor
28. Mineral
29. Pincers
30. —— retriever
35. Orbed
36. Impediment
37. Stretch forward
38. Sinbad, for one
40. Authenticated
41. Drowse
42. Minnesotan
43. Singing group
47. Gossip: Colloq.
48. Lincoln Center unit
49. Confirmed
54. Constant
56. City in Vermont
57. Formerly
58. Gudrun's spouse
59. Light: Prefix
60. Cheers
61. —— noire
62. Force, as payment

DOWN

1. Aromatic plant
2. Winglike parts
3. River bank: Lat.
4. Do a newspaper job
5. Winter cruise area
6. Fall
7. June figure
8. Old slave
9. Thrash
10. Asian capital
11. Amphitheater
12. Put in a new place
13. Sham gem
19. Subtle
21. —— the mark
24. Sphere
25. Skid
26. Sheer cloth
27. Folio
28. Rowing equipment
29. Word of request: Abbr.
30. Malay gibbon
31. Irish expletive
32. Valley
33. Extraordinary person
34. Florid
36. Garden plot
39. Disintegrate
40. Classify
42. Little miss, familiarly
43. Deep sleep
44. City in the Congo basin
45. Precarious spot
46. Corners
47. Treated (with "with")
49. Adduce
50. —— pas
51. —— la Douce
52. Norse pioneer
53. Fender damage
55. Apprehend

79.

ACROSS

1. Plus item
6. Go to ——— of trouble
10. Munich's river
14. Offense
15. Australian parrot
16. ———contender
17. Cease-fire
18. Introductions
20. Guarantee
21. Word for a ship
22. Power
23. Razor mishap
25. Navigational aid
27. Where Tottenham is
30. Airman's initials
34. Soho residence
35. Some time
37. Outside: Prefix
38. Hostilities
39. Through: Prefix
40. Gershwin
42. Early Mongolian
43. German river
45. Dictator
47. Fort near Monterey
48. Took a bus
49. Shakespearian heroine
51. Tournament
54. Chemical ending
55. City on the Somme
58. Grazed
60. Ridicule
63. Asylum
65. Exclusively
66. Pay phone feature
67. Korean name
68. ——— incognita
69. Sawbucks
70. River to North Sea
71. Small fry

DOWN

1. Flats, for short
2. Word of respect
3. Wasted
4. Famed geometrist
5. Golfer's adjunct
6. Xanadu's river
7. Famed siren
8. ——— y plata
9. U.S. President
10. Dramatic role
11. Turn bad
12. Shake ——— (hurry)
13. Optimistic
19. ——— diet
21. Slanted
24. Applaud
26. Primroses
27. Yard implement
28. Insect stage
29. Tatters
31. Student's chore
32. Done to ———
33. Stage and movie name
36. Deteriorated
41. Solar disc
44. Culls
46. Unleash
50. Variegated
52. Neighbor of Que.
53. Loan shark's line
55. Right-hand man: Abbr.
56. Man or boy
57. Participating
59. One who peeks
61. Regarding
62. Bohea and oolong
64. Exclamations
65. Appended: Abbr.

80.

ACROSS

1. Like some hay
5. Snake
10. Centuries
14. Exchange premium
15. Pintail ducks
16. Migrate
17. "Recessional" word
18. Mets and Reds
19. French husband
20. Lukewarm
22. Woe
24. Mince or humble
25. Fiascos
28. Flower cluster
31. Repast
32. Wing
33. ——— a time
37. Plane-boarding staircase
41. Kern musical (with "The")
45. Organic compound
46. Flogged, in a way
47. ———clear
48. Raises the pot
51. Piece of jewelry
53. In an arrogant way
59. Metric measure
60. Presumes
61. Difficulties
65. Air
67. Cleanse
69. "What's ——— for me?"
70. Cuban money
71. Organic compound
72. Heart
73. Large number, informally
74. Strokes in a game
75. Skier's quest

DOWN

1. Fountain order, for short
2. Molding
3. Mere indication
4. Observe
5. Chicago time: Abbr.
6. Alpha's companion
7. Sustains
8. Forgive
9. Declare
10. Air: Abbr.
11. Diagram
12. Weird
13. Hits a towering fly
21. Famous friend
23. Rival
26. Nurse
27. Friend, out west
28. Derby, for one
29. Dog in heraldry
30. Pompey supporter
34. Relative of et al.
35. Villain's cry
36. A scholar's hour
38. Aleutian island
39. French miss: Abbr.
40. Trapper's prize
42. Astringent
43. Tumbled
44. Images
49. Stuff
50. Gazes
52. Misanthropes
53. Moistens
54. Protruding window
55. Graylags
56. Type of coffee
57. Omnibus of quotations
58. Useful quality
62. Shortly
63. Whirlybird, for short
64. Mulligan
66. Immediately
68. Hesitations

81.

ACROSS

1. House pets
5. Word for a strikebreaker
9. Low places
14. Greek peak
15. ——— Longa, ancient city
16. Stay
17. Desserts
19. Thrust
20. Seaman
21. Bread spread
23. Iowa town
24. Sloths
25. Thespian
28. European capital
30. Crowlike bird
33. Ancient raiment
34. Thirst quencher
36. Shortly
37. A profession
38. San ——— Obispo
39. Lacquer
42. Minute amount
43. Arch
44. Taking repose
45. Household helper
46. Mailing address

47. Berlin's forte
48. Yuletide treat
53. Vegetable
56. Calcutta celebrity
57. Fruit dish
59. More experienced
60. Irish hill
61. Merganser
62. Secures a ship
63. Overwhelm, informally
64. Gridiron thrill

DOWN

1. Egyptian
2. Addled
3. Monarch
4. Illinois Indian
5. Military engineer
6. Fasteners
7. Steelworkers' leader
8. Low
9. Appraising
10. Touches
11. Fluffy stuff
12. "The Razor's ———"
13. Farsighted one

18. Harness parts
22. Storage place
23. Guam's capital
25. Direct insults
26. Of sound
27. Torment
28. Trimming
29. British title
30. Cow
31. Italian river
32. North Sea tributary
34. Woodwind
35. Choice part
40. Sleepyheads
41. ——— ben Adhem
42. Ringing sounds
45. Source of light
46. Eastern notable
47. Headdress
48. College event
49. French composer
50. Bring to ruin
51. Store areas: Abbr.
52. Transaction
53. Arizona city
54. Ashe's specialty
55. Gulls
58. Serpent

82.

ACROSS

1. N. or S. ———
5. Dutch painter
9. Fools
14. Biblical weed
15. Curved molding
16. Pare leather
17. Malay coins
18. Nothing, in France
19. San Francisco stadium
20. Tax men
22. Horne
23. Smiling word
24. English poet
27. Biscuit of a sort
30. "One ——— under God"
33. Hoedown feature
35. Certain political people: Abbr.
39. Sandwich order
40. Apollo's mother
41. Overloads, in a way
43. Invisible
44. Status
50. Requires
52. Oklahoman

53. ——— were
55. What cie. stands for
58. Hurdles
60. Broadway hero
61. Smitten: Colloq.
62. French Impressionist
63. Sunbathe
64. Number suffixes
65. Evaluate
66. ——— -mell
67. From himself, in law

DOWN

1. Glue on
2. Actress Hunt
3. Chalk's partner
4. Plant over
5. Cut up
6. Exchange premium
7. Nasty look
8. Objects of perception
9. Request
10. Like framework
11. Clementine's footwear

12. Man's name
13. Body fluids
21. Initials for supersonic plane
25. Mesmerized
26. An elder
28. Neighbor of Mass.
29. Middle East people
31. Month: Abbr.
32. Prefix for classic
34. Russian reply
35. Baton Rouge initials
36. Motel of yore
37. Balkan people
38. Flower
42. ——— red
45. Free of taboo, in Hawaii
46. Shadowed
47. Native
48. Stable sounds
49. Fat
51. Pelt of sorts
53. Campus first name
54. High waves
56. Hautboy
57. English philosopher
59. Eye affliction

83.

ACROSS

1. With 26 Down, Israeli statesman
5. Priest's garments
9. Burn in a way
14. Flower, for short
15. Irish fuel
16. People of central India
17. Relatively new industry
19. Muse
20. Sioux City gal
21. Kind of securities sale
22. Burns brightly
23. Glaring light
25. Some pets
26. Lily maid
28. ——alive!
29. Hail-fellow-well-met
31. Bullfight cry
34. Late writer and critic
35. Chill
36. Claim
37. Signal of approval
38. Intend
42. ——state stereo
43. Brings into play
44. Trifling
47. Sound of silk
48. Soap plants
49. Swallow hastily
50. Goal
53. Fasten a rope
54. Had meaning
56. Model railroad measure
57. Scandinavian name
58. Drinks
59. Revealed
60. Fog
61. Advantages

DOWN

1. Turkish leaders
2. Cordon——
3. Brazen
4. Stir
5. Clothing
6. Realty matter
7. Organist
8. ——Jeanne
9. After helter
10. Weight units
11. Astonish
12. Grow less early
13. Refuse
18. Trumpeters
22. Boy's vehicle
24. Find agreeable
25. Greek letter
26. See 1 Across
27. Lake: Sp.
28. Caught sight of
30. Certain chorus
31. Tennis strokes
32. Baltic native
33. Cupid
36. Some votes
38. Sweetened
39. Oh, dear
40. Liberal movement of the 1960s
41. Auditorium signs
42. Fodder
44. Wealthy man
45. The last
46. Tooth
47. Drinks
49. Pacific island
51. Words of comprehension
52. Army hall
54. Household figure
55. Cologne water

84.

ACROSS

1. Hawser
5. Ten: Prefix
9. Confronted
14. Auricular
15. Words of confidence
16. Alpaca's neighbor
17. Name of Attila
20. Arranged
21. Egyptian dancing girl
22. Airline posting: Abbr.
23. Chemical suffix
24. Labor initials
25. Greek god
26. Table: Lat.
29. Constituent part
31. Like Swiss cheese
32. Connectives
33. Determined
37. Three: Prefix
38. Agent
39. Little one
40. Iowa college
41. Summit
43. Human
44. Antarctic sea
45. Vibration
47. American poet
48. Be down in the dumps
51. Man's nickname
52. California fort
53. Supplement (with "out")
54. Diagonal
55. Wild sheep of Tibet
59. Daughter of Francis I
62. Aftersong
63. ". . . come at ——'clock"
64. Above
65. Baseball hit
66. North African port
67. Female deer

DOWN

1. Decays
2. A Holy Roman emperor
3. Wharf
4. Rapture
5. Electron tube
6. Old French coin
7. Venezuelan city
8. International language
9. Arctic sight
10. Landon
11. Basketball player
12. Act in a way
13. Baby words
18. Dinner in ancient Rome
19. Anger, for one
25. Knack
26. French battle site
27. Judicial circuit
28. No, in Munich
29. Small——
30. Canadian province: Abbr.
32. Daughter of Polonius
34. Business course: Abbr.
35. Margin of victory, sometimes
36. Exam
38. Ship: Abbr.
39. Viscous liquid
42. Inhabitant: Suffix
43. Dragon, for example
44. Carrottop
46. Intend
47. Cereal
48. Baltic port
49. Giraffe's cousin
50. Former dictator
52. Pearl or Bermuda
54. German export
56. Preminger
57. Western Indian
58. Corded fabrics
60. European food fish
61. Not——bet

85.

ACROSS

1. Came down
5. Baseball term
10. Fruit
14. Function
15. Family member
16. Semicircular recess
17. Impudence
18. Tips
20. Branch
22. Protective device on a shoe
23. Bikini, for one
24. Word with Pro or Super
25. Former tourist mecca
27. Famous painting
31. Venerate
32. A people of Sonora
33. Grandparental
34. Predatory fish
35. Tonality
38. —— Faithful
39. Like some cheese
41. Johnnycake
42. Elan
44. Attack warning
46. Arizona sight
47. Hume contemporary
48. Of a Hindu culture
49. Track and tie
52. Phrase of daring
55. Pennsylvania Ave. building
57. A horse
58. A Chaplin
59. Mrs. Hobby
60. Part of SEATO
61. Sediment
62. Of a foot
63. Prow

DOWN

1. Southern constellation
2. Dillydally
3. Ugly
4. Communications satellite
5. African country
6. Innsbruck's province
7. Throb
8. Statute
9. German
10. Kneecap
11. Iliad, for example
12. Cruising
13. Defendant in a suit: Abbr.
19. Midwest state
21. Sharpening devices
24. Endured
25. Ishmael's mother
26. Saying
27. Signified
28. West African area
29. Burst of gunfire
30. Famous Pilgrim
32. Drink of redeye
36. Labor term
37. Shirk
40. Sioux
43. Puzzles
45. Overdue
46. Breakfast item
48. Wax match
49. Military offense: Abbr.
50. Brogan
51. Movie: Prefix
52. Having color
53. Scene of Perry victory
54. Suture
56. Egg: Prefix

86.

ACROSS

1. Horse
5. Holiday mail
10. N.C.O.'s
14. Enthusiasm
15. Oil source
16. Bronx cheer
17. Tatterdemalion
19. Ferber
20. Earthy
21. Offstage man at Scopes trial
23. Explosive
24. Refugee
26. Diamonds
30. Designate
33. Sky god
34. Brad
36. Ecological communities
37. Mute
39. Misses
41. Celestial bodies
42. Bower
44. Ship part
45. Jeanne or Marie: Abbr.
46. Did over, as a letter
48. First name at Chequers
51. Words in a salad recipe
53. Vote
54. Shrewdest
56. Vegetable
61. So long
62. Neckpiece of sorts
64. Large bird: Var.
65. Win a few, —— few
66. Reconcile
67. Groucho
68. Perfume
69. Spanish miss: Abbr.

DOWN

1. Emcee Griffin
2. Jai ——
3. Teases: Colloq.
4. Performs, as a role
5. Suing
6. ——, Bravo, Charlie
7. Ransack
8. Sixth century date
9. Remit, as a boxtop
10. Amontillados
11. In ——
12. Diminutive of Antoinette
13. Baseball's Man
18. Bill of fare
22. F.B.I. men: Abbr.
25. Ripen
26. Kind of antenna
27. Habituate
28. Pinter play (with "The")
29. Asian capital
31. Slowly: Music
32. Eat: Ger.
35. Type of verb: Abbr.
38. French port
40. Goes for the ball, as a batter
43. Hot ——
47. Sums
49. Vineyard valley of California
50. Undines
52. Rent
54. Restrain
55. Asian monk
57. See 22 Down
58. Copycat
59. Arctic Circle location: Abbr.
60. Tissue layer
63. One of the dwarfs

87.

ACROSS

1. Feeler
5. Goads
10. Vamp of the silents
14. Nautical term
15. Reinforce an embankment
16. Seed covering
17. "Streetcar" role
18. Bizet work
19. Catchy tune
20. Weed
21. Monetary
23. During passage: Lat.
25. French name
26. Follower of John Wycliffe
31. Fender mishaps
34. Pried into
35. Reluctant
36. Popular dance of early '60s
37. Submerge
40. Tries over
42. Son of the soil
43. Wife of Cuchulainn
44. Wash basin items
48. Cleansing
51. Algerian seaport
53. River to the Moselle
54. Caruso, for one
55. Major or Minor
56. Otherwise
57. Sawtoothed
58. Six: Span.
59. —— slicker
60. Sand hills: Brit.
61. Feminine name

DOWN

1. Over
2. Mongolian range
3. Ascertain
4. Enters
5. Desecrate
6. Complains
7. Hot places
8. Jumps the track
9. Lincoln's Secretary of War
10. —— h'ai
11. Solo
12. Small stream
13. Height: Abbr.
22. Women's skirtlike trousers
24. Express differently
27. Legislative body
28. Egyptian sacred bull
29. Remainder
30. Insecticides
31. Faux pas
32. Arrive
33. Incarnation of Vishnu
38. Made a horsy sound
39. Whatnot
40. Rudolph's beacon
41. Certain refugees
45. Western evergreen
46. Sinned
47. Blackbuck of India
48. Spanish painter
49. Bridge position
50. Low card
52. Space agency
53. Dry

88.

ACROSS

1. "—— Song in My Heart"
6. Angle
10. Church sector
14. Robin —— of old song
15. To the center
16. Thick slice
17. Huntley or Reasoner
19. Nimbus
20. Auto part
21. Philippine islander
23. Charge
25. TV offering
26. British prince
29. Having money: Colloq.
31. Watchful
32. Warren
34. Total
37. —— port in a . . .
38. Craftsman
40. Pronoun
41. Pleasure craft
43. Distant
44. Make fun of
45. Early musician
47. —— criticism (vulnerable)
49. Theaters
51. Residence of a mandarin
53. Unkempt
55. River in Texas into the Colorado
59. Actress Foch
60. Where bibliophiles browse
62. Unique person
63. Jane ——
64. —— a minute
65. British party
66. Put down
67. River feature

DOWN

1. Chinese emperor
2. Inspiration
3. Marbles
4. Chronicle
5. Secret
6. Minnie Maddern ——
7. Banking abbreviation
8. Footfall
9. Greeley
10. Compunctious
11. Soft-pedaled
12. Side dish
13. Heavy wood
18. Respond
22. Actor Lloyd
24. Frugal
26. Farthest from hole, in golf
27. Novel by Zola
28. Busy man after a rain
30. Miss Lanchester
33. Mindanao tribesmen
35. One
36. Southern fish
38. Rose oil
39. Odors
42. Imre Nagy's country
44. Two quintets, in Scotland
46. Girl's name
48. Five days
49. As like —— (probably)
50. Zoo animal
52. Invited
54. Great name in art
56. Seed husk
57. Suspenders stand-in
58. Bewildered
61. Mouth: Prefix

89.

ACROSS

1. Ladies in Lyons
5. Rascal
10. Partly open
14. Staff member
15. Potato
16. Words of impossibility
17. Cheap liquor
19. Secret society
20. Member of the Met.
21. Brewers
23. Repute
25. Like ghosts and ghouls
26. Hairpiece
29. "Citizen ——"
32. Odds makers' words
33. Chopper
35. Scoreboard trio
36. Circle
37. Low, hard-hit ball
38. Predecessor of MVD
39. Article, in Arles
40. Jurors' group
41. Clumsy
42. Spring time
44. Astronaut's big moment
46. On —— (busy)
48. Monday mood
49. Wheedling
52. Have —— on
56. Power source
57. Barbecue offerings
59. Okinawan city
60. People, poetically
61. African port
62. Austrian town
63. Clothe
64. Strip

DOWN

1. Bulk
2. Kind of skirt
3. Where figleaf was skirt
4. Maritime
5. "Nat Turner" author
6. Sports trophy
7. Encourage
8. Allots
9. Oldtime circuit man
10. Mideast capital
11. Flag of a sort
12. "I want —— just . . ."
13. Nessen and others
18. Anchor
22. Boxing champ in 1934
24. Famed sculptor
26. To —— phrase
27. Artillery rocket
28. Forty-
30. Drenched
31. Self-appointed adviser
32. Precise
34. V.I.P., for short
37. Gifts
38. Alert
40. Strip
41. —— event
43. Apostle
45. Pass
47. Popular material
49. Sugar source
50. —— impasse
51. —— be surprised
53. Dumb girl
54. Equipment
55. Serf
58. Noun form: Abbr.

90.

ACROSS

1. Both; Prefix
5. Cut away
10. Ives
14. Cousin of the bay
15. Supra
16. Unicorn fish
17. Lily plant
18. Embankment
19. Mauna Loa output
20. Dainty
22. Went flat
24. Shoots of a woody plant
25. Fowl
26. Mineral salt
29. Permanently
33. Labor initials
34. Leading
36. Monster slain by Hercules
37. Vetch
39. Western capital
41. Shield
42. —— on
44. Fong of Hawaii
46. German river
47. Mikado's son
49. ——-woolsey
51. Thought: Fr.
52. —— Grande
53. Flag
56. Uneven
60. —— of roses
61. —— Oro
63. French composer
64. Soviet river
65. Stranger
66. English town
67. Learning
68. Follower of a belief
69. Man from Korsor

DOWN

1. Jejune
2. What Oliver Twist wanted
3. Handle of a pail
4. First name in India
5. Knights of old
6. Urges on
7. Range
8. Poetic time
9. More profound
10. Direct hit
11. Single
12. Cleave
13. Go ahead
21. Western state: Abbr.
23. Egyptian symbol
25. Optimist
26. Take steps
27. Tropical vine
28. Mohammedan bible
29. Page number
30. Borders
31. Certain TV time
32. See 40 Down
35. Western lake
38. Light up
40. Saucy
43. Caper
45. Do without
48. Sam's friend
50. Caught
52. Zip, et al.
53. Pry
54. Spanish river
55. Intimate
56. California city
57. Filed material
58. N. C. college
59. Over
62. Chemical suffix

91.

ACROSS

1. Welshmen
6. Feast
12. Staying power
14. Of a founding apostle
15. Canadian city
16. Inaugurated (with "in")
17. Grandiloquize
18. Confined
20. Lake in Africa
21. Riparian setting
23. Fellow: Slang
24. Knot in wood
25. Furrows
26. Sovereign
27. His: Fr.
28. Dossier
29. Perry, e.g.
30. Procession on wheels
32. Natty
34. Resiliency
35. High: Mus.
38. Roman garment
39. Faisal's brother
40. Attach in a way
41. Actress Jessica
42. Albee play
44. Being: Sp.
45. Dismissed
46. Jesters
47. Man
49. Obvious
51. Talc or spar
52. Education officials
53. Caught
54. Shot of redeye

DOWN

1. Desert sight
2. Scenery chewer
3. Ship or plane
4. Explosive
5. Brazilian city
6. Remainder
7. Anglo-Saxon letter
8. Prevent
9. Whale's spouter
10. Sports shoe
11. Farming machine
12. Wading birds
13. City on the Po
14. Ruffians: Colloq.
19. Amuse
22. Mai ——
23. Newlywed
28. Raid
29. Brittle, for one
30. Sailing problem
31. Salesgirls' milieu
32. Replacement
33. Western state
35. Food
36. Luminous
37. Small anvils
38. Vapors
39. Fill with resolution
40. Type of aircraft
43. Friend in Tijuana
45. South African village
48. Wrath
50. Italian city: Abbr.

92.

ACROSS

1. Fishing gear
5. Body of Kaffir warriors
9. Russian lake
14. East Indian vine
15. Mournful sound
16. Credulous
17. Where La Chine is
18. City on the Plata
20. Begin
22. Look attentively
23. Traveler's stop
24. Bangalore's state
26. Malayan dagger
28. Certain basehits
33. Blue grass
35. Greek wine flask
36. Balanced
37. Hybrid primrose
39. Kennel sound
41. Have an —— (mean)
42. Means of enforcement
43. Counterfeit
45. Ordinance: Abbr.
46. Naturally
50. Pastiche
51. Outranking
53. Estuary
56. Part of M.I.T.: Abbr.
58. Machine part
60. Agitation
63. Rowdy: Slang
64. Family member
65. Olive genus
66. Apollo's mother
67. Unburdens
68. O'Casey
69. Whilom

DOWN

1. Capricorn
2. Roll-call answer: Lat.
3. Children's delight
4. Strip blubber
5. Wicked
6. Pasture sound
7. Torment
8. Opening for fluid in a pipe
9. Act of alluring
10. Chou en ——
11. South of France
12. Unruffled
13. —— light
19. Pound
21. Bowmen
25. Detect
27. Chop ——
29. Minimum
30. Alternative
31. Network
32. Plod heavily
33. Black Sea port
34. Farm animals
38. Tell —— the . . .
40. Greek letters
44. Old Iranian language
47. Indians or Braves
48. Fall-blooming annual
49. Subject
52. Implants
53. Descartes
54. Corn lily
55. Experts
57. Prefix with scope and vise
59. Farmer of India
61. Weather word
62. Teachers' org

93.

ACROSS

1. Composer
5. Style of art
9. Western Indians
13. Monarch in Norse legend
14. Part of a fairy tale beginning
15. Weight unit
16. Middle-class
18. Sports place
19. Plants firmly
20. Dregs
22. Bon ——
23. Four-baggers: Abbr.
24. Be useful
26. Certain poetry
28. Type of violin
29. French coin
30. Scarves
31. Spanish fellow
35. Racing-chart comment
37. Distribute
38. Doctors of Muslim law
39. ——Nostra
40. Wedding-notice word
41. Plead
43. Flower places
44. Dancer and Prancer
47. Reddish wood: Abbr.
48. Priestly garment
49. Gaelic
50. Not alert
53. American-born Japanese
55. Reckon
57. Thinker's aims
58. Descendant of Gilead
59. Ferber
60. Transmitted
61. In —— (existing)
62. Ruler

DOWN

1. Ruth or Herman
2. Particle
3. "19th hole"
4. Personnel men
5. Certain payments
6. Military address
7. Ornamental mats
8. Former Archbishop of Canterbury
9. Italian island: Abbr.
10. Rocky ridge
11. Kayak or proa
12. Run, in England
15. Great lover
17. Merchandise: Abbr.
21. Old Testament writer
24. Partner of Ollie
25. —— of the game
26. Biblical name
27. —— tax
28. Bar appurtenance
30. University in Waltham, Mass.
32. Stupid ones
33. Regretted
34. French summers
36. Soothsayer's need
37. Tibetan gazelles
39. Certain foods
42. Coast Guard activity
43. Villella's forte
44. Oriental princesses
45. Slur over
46. Norwegian dramatist
47. East Lansing campus: Abbr.
50. Zenith
51. Lava source
52. Fruit
54. Consume
56. —— Vegas

94.

ACROSS

1. Thin tufts
6. Faulty
9. Fat product
13. Hokkaido port
14. Deep —— well
15. Craze
16. Make a second plan
17. Small island
18. Sluggish
19. Long time
22. White cotton
23. Have this —— (our treat)
24. Addresses: Abbr.
26. A tense: Abbr.
27. French pronoun
30. Composer of "Good-bye"
33. Distance measurers
36. Revoke
37. Zero
38. Stopover spot
39. Proofread
41. Proverb
42. Three, in Italy
43. Kind of Asian cattle: Var
44. —— jiffy
45. Peak near Banff Park
48. Slangy response
51. Old-hat female
55. Expiate
56. Group: Abbr
57. . . . and —— grow on
59. Openings
60. Parisian's one
61. Guzzling sound
62. Persons
63. Home: Abbr.
64. Certain needles: Slang

DOWN

1. Venerating: Abbr.
2. Particulars
3. South Pacific isle
4. Joker
5. Overseer: Abbr.
6. Breakfast item
7. —— place to hide
8. Time past
9. Rubs in a way
10. —— penny
11. Breezy
12. Taps gently
15. Revolutionary soldier
20. Exclamations
21. Word on a quarter
25. Global divisions
27. Prefix for tarsus or phor
28. Western state: Abbr.
29. Capri
30. Diplomacy
31. Repute
32. Withered
33. News time
34. Shaping device
35. Sale words
40. —— war
44. State: Abbr.
45. Geometrical shapes
46. French river
47. Celestial beings in France
49. Deplete
50. Stone: Prefix
51. Toadfish
52. British school
53. Center
54. —— ha-Shanah
58. Ceres' mother

95.

ACROSS

1. Johnny Appleseed's name
8. De —— (in reality)
13. Halo
14. Strands
16. Mistake of a sort
18. Ach!
19. River through Lake Geneva
20. Dramatis personae
21. Suffix with press or moist
23. Charlotte ——
25. Pops the question
29. Hayseeds
33. L. P. for one: Abbr.
34. Emulated O'Toole
36. City near Lisbon
37. Antony's phrase for Brutus
40. Polo
41. "Olympia" painter
42. First word of "Home, Sweet Home"
43. Quarterback play
44. Set apart solemnly
46. Straight muscles
49. Car of the '20s
50. Jai ——
53. —— mañana
55. U.S. agency: Abbr.
59. Very special
62. Fred from Omaha
63. Not so neat
64. Sample
65. Goes up

DOWN

1. Señora's place
2. Pea pod
3. "Un bel di," for one
4. Invigorates
5. Barn sound
6. Open-air
7. Where Haarlem is: Abbr.
8. Gruesome threesome
9. Nigerian native
10. Fancy
11. Forum garb
12. Obligation
14. Cafe card
15. Term in new math
17. Condiment
22. Raleigh's island: 1585
24. Pony
25. Hyde Park vehicles
26. French author: 1823-92
27. Artist's pigment
28. Garden: Suffix
30. Slight pause
31. Cobra's cousin
32. Earl of Derby fame
35. Hamlet
38. Cousins of harmonicas
39. Clothes
45. Links
47. Milking, for one
48. London gallery
50. Desert coat
51. All at sea
52. City in N. W. Greece
54. Melodic subject
56. Ballet maneuver
57. "—— Three Lives"
58. Pulpit talks: Abbr.
60. Small bird
61. Alma mater of O. J. Simpson

96.

ACROSS

1. Trifle in love
7. Noted Ohio family
11. Vichy
14. Smith graduate
15. Go beyond
17. American author
18. The Mauve Decade
19. Sicilian city
20. Requirement
22. Uncle Miltie
23. Flowers
25. Still and ——
26. Boorish
28. Atlantic nation
32. Psychic initials
33. Put aside
35. Caucasian language
36. Aide of a sort
38. Red or White
39. Pair
40. German river
41. Styron subject
43. New Deal initials
44. Eye parts
46. Frequented
48. 1920 Presidential candidate
49. I.D. for a G.I.
50. Collect
53. Chinese weight
54. —— Strip
57. Generated
59. Tidal bores
61. Obstructions in nasal passage
62. Busy
63. Bishopric
64. Condition
65. Tension

DOWN

1. Appeared
2. Pearl Buck heroine
3. One of five
4. Diacritical mark
5. Direction
6. Sully
7. Hues
8. Greedy
9. Boggy land
10. Hi-fi setting
11. Excite
12. British statesman
13. Building recess
16. Bright
21. Site of one of Seven Wonders
24. Careen
25. Tennis point
26. Crowbar
27. River to the Missouri
28. Scott novel
29. Out front, as in art
30. Mother-of-pearl
31. Face with reluctance
34. Gaelic god
37. Norse explorer
39. Dry, as champagne
41. Censure (with "with")
42. Young birds
45. Fresh-water algae
47. Faultfinder
49. "—— Macabre"
50. Down with: Fr.
51. Ancient Persian
52. U.S. author-critic
53. Kennedy and Sorensen
55. Olympian
56. Vipers
58. Aunt: Sp.
60. Small island

97.

ACROSS

1. Naval historian
6. Start of soliloquy
10. ——were
14. Place of action
15. Soon
16. Hair style
17. Kind of vote
18. Arm of Black Sea
19. Strong wind
20. Doldrums
23. France's St. ——
24. Slangy affirmatives
25. Track event
28. Stout's cousin
31. Record again
35. In the style of: Fr.
36. Comb: Prefix
38. Girl's name
39. Parental advice, old style
42. Join
43. Debacles
44. Regret
45. Mariner
47. Baton Rouge campus
48. Pare
49. ——about
51. Degree
53. Emotion of a kind
60. 0900, for example
61. Iris part
62. "Just . . ."
64. Greek mountain
65. Focusing device
66. Wagner character
67. Power unit
68. Was: Lat.
69. Defeated narrowly

DOWN

1. Concern of editors
2. Relative of cortisone
3. Sandwich
4. Denier of authority
5. Gossipy
6. South African language
7. Spanish weight
8. Spoils
9. Jealous one
10. Queen Anne's literary age
11. Nail
12. Trifling
13. Digits
21. Muse
22. Greek letters
25. Women: Slang
26. Straighten
27. "The Secret of —— Vittoria"
29. Their: Fr.
30. Enter
32. Kostelanetz
33. Dress goods
34. Canvas holder
36. Rostand subject
37. Work
40. Party man
41. Dwarf
46. Lump
48. Scheduled
50. Bronx or East
52. Card, as wool
53. Dog
54. Sub ——
55. Eject
56. Horne
57. Middle or Far
58. Opera cycle
59. Glut
63. Reckless

98.

ACROSS

1. Good wood for rafts
6. Yellowish brown
11. Occasional sky sighting
14. Rod of a certain shape
15. Artless
16. Pester
17. Grocery's descendant
19. Fizzle
20. Journals
21. Good, in Rome
22. Decimal rate: Abbr.
25. Egyptian dancing girls
26. Revived an old film
27. Babylonian god
29. Weight unit
30. Baltic native
31. Fruit
33. Predatory
37. Formed on earth's surface
39. Firm
40. Put through the washer again
42. Ancient Italian city
43. Otherwise
44. Tatter
46. Agitate
47. Trojan War figure
49. Participant in a child's game
51. Foxy
52. Bows
53. Some literary works
55. Depot: Abbr.
56. Barber, modern style
60. Pronoun
61. Get along
62. Down
63. Cleopatra's finis
64. Works by a Spanish master
65. Hard

DOWN

1. Vehicle
2. Sumerian deity
3. Cut off
4. Coaster
5. Roman courtyards
6. Without weaponry
7. Lady in "Measure for Measure"
8. Two-wheelers
9. Poetic times of day
10. Soak, as flax
11. Doesn't brown enough
12. Flora's friend
13. City in Utah
18. Ingredient of beer
21. Early
22. Collector for those who dance
23. Gift-wrap paper
24. Place for some tourists
26. Summary, for short
28. Bighorn sheep
30. Chap
32. Writer of children's books
34. Pleasant places
35. Up to
36. Floor
38. Compass mark
41. Former Italian colony in Africa
45. Girl's nickname
47. Eastern title
48. "—— long, life is short"
49. Well fuzzed
50. Spanish kings
53. Pudding starch
54. Hong Kong skirt feature
56. Crone
57. Form of Esperanto
58. Change from a yen
59. Do a judge's task

99.

ACROSS

1. Derby winner, 1935
6. Carson's predecessor
10. Tusked animal
14. Airman
15. Spanish jar
16. Sea bird
17. Put forth
18. Nests
19. Phoned
20. Maria Tallchief, in a way
23. Waist band
26. Acclaim
27. Giggle
28. Timers' necessities
30. Conjunctive
32. Superlative ending
33. Mediterranean island
34. Ukrainian river
36. Hat for Governor Nunn
42. Mideast motel
43. Son of Aphrodite
45. Have a bite
48. Coed's pride
49. Silk-clad men
52. Uneven
54. Middle East people
56. Misery
57. Statue of Fred Astaire, in a way
60. Time —— half
61. Particle
62. What some races are won by
66. Row
67. Old name for one of 54 Across
68. Man and horse contest
69. Early western name
70. Part of a sentence: Abbr.
71. Derby winner, 1955

DOWN

1. Reveal, old style
2. Tom ——
3. Beverage
4. Southern cape
5. Append
6. Bangtails
7. Existing
8. Breed of cattle
9. Police action
10. European capital
11. Spinach-like plant
12. Years: Fr.
13. Derby winner, 1915
21. Article
22. Up ——
23. Be in the red
24. What some horses do
25. Let ——
29. Receptacles
31. Command: Abbr.
34. Runner
35. Journey
37. Primitive home
38. Swiss canton
39. Small box
40. Concoct
41. Toy
44. Compass point
45. Unflappable
46. Muse of astronomy
47. Derby winner, 1949
49. Fouled up
50. "—— Sunday afternoon"
51. Smokes
53. Steep slope
55. —— Oro
58. Incline
59. Omar word
63. Room in a harem
64. Take apart: Abbr.
65. Greek goddess

100.

ACROSS

1. Relative of telepathy
4. Wild party: Colloq.
9. Defraud
13. Yankee: Abbr.
14. Eastern woman
15. Inter ——
16. Brokerage employe
19. Period of human culture
20. Arrange, as papers
21. Spiro
22. Kitchen gadget
23. Man's nickname
24. Put away
26. European capital
30. Procession
32. Performed a flying stunt
34. Confrontation point in a game
38. —— Fidelis
39. Roof parts
40. Scottish inventor
41. Multitude
42. Townsman: Colloq.
45. Concede
48. —— man to another
50. More spacious
53. French artist
55. Locking, as of fingers
57. Chow ——
58. Characterless
59. No other than
60. Direction
61. Coincide
62. Born

DOWN

1. Appear
2. Assist
3. Trim
4. Guardhouse
5. Recent
6. Some
7. Manatee
8. General direction
9. Dance halls
10. Russian first name
11. —— price
12. Smith
13. Kind of flu
17. Unpolished
18. Cakes' companion
22. Lincoln Center event
24. Bank fixture
25. "—— the season . . ."
27. Evian or Baden
28. Hoof it
29. Form of verse
30. Covenant
31. Bosh!
32. Roman historian
33. Cockney's flat
34. Gresham's, for one
35. Lupino
36. Trawler gear
37. L. A. footballer
41. Exposing
42. Mathematics term
43. Boot part
44. Small
46. Executive: Abbr.
47. Communications word
48. One —— time
49. Squelch
50. Frost
51. Draft classification
52. Colonial patriot
53. Hidden explosive
54. To ——
56. Fish

ANSWERS

1

```
BEEP  ICAME  FFFF
ABLE  GOBEL  ROLE
BOSTONBULL  EXIT
ENESCO  TOILETTE
    TARP  SPILE
NAPOLEON  SMYRNA
AGORA  ROBIN  RUG
MAME  GENUS  HILA
ETE  BODES  FEELS
SERIES  TEARDROP
   ANEST  STAG
HANDSAWS  ONEILL
ABIE  MELANCHOLY
IRAN  ERICA  OLDE
RANT  REPEL  PASS
```

2

```
GODS  JORUM  STAD
ABET  UKASE  TARO
LIAR  DAZED  AXIS
STRUNG  EULOGIZE
    CAMP  PANG
PICKMEUP  RIENZI
UNA  ENTER  TROIS
FURS  TUTOR  SUBS
FREAK  PEWEE  NEU
YESMAN  REQUESTS
    PLEA  DUES
HOTHEADS  IRKING
ALUI  ROPER  IDEA
REAR  BRAVE  MOLL
DONE  YESES  OLLA
```

3

```
AHA  STEAM  IBID
VERB  KOALA  NOSE
ERAL  ERRED  HOLM
CABARET  REBATES
    RATS  TAAS
BLUETS  BETTOR
LINDA  BREEZEWAY
OLD  BOAST  ITO
BLESSINGS  FACET
SERIES  MITERS
    BACK  SORA
BULLRUN  HUMBUGS
ALAI  IOTAS  APIA
TARN  TWINE  LOLL
SNAG  SNEER  NAT
```

4

```
FRAPS  PEDI  CAMP
RESET  OMEN  OLEA
INTRO  SCENARIST
ZOROASTER  GNATS
ONTIME  MISSAY
BEN  SPA  BOOT
ALAE  SWAN  ARTS
ABUT  STORK  LEAP
LATE  HEWN  KALE
REAR  SAL  CID
VAINLY  ATBEST
ANNAS  AVOCATION
REDLETTER  DRONE
ANIL  DERM  MINCE
STAY  SETS  EASED
```

5

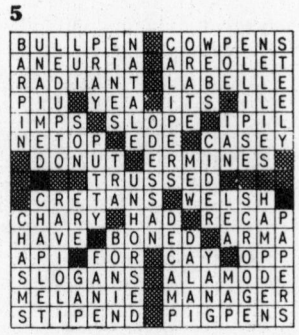

```
BULLPEN  COWPENS
ANEURIA  AREOLET
RADIANT  LABELLE
PIU  YEA  ITS  ILE
IMPS  SLOPE  IPIL
NETOP  EDE  CASEY
DONUT  ERMINES
    TRUSSED
CRETANS  WELSH
CHARY  HAD  RECAP
HAVE  BONED  ARMA
API  FOR  CAY  OPP
SLOGANS  ALAMODE
MELANIE  MANAGER
STIPEND  PIGPENS
```

6

```
DESK  HANKS  CHAP
ACTE  ORION  HALO
SHAY  TALKITOVER
HOTHEAD  OVEREAT
    OPIA  ELIA
SAILOR  SILENCER
OGLED  TARE  EINE
DEL  EARMARK  GAY
ANAT  NEON  ADARE
SADSACKS  SPARES
    VALE  SPUR
FAIREST  ARTLESS
ASSISTANCE  ILYA
WIEN  OPERA  NESS
NADA  RAVED  GETS
```

7

```
JEEP  POETS  RASP
ARNO  ULTRA  ECTO
BIDS  MATIN  SHUN
SCREAM  ENDTOEND
EULER  EARN
MISRULES  LEASED
ECU  MEMEL  ENTRE
LOLL  DUELS  TANA
ENTER  SPATS  LIL
ESSAYS  SMITHIES
    DONA  ALLEN
CHASTENS  LOGGED
LOCO  ATIME  IRMA
ALEF  KITES  RAMS
DEAF  SCENT  ADAH
```

8

```
DESC  ODORS  SHAM
UTAH  RAMIE  POLE
MANU  DREAR  ERIN
PLANTAIN  ISLAND
GAIN  BATTLES
OLDKINGCOLE
AVAIL  RESTATES
FIRN  AAR  WADI
SINGSONG  SATIN
    THESNOWKING
REPLAIT  ERIE
ARROYO  REIGNING
TOAD  ABIDE  INEE
ESTE  NAVEL  NILE
SEES  SLEDS  GALS
```

9

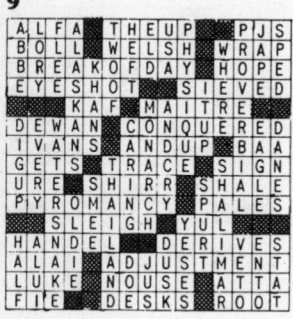

```
ALFA  THEUP   PJS
BOLL  WELSH  WRAP
BREAKOFDAY  HOPE
EYESHOT    SIEVED
     KAF  MAITRE
DEWAN  CONQUERED
IVANS  ANDUP  BAA
GETS  TRACE  SIGN
URE  SHIRR  SHALE
PYROMANCY  PALES
    SLEIGH  YUL
HANDEL    DERIVES
ALAI  ADJUSTMENT
LUKE  NOUSE  ATTA
FIE   DESKS  ROOT
```

10

```
MISC  RAMA   COLA
UNTO  ANIL  RAMAN
STAR  ZENO  ERECT
CHINTZ  THEWORKS
AERIALS   AXIL
    STEAM  TRYSTS
CATHEDRA  RENTAL
IDA  AKITA  ABA
TABRIZ  LIVEITUP
ERSATZ   STAND
    FELL  OGDOADS
MISTREAT  ASLEEP
ADIEU  ZOON  IDIO
ALARM  ELIZ  ZEST
MENS  DADA  ESTS
```

11

```
STAB  CABOT   ALP
LOBO  ABATE   BEL
ADEN  PERON  NOVA
GOLDSTAR  DEADEN
    COMET  SKEET
LOCKER   LEASE
ALLIN  HOSS  DUPE
PLANETOFTHEAPES
SANG  ARMS  APORT
    KIDDO  TRENTE
SETON   ENDUE
CRANKS  KINDNESS
RANG  OLEAN  ALTA
USE   BEYLE  ISAR
BEY   SASSY  LARD
```

12

```
FLAM  STEAM  WHIP
EURE  UINTA  HIDE
EXAM  FADED  ILLE
LETOFF  STROLLER
    RUIN  EINS
LOUISXIV  GOTOFF
APRES  CIGAR  KEA
BIGS  GHOUL  TALL
ONE  QUELL  PEPOS
RESCUE  ALKALINE
    AIRS  YIPE
BRANDNEW  LAGGED
RANI  STEAL  RAZE
ATEN  ETAGE  ATIP
TETE  YOKED  MOOT
```

13

```
STAR  DAMN  TAFTS
COLA  ALAI  ORION
ALLFORONE  TOSTI
DEE  VIGILS  SHOP
STYLE   PLEBES
    ONEALONE  TIM
BELG  TIE  ALLONE
AVAILED  ATLARGE
RANCOR  TMO  NYET
END  ONEHORSE
    ONSALE  OSCAR
ALFA  LIKEAS  ODE
LUNCH  ONEFORALL
ADORE  TORI  OTEA
SIDER  STYX  WIRY
```

14

```
 CHEATS  SHAFTS
SHADROE  CURIOUS
NANETTE  IRONAGE
ORD  SARGES  SAN
OLLA  LEANT  OTRO
PEERS  SIC  GREER
SYSTEMS  EDUARD
    INA   EIN
MISTED  COLGATE
MANTA  ETE  DECAL
ANTE  ALAND  SAL'A
RTE  DARTED  CLI
ALREADY  IBERIAN
TENSILE  MILEAGE
DEEDED  OTIOSE
```

15

```
IOTA  CARD  CASTE
SPAT  OMAR  OSCAR
MILL  DANA  SHALE
SECONDSIGHT  ROC
    OILS  REAGENT
TOUSLE   HALLO
AGREE  LACE  UTAH
LESE  RAVEN  PARA
LEAN  IDES  LIBEL
    DRAIN  MANUAL
PULSATE   YAKS
ANE  PASSAREMARK
SCAUP  MILK  ORAN
TASSE  ATTU  KITE
ASTOR  NEAP  ELSE
```

16

```
 SMEES    CLEAT
STALLMAN  HARDER
PAULMUNI  ANGELA
EGG  ATINGLE  NEB
CARL  STEAK  SAGA
STEAM  RRS  SPURT
    BOLAS  KOREA
STOLES   REFORM
    PARED  BANTU
CARES  HER  STASH
ONER  FUGIT  STLO
ANN  DIGITAL  TAM
SETTER  NAMESAKE
TRUANT  SNEAKIER
    SMITH  SPINS
```

17

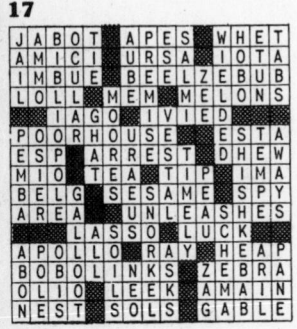

```
JABOT APES WHET
AMICI URSA IOTA
IMBUE BEELZEBUB
LOLL MEM MELONS
    IAGO IVIED
POORHOUSE  ESTA
ESP ARREST DHEW
MIO TEA TIP IMA
BELG SESAME SPY
AREA UNLEASHES
   LASSO LUCK
APOLLO RAY HEAP
BOBOLINKS ZEBRA
OLIO LEEK AMAIN
NEST SOLS GABLE
```

18

```
PISA COWLS TACO
IRIS OBEAH AWOL
LAOS LONGISLAND
EQUALLED FOLIES
   XIII STUNTS
UNCLAD  WHERE
POI REPAID SKEP
TOTES LIL ASAMA
ONYX DULLES LIP
   PRESS STRATA
  PLEACH SEAM
ALONZO REARWARD
JERSEYCITY EZIO
ABIE EAGRE SONG
MESS DRIED TOGS
```

19

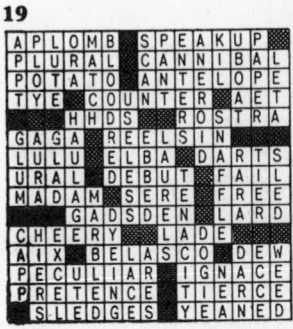

```
APLOMB SPEAKUP
PLURAL CANNIBAL
POTATO ANTELOPE
TYE COUNTER AET
   HHDS ROSTRA
GAGA REELSIN
LULU ELBA DARTS
URAL DEBUT FAIL
MADAM SERE FREE
GADSDEN LARD
CHEERY LADE
AIX BELASCO DEW
PECULIAR IGNACE
PRETENCE TIERCE
SLEDGES YEANED
```

20

```
PALADIN ARARAT
OVERICE PARAPET
REVERIE PLATINA
TRITE BALL CAN
MATERNALLY PANG
AGA ORAL MALTY
NETWORTH PAP
DERIVE FOREST
ASO DISCREET
PRATE MISS PEA
OUCH CONTESTANT
LIT GALE HERAT
ANIMIST PEONAGE
REVERSE STUTTER
DEADEN TETHERS
```

21

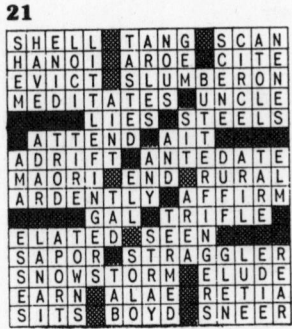

```
SHELL TANG SCAN
HANOI AROE CITE
EVICT SLUMBERON
MEDITATES UNCLE
   LIES STEELS
ATTEND AIT
ADRIFT ANTEDATE
MAORI END RURAL
ARDENTLY AFFIRM
   GAL TRIFLE
ELATED SEEN
SAPOR STRAGGLER
SNOWSTORM ELUDE
EARN ALAE RETIA
SITS BOYD SNEER
```

22

```
SHAPE SHOP CAST
LOGAN TARO ALAR
ICERS ORAL RIVE
THEAUTUMNLEAVES
   GRITS ENTERS
SORREL ADD
AREA EBAN SNOBS
LEAP STUNG OTOE
ALPHA USER VIAL
   LPS EJECTS
SPACER STEEL
TABLEOFCONTENTS
OLEO SEAT STORE
NETS ETRE ETNAS
ESSE REED TEEMS
```

23

```
QUININE QUARTOS
UNRAVEL UNIFORM
ANIMATE AIRLINE
NED NOVELTY LIL
TRIG PALMY LETT
UVULA TIS LITHE
MEMORIES CENSOR
   REDS QUAG
QUOITS QUIVERED
UNDEE SUI ERODE
ATES THINS SPUR
SWS CROATIA ICI
HISTRIO INSTEAD
ENAVANT LACOSTE
SENATES ELECTED
```

24

```
TACO STEPS ABET
OVER HAVEN MOXA
FARM ONICE YSER
FLOORWALKER WAD
   LOB SZIGETI
SEQUOIAS YOWL
ELU FLINT TELIC
ABEE LLOYD NINO
SEETO SORRY ARR
   NUNS DEJEUNER
ASSIZES ELM
BAT ATTACKPLANE
AXON SADLY ALOT
TOWN ARAIL USNA
ENNE TYROL TOOL
```

25

```
COHAN AYAH FLAG
OHARE LANA LUTE
INLAW ENGR OCHS
FOOTLOCKER RIOT
    EASE IDEALS
SLOVAK ELGIN
PILAF ADIANTUMS
ARAU SPOON IFAT
DANDELION GNOME
  EMEND SEESAW
PREVUE LAGO
LEVI PRESSROOMS
ANIL SOBS GRAMP
ITAL ILOT ENTER
DENE NEYS MESSY
```

26

```
THAR SWAPS SHAG
AURA THERE COPY
PRIG EISENHOWER
STANDAT SOARED
   AIDES RUE
SNARKS THATSALL
CANOE PRASE LEI
RINK HOI PLAN
AVA SPILL CEASE
PELLMELL CONNED
   OIL SCOLD
HOGTIE ROTATED
COUGHSYRUP NOLA
APSE SEINE TRIM
PIER EDGAR SNAP
```

27

```
ATOM FOCAL CHUB
SEPT OPERAHOUSE
IRES REDASABEET
ARN RENE BASRA
   EMBOSS SOIL
CHALET CHATTELS
AARU STROKE LET
DUKES AAR DALAI
ETE CARING GAVE
TETRAGON ADORES
   ALAS BROGAN
SALVE CLOG ILE
ALIENATION ONER
MINNESOTAN LESS
PIGS PASTE ESSE
```

28

```
AMPS SPCA MEADE
BARE CLOS DATED
BLUEJEANS STOPE
YAN UNITES ENOS
 PERMANENTPRESS
ORLOPS STAR SEA
BOLOS TETES
SPATULA DESPOTS
  SIEGE SACHA
ATT TART RUTTED
DRESSREHEARSAL
DINE SEANCE GIS
EVADE INDISPOSE
RINGO NOUN ANTE
SATES GLEE USSR
```

29

```
BOFF GLOW OBEAH
ABIE RUNA YALTA
CORD ACES ELBOW
HESERVESHIS ARK
  STRAY TENON
FAY PARTYBEST
CALL PAR REALTY
WHO CRY LOS AAR
TOODLE TIS CETE
SERVESTHE MAO
  INTHE PARMA
ENG COUNTRYBEST
TORAH MORO ITTO
CRATE BSMT NERO
HAYES SESS ERAT
```

30

```
DONT PIPE CABRA
UTAH RTES ADREM
LOVEBEADS REINE
LEA ELLE SISTER
  LURAY CLOTHES
GOBLET SHALE
INATTENTIVE BON
ALSO IRE VEGA
NYE BENEFICIARY
  ARROW VALUES
CARTOON SALEM
ADORNS MINE ORI
TOLET WISHBONES
OBESE INSO IDEA
NESTS SKYE LELY
```

31

```
OSSA TAROT ROAM
AHAB OVINE ARNO
FELLOWAMERICANS
SPEEDERS NILES
   ORE FOPS
UPPERS DILATERS
NEIL SAVER REA
FELLOWCREATURES
EVE ROUTS FEDS
DESSERTS WOODSY
   AGES COG
ALAMO ZILLIONS
ROBINGOODFELLOW
TRET ALLEE LENA
SOLE BEARD AGOG
```

32

```
DOOR TALC BOLA
ALAE JUROR ETAL
WITHMALICE FIND
SCHOOLS KARASEA
  BINAL MEL
LENORA IDEALMAN
EMOTE KNURL ORA
WITH DACES PITT
ILO MINOS BEREA
SENTINEL FORALL
  ADE NILUS
CHARITY HANOVER
HINT TOWARDNONE
ALGA ELATE ALTI
DOER SKYE ETON
```

33

```
LOKI  CAJUN  SAGO
ERIN  AGORA  MEED
ALEC  UNLITTERED
REVERSALS  RAISE
     PIETY  CAREER
TARTS  EGRESS
BROOKS  OARS  FAT
AMOR  CRONE  BARE
RAM  LAID  SAUCER
  CARAFE  GLEAM
ARCADE  EXPEL
LEASE  ALTEREGOS
BESTSELLER  TAXI
USER  STORE  ITEM
MESO  TOWNS  NEAP
```

34

```
SAPA  SPUNK  CHOW
KNOB  PUREE  HARE
ITIS  EMBONPOINT
MINORCAS  YERKES
     TROTS  DART
BUBBLE  SINCLAIR
ELL  ERRED  HEPTA
STAG  SUETS  SPAM
ORNOT  STOPS  OLE
MAKEUPTO  ONFILE
     SAIS  PREEN
UPPING  ARRESTED
POINSETTIA  CITE
TOUT  OUTON  UNUM
ORSO  NEARS  EGIS
```

35

```
BUYS  SLEPT  ROSE
OPAH  AERIE  ELIA
STRETCHONESLEGS
HONDURAS  PEONY
     LER  SUIT
DOFFED  RINGSIDE
OVER  INDO  ORS
PUTONESFOOTINIT
ELI  AVAL  DIVE
SEDATIVE  PLACER
     NILE  GOA
SLIGO  POTHERBS
EATONESHEARTOUT
AGER  MOORS  NANA
SORA  SLOSH  ADAY
```

36

```
BALT  SHARP  EDAM
USIA  EAGER  RENE
ZION  ALATE  RUNT
ZANZIBAR  CEASES
     ANES  DIRT
EVINCE  MOONAND
DORIA  REVUE  YAW
ILIA  MATES  BANE
TED  HOVER  PACTS
SOLIDER  TICKET
     EVES  TUCK
PRICES  THRASHED
ROOT  THREE  OILY
ALTO  LOIRE  FLOE
YEAR  YEMEN  FOND
```

37

```
SPICA  BEAST
QUASARS  PULSARS
UNTRUTH  ARMENIA
ODE  LEADINS  DEG
TOLES  DALE  OISE
AWLS  BIT  TENETS
NATIONAL  CERE
     HANG  ETAL
DIEM  STANDISH
CANTBE  APT  FOOL
RIFE  CALF  LEONE
ALA  GONERIL  NOA
MINEOLA  ONAGERS
PETITES  GAMESET
SERTS  SALTS
```

38

```
BORAH  STAB  OBEY
AMANA  IAGO  FORA
BABYSITTER  FOAL
ARI  BRAE  NUBBLE
     NEAR  AFAR
GREEN  MIRRORED
COHAN  BAKE  AURA
ARON  ALLEE  DRUB
REND  CAIN  SWAPS
KNEEJERK  SHALT
     ROLE  AIRY
JOLTED  ASTI  CSA
UTAH  ALLHALLOWS
SOLA  MUTE  LANAI
TEAL  AGIN  SENTA
```

39

```
SHAM  LAOS  MARC
CHAPE  ETCH  ABEL
LOVED  ALTO  NOVA
EWE  INPERPETUUM
BISCAY  OPIATES
FITTOBETIED
ALOE  SAO  DERMA
SLURS  RNS  ROACH
STEEP  ITA  PROA
  DISCOTHEQUE
PROTEST  RHESUS
LIBERTYBELL  ETA
APEX  IMID  MUSIC
TEST  LITU  EPACT
ONES  SEEP  TASS
```

40

```
DENEB  MOPS  MESA
AROAR  OMER  ILES
MURRE  ZENO  NARK
SCALAWAGS  TINGE
     STOMA  TRADED
COB  HOB  CHIT
OVERT  IRREGULAR
MALEA  QUO  ORALE
BLACKOUTS  NERVE
     KINE  SOO  DAD
ALLONE  SPUME
DOING  SPARERIBS
ANTI  DOIT  TINEA
PERN  ALEC  EDGES
TREG  WISH  RUERS
```

41

```
BEARUP DAD CHIT
ARREST IVE HONE
HATCHETJOB ERLE
STARE ROTTERDAM
   ERMINE PREYS
 CHASES   BUY
IRON LESSER GEN
DONTROCKTHEBOAT
OWI ENTIRE LASH
 DAS   ASTUTE
STOOD SMITES
PULLSOPEN ATIME
ANIL TRUTHSERUM
DEVA OAS AERATE
EDER ETE TRYSTS
```

42

```
CHIC BEVEL PLUG
HEMO ASOKA IONA
INIQUITIES QUID
 STUNTED SAUTES
   ESSE PIPE
SANTE MARTS POR
CHATTY ROUE OSE
AMIE OREAD PICA
LEV PRIN EARLAP
EDE SKATE SOURS
   HISS NEST
SQUASH CURARES
AUNT INTRAMURAL
GIDE ROMES DILO
APOS EROSE ESTA
```

43

```
LABS PYLON RAMS
ALIT ISERE ESAU
RIGI LARGESCALE
KILLJOY DAINTY
 ELATE GLUT
THATIS PIECESOF
WAGON FALSE MUR
ANU FURLS ATA
ISE FAZES ACLAM
NASALIZE SMALTS
 GARY ENOCH
UNSAID VARIOLE
LITTLEBEAR QUIT
ALEE ARIDE URSA
REPS LANED ESTS
```

44

```
CRASS BOSS INDO
RESTE AMOI SEAL
EATEN NEWSSTAND
STANDINGS TAPES
TARO ZSA HEN
  SAV TIMBALE
SPH DEACON URAL
GRANDSTANDPLAYS
TORO TOTEMS BSA
STANDIN OAR
 SEA RAS ELIA
RIDEA LASTSTAND
STANDREWS PARKA
VERS ISEE TIGER
PATE PERT SNORE
```

45

```
SPHER ACTS PETS
INANE SASH LAIC
TEDDY CLEOPATRA
EURE MOI ORISON
 IAGO BETON
CLARISSAS TEAR
AIN SLINKS STLO
VAV TEL ITE HIP
INIT MARMOT ABE
LAIR GIOVANNIS
 EASED ELEF
TRANCE DAS URGE
BUTTERFLY TROLL
ALLO ALEE SAMOS
REIN LADS PLEBE
```

46

```
SNUB CORE STET
HOPO AHUM THOLE
ONPURPOSE ORALE
TEETER HEROINES
 TRAGIC RIKKI
 DACHA PIECES
GRUEL OLDEN EXE
LOPS FITIN STIR
UVA BARON LEYTE
MENTOR SERAC
 DOLED DEPOTS
SHAKESUP LINEAL
LATER CUTANDDRY
AMINO KNOT EDGE
GETS SYNE DYES
```

47

```
BLUEBLOOD HIRES
RUNAROUND AROMA
UNDRESSES HOOPS
NAE WEIR CANTOS
ORRA RAOUL SOWA
 OSTS UPAS FEN
GENOA ASTRO TRI
ACERBIC HATCHED
RCS LOOSE HEEDS
REB ETRE FORM
INRE ANNAL TAMP
STEAMS ANIS TOO
ORATE ATTRACTOR
NITER PORTLIEST
SCHRS CROSSTREE
```

48

```
LAIC TRAMP CALL
ODOR AERIE OLEO
TITI LEAST RATA
STATEOFTHEUNION
   TANS RTE
SEVERS CAPETOWN
ALORS PAPAS ROE
LETS DEMON PROW
EME CARED CHILL
MIRTHFUL BRASSY
 OAF BOER
STANDONCEREMONY
PANG DIANE ABIE
ABOU INNER CONN
TUNE LETTS YEAS
```

49

```
ACTUP TABBY STG
BLASE ISOLA OOO
BAKERSDOZEN UPA
EYED CYR SKEWED
    UFO USELESS
JUMPOFF NEEDS
ONA AFRAID ETRE
VITAL ESQ AREAR
ETCH REBUFF RCA
HEGEL ELAPSES
DUBARRY ORE
EPOPEE SAO LAVA
WAX EDWARDELGAR
ENE COAST REARM
YDS ESSAY STRAY
```

50

```
STAR PARIS OPAL
AONE INUSE REDO
GOAL CABLE CRAG
ATTACK SAPPHIRE
TAUS MALI
SWEETPEA GADGET
OHARA ARDEN ORO
DOTS STERS BONA
OLE TOSCA SAFES
MENTAL AMETHYST
AMID ARIA
LARKSPUR ARMFUL
OGEE EVILS IOLE
BEAR DEFOE ARNE
ODDS STEWS NEAR
```

51

```
SHIMS OWES ARMS
HELIC DICE NEAT
AROMA ITALICIZE
DEVILISH SINES
ESE LETO ABE
SIR URBANIZE
HASTO STOL BEL
INCONSEQUENTIAL
DEA TNUT AISLE
ESTIMATE EVA
NAT SHRI EVE
AVIAN TANGELOS
REDPENCIL ALCIS
CLEO BOOT TOILE
SOOT EONS EDDAS
```

52

```
SURF FARES EDAM
ORAL AGENT RIGA
INFORMEDSOURCES
REFRAINS PRATES
ENNA ELAN
GRANGE SMOLDERS
LANCE SWISS GOT
AMIE SHUTS LAVA
SOS SHINS CEDES
SNEAKING LAVISH
LIVE AARE
URSINE IMPERIAL
SALESRESISTANCE
SCAN EVADE GIRT
REVS DARES ETES
```

53

```
BEATNIK SPUTNIK
ANTOINE TERRENE
UNTASTY ENDORSE
MAYS ESSEN TOOL
TAR AVAST
HOMEPLATE HESSE
OVERRATE EARTHS
IAD ICELAND OUT
STANCE LITIGATE
TELEO FIREEATER
STOUT RRB
BRAT BREST BRET
EARLIER EAGLETS
LICENSE BIRETTA
SNORTED INORDER
```

54

```
GABS ITZA QUAFF
NILE MOOS UNCLE
ADAR PINKLADIES
RECIFE DEER DET
SKALDS DATA
SLEEP PEBBLE
JAM ASIDE RURAL
UNIS NOX TOMB
DATED STEWS WEE
OTHERS CROWN
MILD SAFEST
OWN VEEP PANTED
WHITEWALLS TULA
LANAI LIEU ADAM
STERN SEEP TYRE
```

55

```
ARCA TEMPS TAFT
BEAD URIAH ADAM
BARA RADIO BATE
ADAMANTINE AMAN
SIS ERS
SAAR JOHNADAMS
SADLY INONU PIA
ALAE ENDOW DPTS
GAM IONIC SOLES
ADAMSMITH ONES
NUT SRA
EADS MAUDEADAMS
TREE ALLEN ALOE
NAVE NONES METE
ALES ETAPE SEAN
```

56

```
ATARMS JET ORES
TUREEN UAR NOPE
OFINDUSTRY EXIT
MALT FUEL PSYCH
PFCS DIF
CATERER RIPOSTE
OPENED GOVERNOR
PINTA OAT SCORN
ASSEMBLY STERNE
SHERBET SIESTAS
PLY HELM
ADORE COME OBOE
JOLI PUNISHMENT
AMES IBO IONIZE
ROSE TAR ABIDES
```

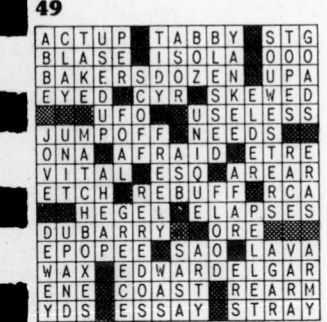

57

```
CAPT  MARAT  SMOG
LURE  OBESE  CAME
ARES  BLASE  ALAN
PASTRY   DATELINE
    SAE   SIEVE
FLATFOOT   RINGER
LOGE  RAHS  LEASE
ARE  RESECTS  LTS
RINGO  TRUE  GLEE
ESTATE   IDEALIST
    SETTO   SAC
BUCKSHOT   SECURE
ABLE  ERATO  IRAN
BEAT  RICIN  ACID
ARMS  SITUS  LIDS
```

58

```
CORAL  AMAS  EAVE
ANISE  WIGWAGGED
DICTA  ARRANGING
STEED  KOALA  LIE
   PRIME  LINERS
JEANNE    ASOLD
ALD  SALLOW  ALEF
MIDI  DIDNT  KOLA
BAYH  OMEGAS  VAT
   ASWAN  IODINE
MENDEL    ALLEN
ALA  DAMON  ERGOT
RICHARDII   RICAN
SHRINKING  ADUST
HUES  SIKH  SEPTS
```

59

```
HEMS  MAST  HEADY
EXIT  INOR  ERNIE
MILA  LENE  RATES
PLAYITAGAINSAM
SENATOR    CREE
   WAN  SHE  RAKE
IDEAL  SCENA  RID
VERYINTERESTING
ELI  CORNY  MIDDY
SENT  TAT  LAG
   OMIT  AUREATE
ROWANANDMARTIN
POLAR  GOOP  COND
APART  ETRE  ANGE
WENDY  MEND  TEED
```

60

```
PALED  TROD  WHAM
ADORE  RULE  HOPI
LIMAS  ADIT  IBEX
AGATE  NEVERMORE
RESORTS    ERIS
   VIAL   SPIDER
COMMENCED  SCALA
UVEA  STARK  ALAN
BANNS  SPINDLING
ELUDED    SEER
   REAL  DEAFEST
CLOAKROOM  SLATE
HAWK  TIKI  TAROT
IDLE  ERAL  IRENE
NESS  DESK  CEDES
```

61

```
NEW  ATTHE  SHOP
ARAB  PERON  TORO
TITO  PAINT  UNAL
OCTOBER  GRACKLE
   TRAY   SUCK
UNVEIL    STUMPS
POISE  JUXTAPOSE
OME  CAKES  THE
LAWNMOWER  SITAR
UNSEEN    THROWS
   ANTE   IRAK
BITTERN  DENIZEN
ADUE  ATSEA  NEVA
FOBS  CROAT  GRIM
FLAT  TELLY  OLE
```

62

```
SIGHT  MOTO  MAWS
TORAH  ARAN  OPIE
ELATE  NEVERDONE
PEN  CULL  FEEDER
   DEARY   SOLS
MADDEN  SPLITSIN
ARUN  SOLIDS  ULE
RECAP  LAC  HOPIS
ICH  AMICAL  MEAT
SAYBROOK  AWARDS
   AIDS   STARS
POLITE  SHEM  EBB
ATANYRATE  PADUA
COZE  NILE  UPEND
KEYS  SLOT  MIDGE
```

63

```
HALE  PLUTO  QUID
ALIT  IONIA  UGLY
HOLE  QUICKFIRES
AHA  PUTT  LOCOS
SACQUES   DIRK
   UPS  LONESOME
CADIS  FIVESIDES
ALEC  ROVED  LENT
BACKDOORS  EVADE
SEATRADE    NAE
   RISS  DERRICK
STINT  MAIS  RHO
QUICKENING  JAIL
TREK  RANCH  EDNA
SERS  SPIES  BEES
```

64

```
CASA  OKLA  DOMED
HULL  RIEN  IRIDO
ARIL  ISTS  ABNER
TIPONESHAND  INA
SCAVENGE   EELS
   ENTO  RAMEKIN
LIBRE  OVER  FIDO
AROW  EDITS  TRIO
SARI  TBAR  AFTON
SKETCHY    ANGI
   SHOE  SCOREPAD
OAT  BLACKBALLER
TRINI  BAIL  DURO
INFUN  ERNE  EMIL
SOFTA  LEGS  REEL
```

65

```
IBSEN  ASHE  HASP
SEATO  DUEL  ASTO
IDIOT  LEXINGTON
SEL  QUIZ  AGONY
   CRUMB  BOVARY
FILLIP    SATYR
ROOST  BETH  DIAS
ATT  EQUATOR  NBA
NAHA  UGLY  HADON
PRIGS  NAGOYA
SYRUPY  JAPAN
AMAIN  SETS  EWE
DOLCEVITA  OUSEL
ECTO  ICON  DRINK
SKAT  ZIPS  YEATS
```

66

```
BOSC  SAGER  SALA
UVEA  CRUSH  ENOS
NAPS  AMATI  NIKE
GLUTEN  MONGOLIA
   LEYTE  POUR
DECLAIMS  STINGY
ACH  SLEEK  STARE
FORK  YENAN  AREA
FLAIL  ROPER  RES
YELLOW  ROBORANT
   OARS  KRAIT
FRAGMENT  ADVISE
LAIR  NARDS  EVES
ETNA  CROAK  REEK
DEUM  HEDDA  ASKS
```

67

```
PRIG  APPT   FLIP
AUTO  SOIR  FLARE
SLAV  SINEQUANON
TELEVISE  URGENT
   RISE  KILO
MAGNET  JUVENILE
ARROW  FADED  LOX
GEAR  HUMOR  JOSE
INS  BUSES  WAVER
CAPSIZES  DIVEST
   HAZE  BONA
JACANA  BOWKNOTS
OVERCHARGE  ECHO
KOREA  CIEL  STIR
EWES  TOYS  EASE
```

68

```
CAMP  CABS  ALTHO
OPAL  OTOE  NEROL
MIRABELLE  SCALA
BACCARAT  HETMAN
   ARCS  GALOP
BOWTIE  PRIMROSE
ACRE  DREAR  SLAT
STA  HAT  ILA
KEPT  LENES  SNAG
STARLETS  PATEDE
   ROAST  TARA
AMOUSE  MARGINAL
DAUNT  CANTONESE
DUNCE  ACTA  ERIN
SIDED  THEN  DONT
```

69

```
ABASE  RHO  EATUP
PALER  EON  STERE
ASPARAGUS  CONGA
SHE  ADAR  SUNDER
   NOTALITTLE
MISHAP  HIE  SAC
ANTA  TABERNACLE
SCORE  NUT  TRAIN
SACERDOTAL  ORES
ASK  EOS  ESSENE
   IMPETRATED
GOALIE  HOPE  YAO
ARMET  BUTTERCUP
SLIDE  ALE  RIATA
PYRES  YES  SOTOL
```

70

```
PALATE   GAFFER
EMINENT  ORIOLES
PINNATE  RATRACE
ODE  MELTERS  TAN
   DEARER  KEPT
MARAN  TILTER
AMIS  SYNERGETIC
SAVEDUP  AUGURAL
CHESAPEAKE  ZAMA
   USESUP  RENAN
RAMP  TRIERS
ACE  BABOONS  POM
POLEAXE  ONETIME
TREACLE  FEDORAS
NETHER  RATERS
```

71

```
ROSS  FLAIL  PLAY
AMAT  OUNCE  LUXE
MAKEFORTHEHILLS
PRIMATES  INLET
   ZED  MAST
BLAMED  BOLSHOI
LORE  SETAE  SNY
EVENSUPTHESCORE
TEA  PROAS  CLOT
ASSENTS  JAMESI
   ACES  BAR
TUTTI  CAPTIONS
ITRIEDMYBESTBUT
DEER  EASER  CODE
ESSE  APTLY  HEEP
```

72

```
BLOB  CHIC  SAME
RAYOF  LOCO  KRIS
AMERICANINDIANS
NEZ  RISK  VINGT
   FENS  DENS
MADAME  CORE  SIP
ACUTE  PLUS  SODA
JAPANESEBEETLES
OREL  SHOT  GRASS
RED  ACAN  BOUNTY
   CLAW  WATT
SEOUL  IASI  VIE
RUSSIANDRESSING
FRAT  TOED  TIETO
DEUS  ERAS  TWOS
```

73

```
GATE  CHUM  ALEC
ORAN  RENO  CAN'T
BALT  I'VE  RIVER
ADORABLE  MOROSE
DON'T  LISA  SITE
   ALA  LIRA
MARC  RESEMBLING
ORATORS  GOTOBED
WINETASTER  VOWS
   ONEO  ADE
SAIC  GNAW  D'ARC
TIRADE  SEMESTER
ANANA  IT'S  OSLO
B'NAI  VERT  LEAP
TILL  AREA  DAYS
```

74

```
TRAS'S  LAIC  RABA
RECIT  OSSA  EDEL
ADANA  CHARIVARI
MONARCHY  AISNE
   DILL  SAGEHEN
HAL  EATSCROW
ALE  TROPES  ENNS
METS  INONE  DIEU
SCOT  SIDING  NOR
   PASTECAN  END
REFEREE  LAMP
UNITE  DISRAELI
SALESGIRL  LINES
EMER  OVIS  ANCON
SIRS  TYNE  TEEST
```

75

```
ETON SHREW JABS
LIMA TEASE ABET
BENI RAISE MAGI
ARISTOTLE PECAN
    HIKE NOISING
OAF LED CURT
DRAPE PERSONAL
ONTO BLISS WOKE
RESTRAIN INDIA
   CORK SIC END
METHANE COOL
OARED WOODNYMPH
TREE TIARA RARE
ETAS ASSET ETAL
LODE METRE SAMP
```

76

```
SWAY IRES JAPAN
TALE RENT OPOLE
ELLS ACTA APRIL
NEO EQUAL NATAL
  TAX TILT LOSS
RAMMED LIRAS
OLEARY SNIP PPH
MONSTER GORILLA
PET EPIS DOGEAR
   ADOBE EPONYM
BERG TRAM ORT
ASHEN OMENS EGO
STONE AINU FOUL
RENDS SLUB RULE
AREAS TESS OSLO
```

77

```
ACTS BOORS GEAR
GHAT INDIA ERIA
TAKEINTOCUSTODY
STERN RECESSES
   PERIL DEER
FRA ULES SPIRAL
AER SITE CEDE
CATCHASCATCHCAN
EVIL THOU RID
DENUDE SALT ERS
   TARA BLOWA
REACTIVE FATAL
INTHENICKOFTIME
VOLE GACID EVEN
EWES ONEND REST
```

78

```
HAREM ABET HARP
ELIDE URSA AREA
RAPID TINNINESS
BEATITUDE MONET
   TOME OPIATE
SPLEEN ORE
PLIERS LABRADOR
LUNAR BAR CRANE
SEAFARER SEALED
NOD GOPHER
SEPTET DIRT
OPERA CERTIFIED
PERENNIAL BARRE
ONCE ATLI LUMIN
RAHS BETE EXACT
```

79

```
ASSET ALOT ISAR
PIQUE LORY NOLO
TRUCE PROLOGUES
SEAL SHE ENERGY
   NICK LORAN
MIDDLESEX USAF
OME AWHILE ECTO
WAR PER IRA HUN
EGER DESPOT ORD
RODE DESDEMONA
   JOUST ENOL
AMIENS FED TWIT
SANCTUARY ALONE
SLOT RHEE TERRA
TENS YSER TYKES
```

80

```
MOWN COBRA AGES
AGIO SMEES TREK
LEST TEAMS MARI
TEPID GRIEF PIE
CATASTROPHES
RACEME TEA
ALA ONEAT RAMP
CATANDTHEFIDDLE
ENOL CANED ALL
   UPS LOCKET
DOGMATICALLY
ARE DARES SNAGS
MIEN RINSE INIT
PESO ESTER CORE
SLEW SHOTS SNOW
```

81

```
CATS SCAB VALES
OSSA ALBA ABIDE
PEACHPIES LUNGE
TAR APPLEBUTTER
   AMES AIS
STAGER BERN DAW
TOGAS ORANGEADE
ANON BAR LUIS
BANANAOIL TINGE
SLY ABED SITTER
   APO TUNE
PLUMPUDDING YAM
RANEE PEARSAUCE
OLDER TARA SMEW
MOORS SLAY PASS
```

82

```
AMER HALS ASSES
TARE OGEE SKIVE
TRAS RIEN KEZAR
ASSESSORS LENA
CHEESE AUDEN
HARDTACK NATION
ROUNDDANCE
LIBS ONRYE LETO
SNOWSUNDER
UNSEEN STANDING
NEEDS SOONER
ASIT COMPAGNIE
LEAPS ABIE GAGA
MANET LOLL ETHS
ASSAY PELL DESE
```

83

```
ABBA ALBS SCALD
GLAD PEAT KAMAR
AEROSPACE ERATO
SUE WASH BLAZES
   FLARE KITTENS
ELAINE SAKES
BACKSLAPPER OLE
AGEE NIP AVER
NOD HAVEANEYETO
   SOLID EXERTS
NOMINAL SWISH
AMOLES BOLT AIM
BELAY MADESENSE
OGAGE OLAF ADES
BARED MIST USES
```

84

```
ROPE DECA FACED
OTIC ICAN LLAMA
THESCOURGEOFGOD
SORTED ALME ETA
   ANE CIO ARES
MENSA FACTOR
EYEY ORS INTENT
TRI SPY TOT COE
ZENITH MAN ROSS
  TREMOR BENET
MOPE LEN ORD
EKE BIAS NAHOOR
MARIEANTOINETTE
EPODE TENO ATOP
LINER ORAN DOES
```

85

```
ALIT ATBAT PEAR
ROLE NIECE APSE
GALL GRATUITIES
OFFSHOOT TOECAP
   ATOLL BOWL
HAVANA MONALISA
ADORE SERI AVAL
GAR SONANCE OLD
AGED PONE VERVE
REDALERT CANYON
   KANT VEDIC
ASCOTS HEREGOES
WHITEHOUSE MARE
OONA OVETA ASIA
LEES PODAL STEM
```

86

```
MARE CARDS SGTS
ELAN OLIVE HOOT
RAGAMUFFIN EDNA
VISCERAL DARWIN
   TNT EMIGRE
REDSUIT ENTITLE
ANU NAIL SERES
DUMB GIRLS SUNS
ARBOR PROW STE
REWROTE WINSTON
   ADDOIL NAY
SLIEST EGGPLANT
TATA ADAMSAPPLE
EMEU LOSEA HEAL
MARX SCENT SRTA
```

87

```
PALP PRODS BARA
ALEE REVET ARIL
STAN OPERA LILT
TARE FINANCIAL
  INTRANSITU
  RENE LOLLARD
SCRAPES SNOOPED
LOATH TWIST
IMMERSE RETESTS
PEASANT EMER
  SOAPDISHES
DETERGING ORAN
SAAR TENOR URSA
ELSE EROSE SEIS
CITY DENES EDNA
```

88

```
WITHA FISH APSE
ADAIR INTO SLAB
NEWSCASTER HALO
GASTANK PANAYAN
  ONSET COMEDY
ANDREW HEELED
WARY EARL ADDUP
ANY ARTISAN ONE
YACHT AFAR TWIT
  LUTIST OPENTO
ARENAS YAMEN
SHAGRAG SANSABA
NINA BOOKSTORES
ONER EYRE AMILE
TORY LAID DELTA
```

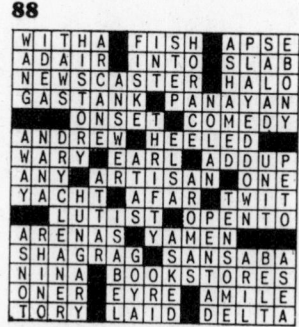

89

```
MIMES SCAMP AJAR
AIDE TUBER NOGO
SNEAKYPETE KLAN
SINGER TEABALLS
   ODOR SCARY
  CHIGNON HEARST
TOONE DICER OOO
RING LINER OGPU
UNE PANEL INEPT
EASTER REENTRY
   THEGO BLAH
CAJOLERY ANEDGE
ATOM SLOPPYJOES
NAHA SOULS ORAN
ENNS ENDUE BARE
```

90

```
AMBI PARED BURL
ROAN ABOVE UNIE
IRID LEVEE LAVA
DELICATE PALLED
   RODS HENS
ALKALI FORKEEPS
CIO ONTOP HYDRA
TARE SALEM EGIS
ONAND HIRAM EMS
NANKIPOO LINSEY
   IDEE CASA
PENNON LOPSIDED
ABED RIODE LALO
URAL ODDER ETON
LORE DEIST DANE
```

91

```
 CELTS REPAST
STAMINA PETRINE
TORONTO USHERED
ORATE PENT CHAD
RIVERBANK BLOKE
KNAR RUTS RULER
SON FILE CIDER
  MOTORCADE
SMART TONE ALT
STOLA SAUD GLUE
TANDY TINYALICE
ENTE SENT MIMES
ADAMITE EVIDENT
MINERAL REGENTS
SNARED SNORT
```

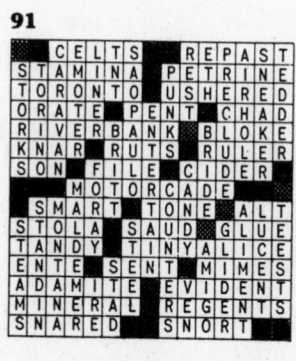

92

```
GAFF IMPI ILMEN
ODAL MOAN NAIVE
ASIE MONTEVIDEO
TURNTO GAZE INN
MYSORE KRIS
  TEXASLEAGUERS
POA OLPE LEVEL
OXLIP YAP EYETO
TEETH SHAM REG
INSTINCTIVELY
  OLIO SENIOR
RIA INST STATOR
EXCITEMENT BHOY
NIECE OLEA LETO
EASES SEAN ERST
```

93

```
BACH  DADA      SACS
ATLI  UPON  CARAT
BOURGEOIS  ARENA
EMBEDS  LEES  TON
HRS  FILLANEED
EPOS  CREMONA
SOU  BOAS  HOMBRE
ALSORAN  GIVEOUT
ULEMAS  COSA  NEE
ENTREAT  BEDS
REINDEERS  MAH
ALB  ERSE  ASLEEP
NISEI  CALCULATE
IDEAS  ULAM  EDNA
SENT  ESSE  TSAR
```

94

```
WISPS  BAD  SOAP
OTARU  ASA  MANIA
REMAP  CAY  INERT
MONTHOFSUNDAYS
SAK  ONEONUS
STS  FUT  MOI
TOSTI  ODOMETERS
ADEEM  NIL  MOTEL
CORRECTED  ADAGE
TRE  ZOH  INA
COLEMAN  YUP
SECONDHANDROSE
ATONE  ORG  ONETO
PORES  UNE  SLURP
ONES  RES  HYPOS
```

95

```
CHAPMAN  FACTO
AUREOLE  MAROONS
SLIPOFTHETONGUE
ALAS  URE  RHONE  CAST
RUSSE
PROPOSES  HICKS
REC  ACTED  EVORA
ANHONOURABLEMAN
MARCO  MANET  MID
SNEAK  DEDICATE
RECTI  REO
ALAI  HASTA  USIS
BORNTOTHEPURPLE
ASTAIRE  MESSIER
TASTE  ASCENDS
```

96

```
COQUET  TAFT  SPA
ALUMNA  OVERSTEP
MAILER  NINETIES
ENNA  NEED  BERLE
TULIPS  ALL
LOUTISH  ICELAND
ESP  SHELVE  AVAR
VALET  SEA  BRACE
EGER  TURNER  NRA
RETINAS  HAUNTED
COX  DOGTAG
AMASS  TAEL  GAZA
BEGOTTEN  EAGRES
ADENOIDS  TIEDUP
SEE  CASE  STRESS
```

97

```
MAHAN  TOBE  ASIT
SCENE  ANON  UPDO
STRAW  AZOV  GALE
HORSELATITUDES
CYR  YEHS
DASH  ALE  RETAPE
ALA  CTENO  TANIA
MINDYOURPSANDQS
ENTER  ROUTS  RUE
SEAMAN  LSU  PEEL
ONOR  NTH
CROCODILETEARS
HOUR  UVEA  ASIAM
OSSA  LENS  SENTA
WATT  ERAT  EDGED
```

98

```
BALSA  UMBER  UFO
UBOLT  NAIVE  NAG
SUPERMARKET  DUD
DIARIES  BENE
PCT  ALMAS  RERAN
IRRA  TON  LETT
PEARS  RAPACIOUS
EPIGENE  ADAMANT
RELAUNDER  PESTO
ELSE  RAG  STIR
PARIS  HIDER  SLY
ARCS  SATIRES  STA
HAIRSTYLIST
HIM  AGREE  EIDER
ASP  GOYAS  STONY
```

99

```
OMAHA  PAAR  BOAR
PILOT  OLLA  ERNE
EXERT  NIDI  RANG
NATIVEDANCER
OBI  CHEER  TEHEE
WATCHES  NOR  EST
ELBA  SERET
KENTUCKYDERBY
SERAI  EROS
SUP  PIN  JOCKEYS
EROSE  IRANI  WOE
DANCERSIMAGE
ANDA  ATOM  ANOSE
TIER  MEDE  RODEO
EARP  PRED  SWAPS
```

100

```
ESP  BLAST  BILK
AMER  RANEE  ALIA
SECURITYANALYST
IRONAGE  COLLATE
AGNEW  CORER
NED  STOW  OSLO
TRAIN  LOOPED
LINEOFSCRIMMAGE
ADESTE  EAVES
WATT  ARMY  CIT
ADMIT  ASONE
ROOMIER  MATISSE
INTERDIGITATION
MEIN  INANE  ONLY
EAST  AGREE  NEE
```

VOLUME 2

Ideally, a reprinted puzzle should be exactly the same as when it first appeared. But times do change; and you can't call Tommy Agee a Met outfielder any more, nor can you refer to "Luv" as a current Broadway play. The result is that an occasional definition has to be tinkered with to keep solvers' eyebrows from being raised. If any anachronisms got by, mea culpa (see Puzzle 30; 52 Across).

WILL WENG

1

ACROSS

1. Rialto offering
5. Urchin
9. Doctor's frequent advice
13. Kansas city
14. Rockfish
15. Used up
17. Odd
19. Repeat exactly
20. Hagen
21. Chemical suffix
22. Large bird
24. Old soldier
25. Ancient ascetics
27. Apartment
29. Feel in one's bones
31. Flowed through
34. Agreements
37. Compensation of a kind
39. Ecuadorean province
40. Loves fatuously
41. Before: Prefix
42. Johnny-one-notes
45. Nicene, for one
47. Spangle
48. Put a vessel in condition
50. Absolute
52. Turn about
56. Primate
58. English repast
59. Compete
60. Propeller
61. Suiting
63. Least bit
66. Animal track
67. Four gills
68. Certain festivals
69. Scraps
70. Droops
71. __ out

DOWN

1. Resentment
2. Bumpkins
3. Pseudonym
4. Baseball nickname
5. Up
6. Period of the late 30s
7. Literary scraps
8. Bundles
9. Brahms work
10. French drink
11. Lincoln hat
12. Head, in Lyons
16. Seine
18. Earth's belts
23. Calliope and others
26. New York time
28. Lacrosse team
30. Share in
32. Common French verb
33. Did a hair job
34. Flowers, for short
35. Indonesian islands
36. William, for one
38. Worthy
40. Recipient
43. Baseball term
44. Giggles
45. Cat
46. Way: Abbr.
49. Boxer's tricks
51. Grates
53. Once-popular children's book figure
54. Soupy of TV
55. Obliterate
56. Nincompoop
57. Squash or melon
62. Won
64. Gov't agency
65. Gaelic name

2

ACROSS

1. Available
6. Commander in Revolution
10. Be off!
14. French river
15. Bandy words
16. Weight deduction
17. Girl's name
18. Evening, in Naples
19. Island land
20. Become upset
22. Every: Ger.
23. Prefix with freeze or body
24. Farthest
26. Where kinder learn to write
30. Wall hanging
32. At __ for words
33. Features of jazz
37. Asian boundary river
38. Enervates
39. Course
40. Openings
42. River area
43. Control board
44. Performed, in a way
45. Note
48. Bolivian Indian
50. Part of a Latin trio
51. Post Office function
57. Year during reign of Henry I
58. Southwest wind
59. Free
60. Wine: Prefix
61. Regarding
62. Prevent
63. Realized
64. Myrna and others
65. Cherished ones

DOWN

1. Cassini
2. __ contendere
3. Pinball word
4. Mars: Prefix
5. Writers of a sort
6. Useful quality
7. Postal service
8. Speedy one
9. Removals
10. Gets at some mail
11. Ponti
12. Seed coverings
13. Stand
21. Noun suffix
25. Brown
26. "__ prayer..."
27. Strike
28. Predicament
29. Seizure of a kind
31. Is sorry for
33. Unmask
34. Barbershop item
35. Feminine ending
36. Food fish
38. Some letters
41. Seafarer
42. Hung loosely
44. Cub Scout unit
45. Kind of gin fizz
46. Allen or Griffin
47. Muskie's state
49. Exasperates
52. __ consequence
53. Month, in Italy
54. "__ boy!"
55. Stravinsky
56. Cuts off

3

ACROSS

1. Thick piece
5. Rosters
10. Retired
14. Kind of dancer
15. In __ (hurrying)
16. Mud puddle
17. Indigo source
18. Disarray
20. Pruning tool
22. Like some castles
23. __ Peter Dunne
25. Old auto
26. "R.U.R." character
29. Periods
31. Cereal bristles
34. With bad intent
36. Vehicle
38. Chit of a sort
39. Most nervy
41. Lettuce type
43. Building wing
44. Court-case figure: Abbr.
46. Grain appendage
47. Timber wolf
49. Hard to find
51. Change
52. Exist
54. Post again
56. Narcotic
59. Game shot
63. Business paper
65. A tide
66. Words of understanding
67. Dervish
68. Nerve
69. Enunciates
70. Candy
71. Scions

DOWN

1. Try: Colloq.
2. Wool: Prefix
3. Leaf angle, in botany
4. Wallet
5. Gaseous element
6. Baltimorean
7. Pachyderms
8. Residue
9. Playwright
10. __ minute
11. Most wavy
12. Gardner
13. Action
19. Legal group
21. Putsch leader
24. Summer mansion in Turkey
26. Insurgent
27. Convex molding
28. Object of a homecoming plea
30. Dry season: Sp.
32. Type of Americano
33. Table item
35. River into North Sea
37. Throw off course
40. Peter, for one
42. Humorist Josh
45. Cook before
48. Papal capes
50. Girl's name
53. W.W. II area: Abbr.
55. Warning
56. Geisha garb
57. Italian city
58. Belongings: Abbr.
60. Gas: Prefix
61. Ark weather
62. Store divisions: Abbr.
64. Adage

4

ACROSS

1. Spread thickly
8. He makes house calls
15. A place for jewelry
16. Far out
17. Tempest in __
18. Mocks
19. Mets or Jets
20. Word with cracker or hatch
22. Like lily pads
23. Don Juan creator
25. Matted fabrics
26. Show of sorts
30. Princess Anne to Margaret
32. Kind of stance
34. New Guinea port
35. "__ silly question . . ."
39. Commended
41. Like a medium
43. Preservative
44. Vex
46. Hubbub
47. Desolate
49. Baltic people
50. Highly flavored
54. English admiral
56. Convict's goal
58. Famous Norwegian
59. Seaweed
63. Astronomy Muse and others
65. Of antimony
67. Easing of world tensions
68. Solar phenomenon
69. Crystal-ball gazer
70. Balkan range

DOWN

1. Fuel soil
2. Better than never
3. Neighborhood
4. Bridge term
5. Exceed
6. Cabinet wood
7. Boomerang act
8. Foot: Prefix
9. Draft animals
10. Attack with repeated fire
11. Stereotyped
12. Award
13. Catkin
14. Sets of boxes
21. Struggle
23. Jerking motions
24. Wagon pole: Dial.
26. Strikes
27. Soup ingredient
28. Telephone tone
29. Voice
31. "L'état __"
33. Eye: Fr.
35. Highest point
36. Close
37. Skirt of sorts
38. Book of the Bible
40. Scott
42. Holiday time
45. Marx
47. Signature on a news story
48. American industrialist of W.W. II era
50. Taters
51. Gay __
52. Disturbed
53. Fur-fiber worker
55. Vessel similar to a yawl
57. Has a bite
59. Make __ for
60. Early Chinese poet
61. Pant
62. Opposite of aweather
64. French adjective
66. World workers' group: Abbr.

5

ACROSS

1. Dance
5. __ Magnon
8. Kind of numeral
14. Brainstorm
15. Scuttle
16. Latin rhythm
17. Home
19. Died down
20. Speechify
21. Rub out
22. Put on
24. Reader
28. Command
30. World area
31. Compass point
34. Agitate
35. Feeling
37. Weather forecast
38. Dividing walls
39. Reputation
40. Include
42. "__ evil . . ."
43. Netherlands commune
44. Word with bahn or mate
45. Seafood item
46. More rugged
48. __ poetica
49. Jelly garnish
52. Moved slowly
54. Spinner of life's thread
56. Potential loser
59. Whigs' opponents
60. Wire measure
61. Pelvic bones
62. Exhausts
63. Tiny
64. Broker's advice

DOWN

1. Offer
2. Stir
3. Sour ingredient
4. Den
5. Mollusk
6. Log-rolling contest
7. Canticle
8. Arabian cloth
9. Miss Peters
10. Tocsin
11. Greek letter
12. Incenses
13. Cipher
18. Mountain retreat
22. Law
23. In stock
25. Continues
26. Needs
27. Peak in Thessaly
29. Whether __
31. One way to ride
32. Certain frontiersman
33. Matriculates
35. Eastern alliance
36. Golf club parts
38. Goad
41. Paired off
42. Swell
45. Interfere
46. Participate
47. Spirit
49. Biblical book
50. Hog food
51. Opening
53. Strife goddess
55. W. W. II group
56. John L. Lewis's org.
57. Iranian export
58. Measure: Abbr.

6

ACROSS

1. Zoo sounds
6. Where Surabaya is
10. Bind tightly, asea
14. French thoroughfare
15. Leaf angle
16. __ mutton
17. Imperil
19. Leap __
20. Reptile
21. Adversaries
22. Badger
24. Douceurs
25. Russian peninsula
26. Took an oath
28. Erring
32. One at __
33. Spheres
34. Jubilate
35. City near Tel Aviv
36. Line up
37. Sharpen
38. Unruffled
39. Single
40. Inert gas
41. Return
43. Saint __ River, to Soo Canals
44. Month
45. Reads
46. Remnant
49. Go to __ of trouble
50. Undertake
53. Caesar's wife
54. Opposite
57. Shakespearean role
58. Control
59. Veni, translated
60. Associate
61. Joining piece
62. Tobacco worker

DOWN

1. Indian ruler
2. Corrida encouragement
3. Drooping
4. Capitol Hill man: Abbr.
5. Marine phenomenon
6. Becomes weary
7. W. W. II powers
8. Namely: Abbr.
9. Pub
10. Certain birds
11. Give off fumes
12. Bedouin headband
13. Reflect on
18. Do a rodeo job
23. Letter
24. Bar offering
25. Afghanistan's capital
26. Stanza
27. Shrivel
28. Fleck with color
29. Sardonic humor
30. Taboo things
31. Verdon
32. Geologic periods
33. Snow leopard
36. Predicament
40. Yellowish
42. Bakery item
43. Debatable
45. Slope: Suffix
46. Russian city
47. Skating leap
48. Scoreboard entry
49. Star in Perseus
50. Ivan the Great
51. Frost
52. Belgian river
55. Modern: Prefix
56. Old French coin

7

ACROSS

ACROSS

1. Eastern church title
5. Coarse corn
9. Super __
14. Martin
15. Muse
16. Site of Expo 70
17. Target
19. Marsh plants
20. Circulating
21. Straddling
23. Intertwined
25. Danish measure
26. Lithe
29. Part of a church period
33. Youth in Greek myth
34. Skiers' lifts
35. Herb
36. Cetaceans
37. River to Moselle: Fr. sp.
38. Girl's name
39. Book of the Bible: Abbr.
40. Memento
41. Neighbor of Leyte
42. Traffic
44. Large dish
45. Foot: Prefix
46. Got along
48. Narrative
51. Woman of fashion
55. Poplar
56. Make an observation
58. First bishop of Paris
59. Mound
60. Seeger
61. Stakes
62. Caen's river
63. Word with stone or star

DOWN

1. River of Italy
2. Laser
3. Fishhook part
4. Greater or Lesser
5. Candle holder
6. Winged
7. Russian village
8. Suffixes in zoology
9. Tobacco plugs, old style
10. Shark of a sort
11. Rotor or radar, for example
12. Pieced out
13. Level: Var.
18. Flaps
22. Weapon, British style
24. Interrogate, in a way
26. Follower of Zeno
27. Left-hand page
28. Outdoor quarters
30. Chagall
31. Emanations
32. Long for
34. Mineral
37. Silken
38. Fundamental
40. Quality of some apples
41. Shoe material
43. Ear of corn, in Africa
44. Air blast device
47. Jordan's capital
48. Russian convention
49. Above: Ger.
50. Signal in bridge
52. Capital of Manche
53. Amphibian
54. Nine: Prefix
57. "The strife is __"

8

ACROSS

1. Technician's milieu
4. Cooling equipment
8. Prosperous
13. Brouhaha
14. Asian cervine
15. Variety of marble
16. Narrow pass
17. Weekdays: Abbr.
18. Inner: Anat.
19. So-so haul of fish
21. Roman official
22. Defame
23. Ruler: Abbr.
25. Man's nickname
26. Volstead's opponents
27. City air problem
29. Canadian province: Abbr.
32. Certain Nevadans
36. Make tight
38. River to the Rhone
39. Interdiction
40. Chinese province
42. Variety of quartz
43. Look over
44. Swabs
47. Direction
50. Malay isthmus
51. Middle East domain
55. Biblical spy
57. Nudes in a Warsaw art gallery
59. Covent Garden offering
60. Wicked
61. Sounds from a corrida
62. Refresher
63. Took a bus
64. Part of a fork
65. Follow
66. Insect
67. Curve of a ship plank

DOWN

1. Type of pneumonia
2. Town in north Italy
3. Directors on a stroll, in a way
4. Truly
5. Menus
6. Great
7. What a fool does sometimes
8. Drinks on the house
9. Farmer's necessity
10. Up to
11. Prepare fish
12. Trojan War name
13. U.S. President
20. Hint
24. Mrs., in France
28. Foundation of sod
29. C.P.A.'s concerns: Abbr.
30. Old French ballad
31. Cask
32. John Hancock: Abbr.
33. Camel's-hair robe
34. Correlative
35. Turf
37. Retaliate with the foot
38. Commune in Saxony
41. Central European river
44. Capital of Yucatan
45. Plain or Spanish __
46. Spot on a card
47. Walter or Barbara Ann
48. Flavor
49. Italian queen
52. Tired
53. Wee
54. Latin infinitive
56. Norse navigator
58. English river

9

ACROSS

1. Military planning
9. Carroll or Josephine
14. Film of the 1960's
15. Oscar-winning film
17. Snakes
18. Shawl, south of the border
19. Cuckoo
20. Good advice
21. Ship: Abbr.
22. Military branch: Abbr.
23. Common vetch
25. Drum
27. Shoshonean
28. Representative
30. Standard
31. __ Gynt
32. Reefs
34. Western characters
36. Fraud
38. Relative of a clarinet
41. Soaked-bread dish
45. Mariner's word
46. Blue or White
48. Less adulterated
49. Highways: Abbr.
50. Head count
52. Noun suffix
53. Mother of 31 Across
54. Partner of 'earty
55. The pike: Scot.
57. Sesame
58. Step
60. Make a sheriff's aide
62. Fine porcelain
63. Hospital personnel
64. Sleeps
65. Eared seals

DOWN

1. Of layers of rock
2. Jurisdiction of Scottish baron
3. In seclusion
4. Fore's partner
5. Pinball expression
6. Put into action
7. Monster with three bodies
8. Time periods: Abbr.
9. Toast
10. Fire __
11. Coin of Laos
12. Person taken from a place
13. Teller
16. Wanderers
21. Framework brace
24. Fire __
26. Small amounts
29. Weather abbr.
31. Opposite of vacuum
33. Cowardly
35. Catch
37. Think: Colloq.
38. Torment
39. Anyone over 30, to the teeners
40. Reticence
42. Italian satirist, 1492-1556
43. Inhabitant
44. Lacking skill
47. City in Oregon
50. West Pointer
51. Coral partitions
56. "__ in the Sun"
59. Tax form abbr.
60. Apart: Prefix
61. Numerical prefix

10

ACROSS

1. Steak tartare, for one
8. Personnel manager
15. Intensify
16. Taint
17. Like some sardines
19. Jungfrau, for one
20. English gun
21. Lumberjacks
22. Slangy replies
24. Detroit product
26. Indian weight
27. U.S. literary initials
29. Combined: Var.
31. Hindu deity
34. Canyons
37. Encounter
39. Slack
40. Ad agency instruction for printing
43. Author Deighton
44. Mountain pool
45. Rotated
46. "... play a part, and mine __ one"
48. Gershwin heroine
50. Flap
51. Former eastern railroad initials
53. Accomplishes
55. Army meal
58. Money, in Madras
61. Bauxite and fool's gold
63. Electronic initials
64. Jet-age merchant of sorts
67. German chemist, 1884-1949
68. Approaching
69. Early ascetics
70. Furs

DOWN

1. Iterate
2. Leg joint
3. Upstarts
4. Isle of __
5. Austrian river
6. Vinegars
7. __ laudamus
8. Laboratory sample: Abbr.
9. Ivy clumps
10. Spanish duke and family
11. Bloom
12. Book by 43 Across
13. Spanish poet's sky
14. Port and vermilion
18. Indian storm current
23. Western plant
25. Draft animals
28. Sassy
30. Camper's home
32. Ceremonial staff
33. Dismissed: Slang
34. River to the Colorado
35. Singles
36. Pierce
38. Race-track figure
41. Angered
42. Streetcar
47. Sprinkle with flour
49. Placid
52. Fasten again
54. Passover festival
56. Play part
57. Marionette family
58. Gullible one
59. Consumes
60. Swing around
62. Stitching edge
65. Beast
66. "Exodus" hero

11

ACROSS

1. Small cactus
7. Common illness
10. Near or Far
14. American Leaguer
15. __ Palmas
16. Battleground in France
17. Famous center fielder
19. Linden
20. Chateau room
21. A coming into view
23. Donder's headwear
25. Do a printing chore
26. Bit
28. Vagrant
29. Hourglass part
30. __ sight
33. Slalom
36. Name for the Babe
39. Long time, out West
40. Skipped lunches
41. Bothers: Colloq.
42. Felt or straw
43. Wheel projection
45. Of the ear
48. Pigeonholes
50. Petty
52. Philippine measure
56. Cans
57. Popular adhesive
59. Storm
60. Lawyer: Abbr.
61. Listed
62. Say yes, informally
63. Grain
64. Vipers

DOWN

1. Hay piles
2. Silkworm
3. Oklahoma fort
4. Kale plants
5. Outlanders
6. Nautical word
7. Blaze
8. Leghorn, for one
9. Shostakovich's land
10. Respect
11. Egyptian symbols
12. Hit a ball in a certain way
13. Window sign
18. Dosage containing honey
22. Surly
24. "__ to the judge"
26. Sambar deer
27. Unusual thing, in London
28. Loot: Slang
29. Shote's area
31. __ King Cole
32. In fact: Fr.
33. See 28 Down
34. A Smith
35. "__ a homer!"
37. Morris K. of Arizona
38. Had a feeling of
42. Admiral of W. W. II
44. Like an ogive
45. Houston player
46. Aleut's craft
47. __ bell
48. Snobbish: Slang
49. Overplay
51. Ivan or Peter
53. Poet's valley
54. Me-tooer
55. Rorem and others
58. Rolled tea

12

ACROSS

1. Italian meal
6. Supplicate
10. Spice
14. Forcefully
15. __ avis
16. Writer Paton
17. Indian title
18. Advocate of Christian unity
20. Cleaners
22. Wrath
23. Lifetimes
24. St. Bernard's burden
25. Victimized
28. Slippery or electric
29. Unrefined
30. Idol's weakness
35. Incompetent
36. Durable wood
37. Church area
38. Perpetual boy
40. Comic-strip character
41. Attention
42. Greek letters
43. Ascended
47. Bock, for one
48. Corday victim
49. Events for Figaro and others
54. Disqualify
56. City problem
57. Spoils
58. Barren
59. Rooms, for Cicero
60. Spooky
61. Somewhat: Music
62. Girls' names

DOWN

1. Paris area
2. Oriental nurse
3. Capital of Yemen
4. Fastener
5. Places of no return
6. Course for future M.D.'s
7. Yonkers events
8. __ for one's money
9. Southern favorite
10. Spiritual nourishment
11. Adjust
12. Boxed
13. Vestibule
19. Furniture period
21. Pointed arch
24. Dante's friend, for short
25. Oval cake
26. Heyerdahl vehicle
27. Canal
28. Wapiti
29. Trophy
30. Container
31. Pass quickly
32. Girl's name
33. Diner's sign
34. __ one's hand
36. Row
39. Hippie's home
40. Persian tiger
42. Shipworm
43. Eye brightener
44. Paddleboat, in a way
45. Warmth
46. Nonclergy
47. __ English
49. Asian finch
50. Commedia dell' __
51. Lass
52. Man's name
53. Red and Coral
55. Vapid writings

13

ACROSS

1. Casa room
5. Fad
9. Prima principia
13. Opposed, Western style
14. Roman road
15. Blazing light
16. Petitioned
17. Famed vaudeville and radio duo
19. Figures in U.S. Revolution
21. Disintegrated
22. In fine fettle
23. Page
24. Covering first, second, etc.
27. Singer Frances
31. Of a church tribunal
32. Schedule: Fr.
33. Mal de __
34. Green isle
35. Prefix for graph or mime
36. Jotting
37. Latin conjugation word
38. Apparel
39. Watch
40. Comic of "Laugh-In" note
42. Upbraid
43. Last word
44. Neighbor of Hung
45. Humperdinck girl
48. Well-known brothers
52. Former comic team
54. Run
55. Yearnings
56. Place for yeux and nez
57. Over: Ger.
58. U.S. missile
59. Impressed
60. Word in a comedy show-biz ad

DOWN

1. Window part
2. Chill
3. Extends
4. Gallagher __
5. Coarse
6. Hum __ (croon)
7. Berliners: Abbr.
8. Sea eagle
9. Conductor's cry
10. Undisguised
11. Algonquian tribe
12. Forward
15. Shelter of a sort
18. Taken care of
20. Tie score
23. Endures
24. Advise, old style
25. Pro __
26. Noun-forming suffix
27. Napery
28. The end
29. Pardon
30. Comic: Fr.
32. Father of Rachel and Leah
35. Myrna Loy's Nick
36. Gay
38. Swains
39. Doublet
41. Conversely
42. Kept afloat, with "up"
44. Tropical timber tree
45. Proverbially, a trifle
46. Full of calories
47. Friend of Narcissus
48. Merganser
49. Ex-isle?
50. Coral formation
51. Bondman
53. R. R. stop

14

ACROSS

1. Wearing apparel
5. Theater part
10. One of the leagues: Abbr.
14. State: Abbr.
15. Finery
16. Rebound
17. Times
18. Rich cake
19. Highways: Abbr.
20. Set aside
22. Yellowish green
24. German article
25. Western city
26. Kiss
31. The Bull
35. Cut grain
36. Car part
38. Hymn
39. Spinner
40. Emit
42. Agnus __
43. Alpena's lake
45. Swallow
46. Shade
47. Twist
49. Let go
51. "__ Three Lives"
53. Poem
54. Seller of chances
57. Bouquet
61. River of Spain
62. Bundle of twigs
64. "J'Accuse" author
65. Southern cape
66. See 64 Across
67. Ogler
68. Unfermented grape juice
69. Fanatical
70. Track event

DOWN

1. Garden tools
2. Soup ingredient
3. European
4. Abated
5. Soak
6. Excess: Fr.
7. Opposite of lv.
8. Everglades denizen, for short
9. Metal ring
10. On edge
11. Program listing
12. Next in order
13. Outdistance
21. State: Abbr.
23. Awkward
26. Straight: Prefix
27. Asian capital
28. Island with a grotto
29. Flavor
30. "This __"
32. Spokes
33. Full of: Suffix
34. English colonist
37. Nut
40. Fishline leader
41. Removed utterly
44. Egg-shaped
46. Beauty-kit item
48. Coat
50. Football scores: Abbr.
52. Vehicle for 5 Across
54. Sports officials: Abbr.
55. Not on __
56. Housewife in Munich
57. __ me tangere
58. Spanish artist
59. Guinness
60. Old nautical term
63. Machine part

15

ACROSS

1. Snowy and spotted
5. Virtuous
10. Mrs. Copperfield
14. A — of color
15. Musical piece
16. Greek goddess
17. Remotely
18. Factotum of a sort
20. Forbearance
22. Irritates
23. German admiral
24. Inscribed
25. Introduces, with "in"
27. Defeat
28. Marienbad, e.g.
29. Hankers
31. Scottish Gaelic
35. Dressler
37. Go to ruin
38. Adjust
39. Sacred chests
40. One with a poor bridge hand
42. Reo or Maxwell
43. Ample
45. Ballot anew
47. Balances
49. Signature on some writings
50. Unrelated to key
51. Converted sea water
55. Geniality
57. Prefix for dynamics
58. Otherwise
59. Long-nosed animal
60. Invalid
61. Loved one
62. Lord Avon and others
63. Carob

DOWN

1. Exam
2. Odin's Frigga
3. Predator of sorts
4. Part of a chevron
5. Most squalid
6. Of the ear
7. Elemental
8. American humorist
9. Treasurer's concerns
10. Poured
11. Speechify
12. Frosted
13. Serpents
19. Eagles
21. Strange
24. Keats and Milton
25. Landmark on the Hudson: Abbr.
26. Mast
27. Pronoun
30. Rugged rocks
32. Man with a story
33. Young oyster
34. To be, in France
36. Hawaiian, for one
38. Sphere of activity
40. Ecclesiastic
41. School supplies
44. Man's name
46. Flying
47. Came secretly, with "in"
48. Georgia river
50. Matured
51. Gull
52. Cork's land
53. One of the Gardners
54. Dispensation
56. Small boy

16

ACROSS

1. Best, in Paris
6. Sicilian tourist sight
10. Jewish month
14. Cursed
15. Call for attention
16. General character
17. Egg-shaped
18. Returned a bridge insult
20. Memos
22. ___ voce
23. Or ___
24. Horatian, for one
25. Win
26. Yellow journal: Slang
28. Bulwark
32. Symbol of strength
35. Litterer
38. ___ Rios, resort in Jamaica
39. "___ Sheboygan"
42. Cupid
43. Splashed
44. Jane ___
45. Many
47. Puerto Rican drink
49. Capek play
50. Pronoun
52. Silkworm
56. City on the Po
59. Tailing
61. Flows over
63. Hair tint
64. Mona ___
65. Fare
66. Caucasian
67. Summers, in Nice
68. Flossy
69. Cubic meter

DOWN

1. Duty
2. Orgy
3. Tests
4. Occupation
5. Garden
6. Kind of seal
7. "I'll be ___"
8. Film-actor Sparks and others
9. Common Latin word
10. Basically
11. Idiot
12. Dill
13. Make over
19. Employs
21. Warmhearted one
25. Reaped
27. Panay native
28. Turkish governors
29. Made sure of: Colloq.
30. Where Lima is
31. "___ so brave"
32. Portent
33. Prefix for flying
34. Speed unit
36. Weather word
37. Dallas college: Abbr.
40. Wives of Nicholas and Ivan
41. Fuss
46. Supply money for
48. Up-to-date
50. Halloween apparel
51. Kind of pudding
53. See 63 Across
54. The ___ man
55. Marble
56. Piece in a game
57. Determinate amount
58. Trick
59. Ado
60. Exclamations
62. Girl's name

17

ACROSS

1. Make fun of
5. Work —
10. Mets' arena
14. Look —
15. Intractable horse
16. Sprite
17. Woody fiber
18. Sound of displeasure
20. Display
22. House parts
23. Upbraids
25. Coffeemaker
26. Home of Kennedy Airport
29. Sudden outburst
34. Family member
35. Unusual
36. Siouan Indian
37. In vain
38. Summer, in Tours
39. Midge
40. P. I. dyewood tree
41. Supports
43. Specter
44. Reserve
46. Yield
47. Jagged line
48. Doc or Sneezy
50. "All the world's — ..."
53. Connect
57. With 59 Across, wild carrot
59. See 57 Across
60. Foregoing: Abbr.
61. Fabric finish
62. Thor's stepson
63. Complete turns
64. Les femmes
65. Watercraft

DOWN

1. Agree
2. Have — to grind
3. Elegant
4. Altogether
5. Certain circuits
6. Piano's opposite
7. Bygone
8. Scoreboard data
9. Character
10. Enigmatic one
11. Yesterday, in Arles
12. Letters
13. Seaport of Scotland
19. Noel
21. Source of harm
24. Made out
26. On even terms
27. Inappropriate
28. Brilliance
30. Part of the fauna
31. English Victorian novelist
32. Dye mixture
33. Musical piece
35. Exigency
39. Iron, for one
41. Thai
42. Hunter's quarry
43. Man's nickname
45. Mexican Indians
46. Sweetens the pot
49. Reporter's question
50. Nimbus
51. Percolate
52. Chemical ending
54. Circle
55. Western campus
56. Jaunty
57. As much as you please: Lat. abbr.
58. Nothing

18

ACROSS

1. Sports name
5. Exclamation
9. Verse
14. College in North Carolina
15. Jester
16. "South Pacific" or "Wayside Inn"
17. Approach, in a way
19. Migrant workers
20. __ the collar
21. Della
22. Upper space
23. __ band
26. Producer, as of books
29. Mild oath
32. Grenoble item
35. Water, at cocktail time
36. Kind of type: Abbr.
37. Hoity-toity
39. Arrange
41. __ hejirae
42. Johnson in-law
44. Norse goddess
45. Destiny
46. Tramp
47. Queen
49. Insects
54. Gielgud vehicle
56. Endures successfully
59. Do a cartographer's job
60. Indicated
61. Musical piece
62. Ego
63. Ruffle
64. German river
65. Hunted animal
66. Bird

DOWN

1. __ de-mer (a pidgin English)
2. Assign
3. Stall
4. Result
5. Among
6. Short message
7. Loving
8. Capitol Hill man: Abbr.
9. __ trooper
10. Use the pool
11. One who conveys property
12. Necklines
13. Sum, __, fui
18. Add value to
24. Required
25. Wrong
27. Peace, in Hinduism
28. Sixth planet from sun
30. U. S. agency
31. Secluded valley
32. Food fish
33. The movies, in Europe
34. Dullard
38. Domestic
40. Did the prunes
43. Sentry
48. Curious one
50. Bet on __ thing
51. Lethargy
52. Interpose
53. Embezzled
54. Attracted
55. Network
57. Useless
58. Flout
60. Cobra

19

ACROSS

1. Serval, for one
7. Tool
14. Looks up to
15. Land area
16. First-hand
17. Substitutes
19. Initials on an airport board
20. Pets
22. Political boss: Abbr.
23. "___ face red?"
24. Groups
26. Stillness
29. Backward, in France
32. Over
33. Run a ___ ship
34. Copies, for short
38. Small shark
39. Stage direction
41. Explorer
42. Nymph
44. Beyond, old style
45. Hindu epic hero
46. "___ the green"
48. Encourage
49. Cuts
52. Lake for 42 Across
54. Exclamation
55. Become attached
58. Author of sayings
61. English poet
63. North Sea port
65. Charms
66. Brought up
67. Kind of eyes
68. Spreads

DOWN

1. Vanish
2. Revise
3. Girl's name
4. Pet
5. Land strips
6. Appraise
7. Fish for trout
8. Entr' ___
9. Seance event
10. Responsive devices
11. Lodging of a kind
12. Well-coordinated
13. Peter's friend
18. Undergraduates: Abbr.
21. Relatives of taskmasters
23. Call in question
25. Experienced
26. Roman statesman
27. One who does: Suffix
28. Easy stride
30. Babe and others
31. Harp on
35. Urchin
36. On ___
37. Word of exit
40. Muscles
43. Concoct
47. Film awards
49. Biblical prophet
50. ___ of steam
51. ___ à manger
53. Place again
56. Indian
57. Pause
58. Pool
59. Over
60. Gambler's concern
62. Drink
64. Pitch

20

ACROSS

1. Mexican stew
5. Arctic gear
10. Alpine gear
14. Well, to a Parisian
15. City south of Amarillo
16. Sicilian resort
17. Improvised
19. Billboard
20. Tennis term
21. Pericarp
22. Exultant
24. Borzoi
26. Arrest
27. Play __
29. Elevates
33. English poet
34. Plant stems
35. Philippine tree
36. Invented
37. Sheltered places
38. Redolence
39. Dessert
40. Juvenile author
41. Yellowish white
42. Reject
44. Until: Sp.
45. Southern sea
46. Opera segment
48. Kept for reference
51. Dartmoor, e.g.
52. Cochineal
55. Ponder
56. Generous
59. Short-eared dog, in heraldry
60. Rocky Mountains of Utah
61. "When I was __"
62. Boor
63. Rocky Mountains of Wyoming
64. Signal flare of W. W. I

DOWN

1. Old Greek coin
2. Biography
3. Pitcher
4. Opposite of syn.
5. Poop deck
6. Clear
7. Hebrew month
8. Contrast: Abbr.
9. Football scores
10. Part of an opener
11. Interlock
12. U. S. dramatist
13. Beach
18. High: Fr.
23. Common suffix
25. River of Normandy
26. More reasoned
27. Concede
28. Trespass
29. Fasten, in a way
30. One way to ride a horse
31. W. W. I vessel
32. Cleveland suburb
34. Phony
37. A kind of sale
38. Algerian city
40. Military truant
41. Pincerlike claw
43. Eastern countries
46. Cub infielder
47. Show-business name
48. Gem
49. I am unwilling: Lat.
50. Dresden housewife
51. Guy
53. Two semesters
54. Famed Hollywood Mountie
57. Pandowdy
58. Defense arm: Abbr.

21

ACROSS

1. Witty saying
6. U.S. sculptor
10. Fellow
14. Pitcher's forte
15. Eastern name
16. Steak instruction
17. Attired
18. Name for certain workers
20. __ loss
21. Set up the pool balls
23. Ancient musician
24. Symbol of curiosity
26. Silly: Colloq.
27. Goodman, for one
28. Midwesterner
32. Very soiled
36. Stowe girl
37. "At __!"
38. Aspiration
39. Word of agreement
40. German pronoun
41. Drawing
45. Scoundrel
47. __ spree
48. Indites
49. Disconnect
53. Sign of obeisance
56. Corrida performer
57. __ Dolorosa
58. Immortality
60. Court defense
62. Feuchtwanger
63. Atlas name
64. Roadside rest
65. See
66. Cowboy's concern
67. Measure of capacity

DOWN

1. Discard
2. Share
3. Word with blight or renewal
4. Common contraction
5. Lowest stratum
6. Opera character
7. Run __
8. In-thing
9. Singing sounds
10. Candia resident
11. Espionage name
12. Clumsy craft
13. Hanger-on
19. Of the cheek
22. Geography word
25. Fresh-water fish
26. Fairy-tale character
28. Form of decoration
29. Lesser: Prefix
30. What some gamblers hope to get
31. Pealed
32. Mrs. Truman
33. Secular
34. Befuddled
35. Certain tales
39. Muezzin's call
41. Work by Massenet
42. Inopportune
43. Go places
44. Encroachments
46. Repetitive chant
49. Sycophant
50. Like a ram
51. Filament
52. Laissez __
53. Vegetable
54. Revolutionary patriot
55. Wallop
56. Musical sound
59. __ Paulo
61. College subject, for short

22

ACROSS

1. Menu listing
7. Team
11. Kind of view
14. Divination
15. French mathematician
17. Good sense
18. Words on a menu
19. Container
20. Operatic prince et al.
22. Portly
23. Fragrant
25. First Hebrew letter
26. Genesis figure
27. Pipesmoker's tool
29. Hasty
31. Partner of Scotch
34. Inlet
36. Shelter
37. Household appliance
40. Apartment-house employee
42. Napoleon's island refuge
43. __ generis
44. Preposition
45. Navy boats
47. Gears' relatives
49. Conceal
53. Late billiard champ
55. Dante
58. More effective
59. Cyrus of Carter's cabinet
60. Kind of mention: Abbr.
61. Good ship
63. Tag on
65. "__ of Venus"
66. Hampton
67. Foot: Prefix
68. Map abbrs.
69. Papal official

DOWN

1. French writer
2. Lines
3. Where Entebbe is
4. German preposition
5. Cookbook direction
6. Irish playwright
7. Lacedaemon
8. Records of debt
9. Cutting remark
10. Sign up
11. Tree
12. Locale of Isle of Man
13. Part of handwriting on the wall
16. Pole used in Gaelic games
21. Rochester's waterfront
24. River in Yorkshire
25. Runway part
28. U. S. President
30. Layer
32. Harvest goddess
33. Card
35. Bon __
37. __ ammoniac
38. Turkey part
39. Eulogized
41. Apple
46. Variety of wheat
48. Statistician's aids
50. Olympian
51. Kitchen tool
52. Gentle
54. Antecedent
56. Cookbook direction
57. Cuttlefish
58. Skewed
59. Viva __
62. Stock market maneuver
64. Utensil

23

ACROSS

1. Cayuse
5. Sends on: Abbr.
9. Nymph who became a laurel
11. Tolerates
13. Omitted
14. Jewelry item
16. Helmsman's order
17. Affairs __
19. Buddy
20. Birds of New Zealand
22. Flowerless plants
23. Raillery
24. Confound
26. Can. province
27. Sight on Martinique
28. Broadway hit, informally
30. Wrinkles
32. Appreciative words
34. Stronghold
36. Seaport of Eire
39. Tendon
40. Sesame
42. La Scala unit
44. Noun ending
45. Aristate
47. Prolific author
48. Kennel sound
49. Beat
51. Denouement
52. Kind of singer
54. Other names
56. City on the Passaic
57. First baseball czar
58. Tore
59. Votes for

DOWN

1. Chemical element
2. Choose
3. Go away!
4. Extinguish (with "out")
5. Campus groups
6. Suffered attrition
7. Coq __
8. Sun Valley gear
9. Social events
10. Relative of et al.
11. Hashhouse
12. Moves sinuously
13. Gives the nod
15. Merriment
18. Submitting
21. Dabble in
23. Shylock's daughter
25. Sound of disbelief
27. Pry and others
29. Owned
31. Greek goddess
33. TV chain
34. Fruitcake ingredient
35. Tidy
37. Beginning
38. __ own
39. Like a popular herb
41. Licit
43. Words omitted in asyndeton
45. Ready to act
46. Setback
49. Patisserie item
50. Enjoy a repast
53. Farm animal
55. Oil city of Oklahoma

24

ACROSS

1. Lincoln's birthplace
6. Winks
10. Over
14. Harangue
15. The Iliad, for one
16. Italian resort
17. Editor's mark
18. Jan van der __
19. Consumer
20. Berliner's upper
21. Remember
23. Volcanic matter
24. Overcharge: Slang
25. Greek god
26. Rose dye
28. Unfamiliar
32. Girl's name
34. Off-color
35. Attention
36. Site of Napoleonic victory
37. Pliny the __
39. Greek letter
40. Capability: Suffix.
41. Roman date
42. Turkish inn
44. Book supplements
46. Tolerate
47. 1101
48. Soon after
49. W. W. II agency
52. Seize arbitrarily
56. Mop
57. Korean name
58. Slangy negative
59. Unkempt
60. "__ we got fun"
61. Eject
62. A slope
63. Up-to-date ones
64. Ball team
65. An ICBM

DOWN

1. Beverage
2. Sheiks and others
3. Hatless
4. Appian Way
5. Final
6. Debase
7. Vertical, as an anchor
8. Row
9. Hollywood worker
10. Ex-coed
11. Unless: Latin
12. One bite ended it
13. News
21. Corned beef and cabbage
22. Ointment
24. Direction: Abbr.
27. Kimono accessory
28. Visualize
29. Chronic idler
30. Entrance
31. Common Latin verb
32. Pelvic bones
33. Convinced: Colloq.
34. Upper British house: Abbr.
38. Grassland
39. Rumanian coin
41. Early Peruvian
43. Handbook: Abbr.
45. Insects
46. Sails
48. Like some coffee
50. Where Galileo taught
51. Bottomless pit
52. Prepare for finals
53. Buckeyes' home
54. Recover
55. St. Peter's feature
56. A kind of belt
59. Depot: Abbr.

25

ACROSS

1. Prohibition
5. Division word
9. Ledger item
14. Above
15. "Silent Night" lyricist
16. Words in handbook titles
17. Kiddie __
18. Frost, for one
19. Skirt style
20. Joy and gladness
22. Cape Horn natives
23. Johnson and Garner
24. Shrouding
28. Riles
32. French appetizers
35. Impressive
36. Veneto or Appia
37. Ages
38. Change
39. Big Top
40. __ vous plaît
41. Standouts: Slang
42. Artery
43. Dawdle
46. Affirm
47. Girl's name
51. Baltic native
53. Explosive shells
55. Smokers' product
57. With the purpose
58. Salamander
59. Put away
60. Former Met star
61. Ablative, for one
62. __ of humor
63. Prefix for cede or date
64. Culbertson and others

DOWN

1. Be silent, in music
2. __ of woe
3. Death Valley product
4. Executes a theatrical ploy
5. Tax
6. Time of day
7. No refunds, in other words
8. Scrap
9. Exclamation
10. Parting words
11. Shift in attitude
12. Sicilian sight
13. __ the mark
21. Suffixes meaning made of
25. Overrun
26. __ vult, crusaders' cry
27. Man or Bermuda: Abbr.
29. Wind-propelled vessel
30. "__ what she used ..."
31. "So long!"
32. Nuisance
33. Forte of 60 Across
34. Long-winded debate
38. Northern Indiana sight
39. Ballerina's routine
41. Spanish pronoun
42. "__ around the house"
44. Chemicals
45. In actuality: Lat.
48. Model
49. Gossipy
50. Western park
51. Miss
52. Villa near Rome
54. Bombast
56. Regard
57. Resort

26

ACROSS

1. Engagement: Abbr.
6. Heavenly being: Fr.
10. Results: Abbr.
14. El __
15. Tusked animal
16. Lamb
17. Famous museum
20. Soul, in France
21. Apart: Prefix
22. Occasionally
23. Hair curler
26. Agnus __
27. Fruit
29. Greek commune
32. Theology degrees: Abbr.
35. Entice
37. "__ gloom of night ..."
38. Melt
39. Greek letter
40. Teas
43. Prefix for med or meditate
44. Spanish pot
46. Hawaiian food
47. Dulling influence
49. Spanish painter
50. Appendages
52. Poet
53. Shoshonean
55. Goad
57. Became serious
61. He is: Lat.
62. Numerical prefix
65. Famous art gift
68. Common contractior
69. Part of a ship
70. Golf nickname
71. Girl's name
72. Gambler's word
73. Rule: Fr.

DOWN

1. Ewe lamb: Lat.
2. Baby carriage
3. Old master
4. Twelfth-century date
5. Bye-bye
6. Degraded
7. __ pros
8. Silly: Slang
9. Part of Q.E.D.
10. Most slippery
11. Art of a certain school
12. Discharge
13. Asserts
18. Nothing
19. British equivalent of co.
24. Previous
25. Works by a French Impressionist
27. Choir members
28. American painting family
30. __ dieu!
31. Therefore
33. Missiles
34. Dry's opposite
36. Familiar negative
41. Mauna __
42. Vehicle
45. Certifies
48. Words of assent
51. Makes plain
54. Speech sounds
56. Take advantage of
57. Playlet
53. 'Arry's steed
59. U.S. satellite
60. Mrs. Eisenhower's maiden name
63. Muddy
64. Arrow poison
66. Legal degree
67. Italian number

27

ACROSS

1. Blarney
9. Composed
15. Being
16. Thin fabrics
17. Military incursion
18. Axilla
19. Miss
20. Bars
22. Brew
23. Lawyer: Abbr.
24. Far: Prefix
25. __ bellum
26. Hebrew letter
28. Leporid
29. Frighten
30. Leaves out
32. Highest point in orbit
33. Word
36. Cordial flavoring
37. Lapel
38. Literary output
39. __ which way
40. Mend
41. Optimistic
45. Indian weights
46. Open-weave fabric
47. Call __ day
48. Distress
49. Flighty
51. Bluster
52. Freeze, in France
54. Condiment plant
56. Quintessence
57. Fodder
58. Altar seat
59. Reached

DOWN

1. Arranged like a ladder
2. Highly adorned
3. Holy days
4. Appendages
5. Depot: Abbr.
6. Yorkshire river
7. Having bristles
8. Besets
9. Scenic view
10. Blunders
11. Political party: Abbr.
12. Natural endowment
13. Linden
14. Looked up to
21. Arena cheer
25. "For every winner __"
27. Baseball thrills
28. Greet the villain
29. Sacred bull
31. Mud-filled
32. Shortly
33. Portends
34. Morning signal
35. Coated
36. Overbearing
38. Cure-all
40. Eastern state: Abbr.
42. Texas V.I.P.
43. Foil
44. Stood agape
46. Actor Peter
49. Conceal
50. Formerly, old style
51. Indonesian island
53. 111
55. Prefix for thermy and lect.

28

ACROSS

1. Took care of
6. Chipped in
10. Put on __
14. Western city
15. Surrounded by
16. Small amount
17. Liquid measure
18. Information
19. Biblical trio
20. Zoo animals
21. Neighbor of Rhodesia
23. Brahms work
25. Gazelle
26. Nearing port
28. Miss Chase
30. "__ but you"
31. In a certain position
35. Artful
36. Picket-line participant
39. Scotsman's denial
40. Place
42. __ the bag
44. Anna's destination
45. Aseptic
47. Convex molding
50. Placed abreast
52. All over
54. Indigence
57. Neat as __
58. School: Abbr.
59. Article of clothing
60. Having proper qualities
61. __ majesty
62. Wake
63. Birds
64. Roman date
65. Available

DOWN

1. Auctioneer's word
2. French companion
3. Gunga Din and others
4. Immediately after
5. Row
6. Like codfish and haddock
7. Dumfound
8. Leafy vegetable substance
9. Cheese
10. Navy V.I.P.
11. Native of Mosul
12. Trickster
13. Sales talk
21. Town: Abbr.
22. Certain stores
24. Doubt
26. Examiner: Abbr.
27. __ contendere
29. Washington & __
31. Diminutive suffix
32. Reversed
33. Fasten
34. Sarazen
37. Spanish relative
38. Wooed
41. Keys
43. Eastern capital
45. Suit
46. Jutting rock
47. Old enough
48. Moisture
49. Constellation
51. Vegetables
53. Spanish painter
55. "Lohengrin" heroine
56. Hard to understand
59. Hit sign

29

ACROSS

1. Add interest to
6. World's highest capital
11. Hindu holy city
13. Dulls
15. Competitor
16. Vesture
17. Round __ ball
18. On top
20. Durocher
21. Out of __
23. Pub serving
24. Billycocks
25. Parcae
26. Waterfront union: Abbr.
27. Praying figures
29. Informal gathering
32. Term in heraldry
33. European area
34. Jut out
36. Wine additive
38. Careless
42. Participant
44. Norse goddess
45. Flying men from Down Under: Abbr.
47. Solid
48. Arab headband
50. Moving
51. Emeritus: Abbr.
52. __ water
54. Adjective suffix
55. Ear shell
57. Candidate
59. Former prisoner
60. Plane-wing devices
61. Stares
62. Copies, familiarly

DOWN

1. Examiners
2. Border lake
3. Roman god
4. Tests
5. Coty
6. Roof
7. British marshal of W.W. I
8. Navy man: Abbr.
9. Danish island: Var.
10. Girl's name
11. Quadruped
12. Binding devices
13. Albanian river
14. Facing a glacier
19. "Buenos __"
22. Shaving of the head
24. Plane sheds
26. "__ body meet . . ."
28. Circular: Ger.
30. Willing: Colloq.
31. Asian country
35. Calendar abbr.
36. Notions item
37. Fanfare
39. Become known (with "out")
40. Silk and cotton fabric
41. People looking for taxis
42. Discard
43. Entertainer Ella
46. Disengages
49. Part song
50. Grant
52. Pier
53. Certain votes
56. Cut off
58. Colombian people

30

ACROSS

1. Nonsense: Colloq.
5. Novarro
10. Undisguised
14. Court cry
15. Ham it up
16. Crystal gazer's words
17. Austrian city on Danube
18. Robin Hood locale
20. Neighbor of Ill.
21. Thrash
22. Varieties of plums
23. Young salmon, in England
25. Realm of Otto I: Abbr.
26. "__ for the birds"
27. Neutral vessel in wartime
32. Tantivy
35. Bricks, iron dogs, etc.
36. Crisp bread
37. Skirt parts
38. Point of land
39. Rolls
41. N. L. team
42. Genoa and Seattle
43. Rialto sign
44. Worldwide: Abbr.
45. Windups for some pitchers
49. Fur animal
51. Commend
52. __ culpa
53. Means
55. Higher, in Berlin
56. Relative of etc.
57. Noted Italian
58. Western nation: Abbr.
59. Piqued: Colloq.
60. Diminutive suffixes
61. Scottish

DOWN

1. Comely, in Cannes
2. Hebrew letters
3. Avesta translations
4. Sleep signs
5. French historian and others
6. With
7. Minutia
8. Hall of Famer
9. Horses, at times
10. "__ On Earth"
11. Tennis star
12. Grasslands
13. Party man, for short
19. Nostrils
21. Name
24. Flatterer
27. Dodge and Dearborn
28. Deer
29. Arizona Indian
30. Philippine dye tree
31. Attention-getters
32. Bows
33. Sheer
34. Off on the Elizabeth 2
35. Parents' word
37. Ederle
40. Shaping-machine worker
41. Incite
43. Neville and others
45. Health: Fr.
46. Remnant of a sort
47. Fishing equipment
48. Army man, familiarly
49. Hep
50. Ivan
51. Afforded
53. Plural suffix
54. Athletic equipment
55. Part of a Greek clan

31

ACROSS

1. Addition and all
5. Shows surprise
10. French lily
13. Impression
14. Wine pitchers
15. Art style
16. Assent
17. __ Youth
19. Affected
21. Caress
22. Gizzard, liver, etc.
23. Delays, in civil law
24. Party
25. Homeland of 4, 30 and 35 Down
28. Shah who built Taj Mahal
31. Magna __
32. Krazy __
33. Asian sea
34. Roast slightly
35. Goddess of youth
36. Duct: Anat.
37. Odysseus's dog
38. Containers
39. Shot __
41. Jack of clubs
42. Handle again
43. Large deer
47. Washington portraitist
49. Word for a poker loser
50. Famous Mongol
52. Ready money
53. Literary fragments
54. Civil War general
55. "I cannot tell __"
56. Indian cymbals
57. Bridge positions
58. Erect

DOWN

1. Resort
2. Drum beater
3. Period in life
4. Famous North African
5. Win release
6. Liliaceous plants
7. Vegetable, familiarly
8. Move, as a camera
9. Start out
10. Expression of amazement
11. Image
12. Umpire's call
15. Shore
18. Artery
20. Well-known Briton
23. Connelly and others
25. Song of joy
26. Man's nickname
27. French summers
28. Coffee: Colloq.
29. Biblical character
30. Brother of 4 Down
31. Army All-American
34. Renown
35. Father of 30 Down
37. Persian deity
38. Complain
40. Closes tightly
41. Colors
43. Gregorian __
44. Street of the Blues
45. Or else, in music
46. Escort
47. Card game
48. Salad fish
49. Dickens, for short
51. Indian ape

32

ACROSS

1. Rock crystal
7. African animal
12. Quite a few
13. Bon —
15. Guardianship
16. Loath
17. Instruments
18. "— horse"
20. Uncommunicative
21. Pastry item
22. Blue Ridge sight
23. Cooks, maids, etc.
24. — antiqua
25. French Revolution figure
27. Kind of voice
28. Comfort
29. Diminish
30. Like a certain hue
33. Canyons' relatives
35. Pay
36. Stringed instrument
38. Kilns
39. Conclusion
40. Ott
43. Hawaiian chant
44. Danish borough
45. Jotting
46. Pique
47. — avis
48. "Private Lives" woman
50. Particular
52. Gifted
54. Lead on
55. — roast coffee
56. Took out
57. British weight

DOWN

1. Soprano Roberta
2. Sports meet
3. Thrash
4. Arm: Fr.
5. Fall behind
6. — stanza
7. Partly round
8. Pueblo structure
9. Park or Madison: Abbr.
10. Cheese
11. Set apart
12. Table item
14. Places of worship
15. Parting words
19. Stepping in
22. Wishes greatly
23. Garb
25. Blanc and others
26. One's companion
27. Church parts
28. Contemptible person
30. Trite saying
31. Clerical title
32. Western or ham
34. Tropical bird
37. Like Kidd
40. Of the chin
41. German port
42. Cargo
44. Bundled
45. Fad
47. Pilaf ingredient
48. King or Arkin
49. Liquefy
51. Trouble
53. Used up

33

ACROSS

1. Duffer's strokes
6. Pequod
10. Opposite of vive
14. Nautical term
15. Philippine cloth
16. Con __ (briskly)
17. See 3 Down
19. Flavoring plant
20. Common contraction
21. Irish dramatist
22. Ancient country
23. Indians of Tierra del Fuego
25. No place for apple eating
26. __ the Covenant
28. Address
30. Try
32. Emotion
33. Rare person
35. Sixth sense: Abbr.
36. Direction
37. Goes flat
40. Decked
42. See 3 Down

43. Postal item: Abbr.
45. Metalware
46. Timetable abbr.
47. Severe
49. Spirit of a people
53. Important alliance
55. Account of a sort
57. Item to be held securely, in superstition
58. Homme d'__
59. Archeologists' tools
61. Indian
62. Wind
63. Tempts fate, ladderwise
65. Henry's fourth
66. First name for an author
67. Children's poet
68. Makes an out in baseball
69. Defeat
70. Geologist's term

DOWN

1. Mawkishness
2. Greek goddess
3. With 42 and 17 Across, a time for caution
4. Wood
5. N. Y. and S. F.
6. Fast man with a dollar
7. Depends, with "on"
8. Violent
9. Exclamation
10. Execrate
11. __ a mirror (tempting fate)
12. Winging
13. News story of a kind
18. Evil __
22. Spring-festival gear
24. Special kind of airport: Abbr.

27. "__ a cold, . . ."
29. Not requiring repetition
31. Apropos
34. This: Sp.
37. Railroad stops: Abbr.
38. __ match
39. Making effervescent
41. __ on (manages)
44. Train
45. Undergrowth
48. __ salt (tempts fate)
50. 17 Across, for one
51. TV Westerns
52. Germ cells
54. Witches' __
56. Containers: Abbr.
60. Pupil's problems
62. Black __
63. Entanglement
64. "Do __ open umbrellas indoors."

34

ACROSS

1. At the drop of —
5. Tapestry
10. French composer
14. Sky sight in Perth
17. Some experts
18. Welds
19. Part of Tito's domain
20. Foot: Suffix
21. First garment
22. Rise again
25. Map area
29. Well-known Nebraska name
32. Divan décor
34. Period
35. Walked unsteadily
37. Merkel
38. Highland garb
40. Soft color
42. O'Neill heroine
43. Belmont customer
44. Cut deeply
47. Early Irish writing system
51. Part of our society
54. Character in "Ivanhoe"
56. Note
58. City sights
59. Disarray
60. Lumber processor's tool
61. French family man

DOWN

1. Misbehave
2. Lena
3. Of a lily family
4. Race track hangers-on
5. Indian mulberries
6. Scottish name
7. Salad item
8. Hewn or squared stone
9. Small porch
10. Football pass
11. Danish measure
12. Pontecorvo's river
13. Greek mountain
15. Nautical direction: Abbr.
16. Ramble
21. Slovenly one
23. Girl's name
24. Quickly
26. Musical mark
27. Scottish island
28. Out
29. Greek letter
30. Algerian port
31. Story
32. Hanger-on
33. Thought: Prefix
36. Scottish village
39. Small drums
41. Adult
43. Excluded
45. Formerly, old style
46. "Do you — ?"
48. Barnacles and graylags
49. Genus of 48 Down
50. Pool-table shot
51. O'Flaherty
52. — d'Huez, French peak
53. Gil —
54. River to the Rhine
55. Spanish bear
57. Native of: Suffix

35

	1	2	3	4		5	6	7	8		9	10	11	12	13
14					15					16				
17					18				19					
20				21					22					
			23					24						
25	26	27				28					29	30	31	
32					33					34				
35				36					37					
38				39				40						
41			42					43						
		44				45	46						
	47	48				49				50	51	52		
53				54				55						
56				57				58						
59				60				61						

ACROSS

1. British title: Abbr.
5. Meadow sounds
9. Commit a crime
14. Nautical term
15. Pilaf ingredient
16. Contour feather
17. Soft-grain sheepskin
18. Visionary
20. Hinged, with "on"
22. Stakes
23. Recompense, old style
24. Bancroft
25. Worn-out horses
28. Omelet ingredient
32. Regarding
33. Stopwatch
34. Winglike part
35. Measure
36. Hard-hit baseball
37. River in England
38. Biblical priest
39. Made public
40. Place of action
41. School session
43. Aches
44. Book of the Bible
45. Retired
47. Arthur Hailey title
49. Splashes
53. Portrays
55. Part of Latin "to be"
56. Common contraction
57. Erudition
58. Place
59. Strong drinks
60. Country, in France
61. Ruler

DOWN

1. Man of 37 Across
2. Drug plant
3. Gather
4. Dwelling of a kind
5. June V.I.P.
6. Backed
7. Scored at tennis
8. Adriatic
9. Fishing lure
10. Did a checking job
11. Grafted, in heraldry
12. Cuckoos
13. Varnish ingredient
19. Mounted soldier
21. Tree sight
24. Intended
25. Tricks
26. Old-womanish
27. Heavy fabric
28. Train unit
29. Shelter
30. "All __, I'm so . . ."
31. Parts of horses
33. Spares
36. Scanty
37. Moment of truth
39. Takeoffs
40. Small barracuda
42. Using up
45. Mimicking
46. Guantanamo and others
47. German title
48. Spread
49. Porch
50. Greek goddess
51. Pro __
52. Abbr. on a spoon
53. Hammarskjold
54. Peak

36

ACROSS

1. Chemical endings
5. Said, of yore
10. Wear out
14. Upcoming
15. Exorbitant interest
16. Roman poet
17. Familiar
19. Unyielding
20. Goes back and forth
21. Peace
23. Where the Adige flows
25. Friendship
26. Annie Oakley
28. Red ink item
30. Italian numeral
31. "__ was saying..."
32. Rebuffs
34. Turkish soldier
38. Siamese
39. Stranded, as a ship
41. Gershwin
42. Show obeisance
44. Wise ones
45. __ grata
46. Auto tag: Abbr.
48. Draw off
49. Tunisian seaport
50. Cliburn's forte
52. Vaquero gear
54. Blameworthy
57. Dolce far __
60. G.I. addresses
61. Terrorist
63. Not taped
64. Heep
65. Curiosity Shop girl
66. Decamped
67. Sample
68. Sly: Br. dialect

DOWN

1. Miscellanies
2. Georgia __
3. Perfected
4. Attention-getters
5. Traitor
6. Gob's monogram
7. Ump's calls
8. Larch or carob
9. Freshwater polyps
10. Polish king
11. Had, in France
12. Squalid
13. Charybdis feature
18. __ loss
22. Corrects
24. Pronoun
26. Organized group
27. __ example
29. W. W. II marine threat
32. Salt marsh
33. Sweeten
35. Red table wine
36. Venezuelan copper center
37. Tailless cat
40. Pain-killer
43. Slipped by
47. European hazel
49. Mugs
50. Eye part
51. "The Man __"
53. Give the __
54. Farm animal
55. Money on the Corso
56. Sponsorship
58. Prefix with vise and cast
59. A Gardner
62. Topper

37

ACROSS

1. Alan of "Shane"
5. Stirred
9. Professional men: Abbr.
13. Sweet spire
14. Pitches
16. Yonkers event
17. Certain pay
19. Get in under the ___
20. Time at sea
21. Contribute
23. Superior
24. In any way
25. Heavy reading matter
28. Light reading matter
31. Habituates
33. Hebrew prophet
34. Taro paste
36. Damon and Pythias, in the vernacular
37. Polytheist
39. Ardor
40. Convene
41. African tree
42. Patron of Venice
44. Important adjunct
47. Primal chaos
48. Baffles
49. Hindu fire god
51. Mention (with "to")
53. Defarge and others
57. Crucifix
58. Wagon part
60. Pentateuch
61. Mount
62. German article
63. Baths
64. Watery fluids
65. Instrument

DOWN

1. Hats: Colloq.
2. Thine: Fr.
3. French numeral
4. Dilettantes
5. Spiral-shelled snail
6. Type of store
7. Malay dagger
8. Tree
9. Freely
10. Diamond thriller
11. Column trims
12. British gun
15. Stadium areas
18. Contract
22. Dutch painter
24. First word of the Aeneid
25. Expense-account item
26. Walking ___
27. Kind of rose
29. Ishmael's mother
30. Zoo sounds
32. Irreproachable
35. Printer's needs
38. Lamentation sound
39. Exacerbate
41. Rebuked
43. French relative
45. Cheeses
46. Barn feature
50. Rigoletto's daughter
51. Study course
52. Chicago area
53. Patella
54. Indian
55. Descartes
56. Germ
59. "___ a deal!"

38

ACROSS

1. Order to a broker
5. Droops
9. Adduce
13. Plains Indian
14. Dickens villain
15. Showiness
16. Distinctive quality
17. Hokkaido indigene
18. Hotheaded one
19. Game
22. Pakistan language
23. Before twa
24. Adorns, in a way
27. Daredevil
32. Silly tricks
33. Spirited
34. Grape
35. Basks
36. Center of activity
37. De —
38. Anger
39. Fervors
40. — eleison
41. F.C.C.'s concern
43. Musicians of a sort
44. Treasury employee: Abbr.
45. Spurt
46. Retrench
54. Completely
55. Course
56. Exclamation
57. Major or Minor
58. Unicorn fish
59. Infamous fiddler
60. Swiss painter
61. Do the floors
62. Ditto

DOWN

1. Take wing
2. Vanity case
3. Forsaken
4. Little —
5. Fragments
6. Vowel lineup
7. Abrupt flexure
8. Related, as a tale
9. Wine
10. Cassio's slanderer
11. Very: Fr.
12. Unearthly
15. Frequent babysitter
20. Host
21. Dismay
24. River valley
25. Pattern to be traced
26. Civetlike animal
27. Zoo attractions
28. Blacktops
29. Diving bird
30. Weight system: Abbr.
31. Scruffs
33. Toucan's feature
36. Wader
37. Storms
39. Cape polecats
40. Father of Saul
42. Mays
43. Urged on
45. Arrive
46. Tool
47. Single
48. Air or sea route
49. Musical work
50. Dog in "Peter Pan"
51. Mother of Zeus
52. Model
53. Brogan

39

ACROSS

1. Wearing apparel
5. Component of Westerns
10. Broadway musical
14. Spanish duke
15. Jacob's brother and others
16. Touch
17. Page
18. French pronoun
19. Cozy home
20. Iron: Prefix
22. Japanese coin
23. Percentage levy
24. Brecht play
27. Biography of Dr. King (with "What")
30. Initials on an audit
33. Part of a Gershwin song title
34. Longing
35. Chairman's place
36. Passage
38. Arid wastes
40. U.S. playwright
41. Sound of woe
43. New York, formerly
44. Novice: Abbr.
45. Type of work
47. Highest of Green Mountains
48. Wash up
51. N. Y. school union: Abbr.
52. Give way
56. Cut of meat
57. Slow down
59. Continuously
60. Prefix meaning height
61. Lease again
62. Make over
63. City of the schnitzel
64. United
65. Sudden sound

DOWN

1. One over two
2. Sailor's direction
3. Type of lift
4. Red fabric dye
5. Authors' group: Abbr.
6. Chilean volcano
7. Fulfill expectations
8. Appellations
9. Compass point
10. The __ the moon
11. Foster
12. Mawkishness
13. Diminutive suffix
21. Auguries
23. Color
25. Skilled worker
26. Restrain, in a way
27. Snail genus
28. Anchor position
29. Civil rights org.
30. Mediterranean tree
31. Upright or grand
32. Ancient empire: Abbr.
35. Former French Premier and others
37. Haircuts
39. Berried shrub
42. Niagara Falls's neighbor
45. Companion of beast
46. U.S. astronomer
47. Opera role
48. Scratch and tear
49. Places
50. Island republic
53. Balanced
54. Mother of Castor
55. Discontinue
57. Bikini part
58. Season, in Nice

40

ACROSS

1. Ropes, hawsers, etc.
8. Civil Defense condition
13. Sir Roger de —
14. Forage plant
15. Menu item
16. Bring back
17. Hot time
18. Implement
20. Elysium
21. City in Arizona
22. Winter wear
24. Delivered
25. Torero's praises
26. Exasperate: Colloq.
27. Bronze Age sight in England
28. Avoid, in a way
30. Diminutive suffix
31. Pasture animal
32. Pronoun
34. Ordinary
37. Sight near Stroudsburg, Pa.
42. Red Square name
43. Muslim title
44. Variety's Green
46. "It's — world"
47. Victimizes
48. Actress Louise
49. Low or ebb
50. Seafood delicacy
51. — Rapids
52. Tooth part
54. New on the job
57. Floating
58. Afternoon party
59. Vogue
60. Orchestrate

DOWN

1. Constrains
2. Excess type, in printing
3. Press statement
4. Endure, à la Robert Burns
5. Height: Abbr.
6. Fetch
7. Peeping aperture
8. Stout's kin
9. One-sided tennis score
10. Plain
11. Vendetta's purpose
12. Thirty: Fr.
13. World: Prefix
14. Western Indian
19. Wear out one's welcome
22. Take on stature
23. Aggressive person
27. Dutch title
29. Laborer
33. Surrounds, with "in"
34. Study group
35. Stepping out
36. Certain musician
38. Galli-Curci
39. Entrance keeper
40. Permanent
41. Expiation
42. Potentially active
45. Roomy
47. Trapper's quest
51. Musical finale
53. Purpose
55. Father of Kish
56. Because: Fr.

41

ACROSS

1. Site of the Quirinal
5. Moroccan port
10. Turnpike feature
14. Seed coat
15. Girl's name
16. Indian
17. Certain worker
20. According to
21. Up and __
22. Images
23. Customer
24. Waiter's offering
26. Intent one
29. Bonanza
32. Instruments
33. Pacific naval base of W. W. II
34. Shred
36. Intimidates
37. Buddhist shrines
38. Night spot
39. Longing
40. Divas' highlights
41. Barbecue spot
42. Jack-o' __
44. Breakfast dish
45. Small: Suffix
46. German's your
47. Fiber plant
50. Electrical hookup
51. Some railroads
54. Indian turnip
58. Pay up
59. Shiraz resident
60. O'Casey milieu
61. Interpret
62. Church plate
63. Part of a Sammy Davis title

DOWN

1. Eastern title
2. Exam
3. Isinglass
4. Leather
5. Jack __ (roof piece)
6. Robin __
7. Haberdashery item
8. "That's __, folks"
9. Do fancywork
10. Piece of china
11. Church calendar
12. Mortgage
13. Between little and least
18. Havens
19. Sports places
23. Containers
24. Lion features
25. Old shields
26. Deacon's vehicle
27. Symbol of defeat
28. Colosseum area
29. Black lacquer
30. Sound off
31. Haitian rum
33. Watered silk
35. Earth science: Abbr.
37. Allowance for waste
38. Protection
40. Biblical warrior
41. Hidden away
43. Long __ turtle
44. Pay one's share
46. Dunne
47. Gates __
48. Harmful agent
49. Proceedings
50. Mountain pass
51. On a grand scale
52. Signore's money
53. British gun
55. Small drink
56. Musical syllable
57. Garland

42

ACROSS

1. Yet
6. Language study: Abbr.
10. Irish body
14. Refuse
15. Streaked
16. Likewise
17. Nest
18. Companion of means
19. Cabal
20. Taking in
22. Dance of sorts
24. Tavern
25. Feminine
29. Quagmire
33. Flirt
34. O'Casey, for one
35. Cry
36. Manner
37. Cinderella's garb
38. Do penance
39. French pronoun
40. Past
41. Euphoria
42. Southern dish
43. Small rodent
45. Uncomfortable
46. Nature
47. Vehicle
48. Norse goddess
49. Floods
54. Sage
57. Indian
59. Frame
60. Wading bird
61. Top-notch
62. Opera-box wear
63. Legal wrong
64. Peel
65. Thrown

DOWN

1. Buck
2. City in Russia
3. Diet
4. World area
5. Schumann's Third Symphony
6. Early astronaut
7. Wagnerian work
8. Besides
9. Aura
10. Speckle
11. Word for a tie, in tennis
12. Equal: Prefix
13. Fate
21. Parts of yds.
23. In __
25. Hired thugs
26. Where Firenze is
27. Shore birds
28. Dissenting belief
29. Desert sight
30. Storms: Fr.
31. Severities
32. Beast
33. Selected
35. Subway entrance
38. Welcome signal
39. Poet's word
41. Stem
42. Clothing inserts
44. Command
45. Neighbor of Ont.
47. Produce
49. Sibelius, for one
50. Greet
51. Brother of Jacob
52. Gull
53. Lava
54. Perception
55. Nigerian tribe
56. Title
58. Reine's counterpart

43

ACROSS

1. Narrow groove
6. Ritzy
10. Six or seven, in bridge
14. Do one's __
15. Kind of sax
16. Hallmark of the good
17. Name for a dog
18. Stern
19. Ardent
20. French river
21. Worsen
23. Harries
25. Aching
26. Fly chaser of sorts
28. Wicker
32. Spread
37. Ship to remember
38. Shaped a certain way
39. Staff men
41. Chemical suffixes
42. Moslem princess
44. Spreads
46. Native of northwest France
48. Glade: Prefix
49. Bufo
51. Extended
56. Do commercials
60. Auto gear
61. Forest animal
62. Olga's boyfriend
63. Snug harbor
64. Other
65. African grassland
66. Range parts
67. Document
68. Time units
69. Exploit

DOWN

1. Part of Las Vegas
2. Pronoun
3. Tears
4. Like neon
5. Consent
6. Sponging
7. Cassini
8. Pollards
9. __ story
10. Slang for an officer
11. In Hawaii it's called aa
12. Descended
13. Way
22. Ancient Syria
24. __ avis
27. Flirted with
29. Time's companion
30. Dill herb
31. Cape
32. Irvin S. or Ty
33. Done
34. Old-time sorcerer
35. Flapped
36. Clergymen
40. Star-spangled, in heraldry
43. Othello, for one
45. White-line straddler
47. Indigenous
50. Swan expert
52. Hanker
53. Homes of a sort
54. In any __
55. Word for a jungle
56. Resting
57. Relief, in Britain
58. Place for a rose
59. Room in a casa

44

ACROSS

1. Dollar: Slang
5. Seal
10. Federal agents
14. Baltic gulf
15. Dispatch boat
16. Rodent
17. Love, in Lima
18. Feline protest
19. Opera bit
20. Certain experts
22. Bettors' I.O.U.
24. Baubles
25. Port of Iraq
26. In the __
28. Scratches
31. What veni means
32. Stall, with "out": Slang
33. Social doing
34. One of a pair
35. Ducts
36. Time periods
37. Copy
38. Rows
39. Actress Elsie
40. Price slash
43. "__ sow . . ."
44. Nut parts
45. Kind of Susan
47. Old warning
49. Ski novice's memento
53. Porsena
54. "I wasn't there," for example
56. Soviet lake
57. Tad
58. African badger
59. Netman Lacoste
60. Parisian suburb
61. Showed obeisance
62. Smith

DOWN

1. Stuff
2. New World capital
3. Seaweed product
4. Wait
5. Davis
6. Vines
7. Part of Menotti's name
8. Prefix for bar or tope
9. D's and F's
10. Indian carriage
11. Caesar's friend
12. Pennsylvania city
13. Close
21. __ fun!
23. Emulate Socrates
25. Poisons
26. __ Flow
27. Philatelist's concerns
28. Grieve
29. Aladdin's friend
30. Lip
31. Islamic priest
32. Tears
35. Clue on an Indian path
36. Dupe
39. Music form
41. Woolen cloth
42. Family member: Abbr.
45. Defamation
46. With lance in hand
47. Prefix for meter or tude
48. Ballads
49. Place
50. Disaster __
51. Bombast
52. Swiss painter
55. Chinese weight

45

ACROSS

1. Object pettily
6. __ Bones
10. Twist
14. Treatment
15. Midwestern school
17. Limitation
18. Handsome horses
19. Corruptive
21. As to
22. Tree dweller
23. Marionette man
25. "The __ Game"
28. Zone
29. Spanish article
32. Mixture
33. Began
36. Delineates
38. Inlet
39. Rumor about
40. Hospital item
43. College sport
44. Shade
45. Long periods
46. Listings in a travel guide
48. Walk or pace
49. Hawaiian port
50. Fishing gear
53. Large baboon
57. Perceptive
60. Girl's name
61. Feature of the Met
62. __ of skill
63. Mind
64. Tree of Java
65. Love __

DOWN

1. Talk, in a way
2. Italian city
3. Ineffectual
4. Car parts
5. Pretends
6. Certain animal
7. Storm sound
8. Night __
9. Chinese great
10. Apiary hazard
11. Drury, for one
12. English town
13. Field's co-star
16. Make spruce
20. Labels
23. Eastern inn
24. High in pitch
25. Dental concern
26. Adjust
27. Dated
28. Torments
29. European river
30. European thrush: Var.
31. Menu favorites
34. English river
35. Some collegians' aim
37. Second-story man
41. Hawaiian yam
42. Chatter
47. A name for father
48. Frozen
49. Netherworld
50. "__ la vie"
51. Be important: Colloq.
52. First Governor of Alaska
53. City in Arizona
54. Irritates
55. Cant
56. Old Riga coins
58. Small shield
59. Pacific islet

46

ACROSS

1. Australian city
6. Kind of race
10. Formerly, old style
14. Siren
15. Cleric: Abbr.
16. ___ kick out of
17. Hits, as a car
19. Cards
20. Pretense
21. Time
22. Skilled
23. U.S. money used abroad
26. Double agent
27. Commutes
28. Decree
30. Routing word
33. Old instrument
34. Happen to
36. Football plays
38. Annoy
39. Storied island
40. Trevino's game
41. Letters
42. Suit
43. Shaded area
45. Publicize
46. Ornamental tree
51. Collect by bits
53. Stalemate
54. Taste: Fr.
55. Arena
56. Produces in abundance
58. Do art work
59. Celeste
60. Unaired
61. Hurricane areas
62. Angers
63. Appropriate

DOWN

1. Like the twist or hula hoop
2. Yale
3. Warship equipment
4. Vibration
5. British seagoing initials
6. Some poems
7. Rebuff
8. ___ barrel
9. Game scores
10. Hoople oath
11. Withdrawn
12. Intervened
13. Savory
18. Mysteries
22. Requested
24. Thinning
25. Mingle
29. Supped
30. Old-timer
31. Lack of capacity
32. Fidelity
35. Certain transportations
37. Moroccan range
38. Soldiered
40. Cloture
44. Stew
45. Approve
47. In ___ -bed
48. Scandinavian
49. ___ -percha
50. Antiknock gas
52. Egyptian souls
56. Greek letter
57. Some radios

47

¹	²	³	⁴	■	⁵	⁶	⁷	⁸	⁹	■	¹⁰	¹¹	¹²	¹³

ACROSS

1. Menu offering
5. Century plant
10. In __
14. Asian range
15. Authentic
16. Queued up
17. Dropping abruptly
19. Reading, for one
20. Stationery item
21. Square footage
22. Incident
24. Hungers
26. Domestic science
28. Corporation V.I.P., for short
30. Refuse heaps
33. Money of Turin
36. Run out
38. Vote for
39. Trim
43. "__ was saying . . ."
44. Geographical feature
45. Man's nickname
46. Optimistic
48. Grammarián's abbr.
51. Hospital staffman
53. Coast Guard role
57. Provoke
58. Impression
60. Common word
61. Today: It.
62. Semblance
65. Evade
66. Deride
67. Grammatical term
68. Record
69. Blank
70. Clears

DOWN

1. Blithe
2. Berlin avenue
3. Bath, in Helsinki
4. Pronoun
5. Disinclined
6. Paid attendance
7. Word on a post office wall
8. Bistro offering
9. In a certain position
10. Stub
11. Soft drink
12. Street sound
13. Bird
18. Cat
23. TV term
25. Gather
27. Realm
29. Resourceful
31. U.N. vote
32. Desiccated
33. Fabulist
34. __ many words
35. Rearing
37. Mimic
40. Rattle on
41. Well-read
42. Tachometer readings: Abbr.
47. Jet
49. Pact
50. Time unit
52. Caper
54. Birchbark
55. Word for some gems
56. Elysiums
57. Turkish leader
59. Tooth, in Tours
61. East: Ger.
63. Jack of clubs
64. __ Arbor

48

ACROSS

1. Music style
5. Short-story writer
8. Fish
12. Boating term
13. Step of a sort
15. Sundae ingredient
17. Stain, in a way
19. Expel
20. Rails
21. Time periods: Abbr.
23. Collections of anecdotes
24. Aphoristic
27. Mats. __ and Sats.
30. Owing
31. "Never __ of money spent"
32. Tool
33. Timid one
35. Appear
38. Locale of yore
40. Punished
43. Ancient unit of weight
44. Follow: Lat.
46. Locale in Iraq
47. Egg: Prefix
49. In a __
50. Body of water
51. Users of crops
55. Benumb
56. Barnyard sound
57. Emotional signs
60. Marx
62. Youth
65. Bishop's headdress
66. Ukrainian city
67. Grimace
68. Give up
69. Iowa college
70. Where supplies are kept: Abbr.

DOWN

1. Preserve
2. Word of regret
3. Thermometer reading
4. Zoo inhabitants
5. Military post
6. French reply
7. Organic substances
8. Direction
9. Certain criminal
10. Sports area
11. Of a titled person
14. City near Leipzig
16. Measures: Abbr.
18. Permissive
22. Train stop: Abbr.
25. Dismisses
26. Japanese immigrant
27. Service branch
28. Students' moment of truth
29. Prefix for tasse
33. Drudge
34. Indian of Mexico
36. Imitate
37. Inferior
39. Proclaimed
41. Changeable
42. Performed
45. Unpredictable
48. Theory
50. Bible book
51. Body of principles
52. Wholly
53. Burden
54. Fiber knot
55. Graduate degree
58. Disturbance
59. Cozy
61. Western state: Abbr.
63. Early car
64. Horse driver's command

49

ACROSS

1. Plant fluids
5. Radio term
10. New Mexican landmark
14. Sharp sound
15. Sidestep
16. Tip
17. Feminine suffix
18. Man's man
19. Prefix for crine
20. Separate
22. List
24. Jade
25. Spring
26. Predicament
29. Theoretical
33. Winged
34. Headquarters
35. Got saddle sores
36. A kind of motive
37. Some theaters
38. Kind of road
39. Continuously
40. Exchange discount
41. German river
42. Kind of pronoun
44. Procrastinates
45. Places
46. Fabric
47. Modern author
50. Jaw
54. Radio term
55. Lasso
57. Carol
58. Did a bank job
59. Post
60. Small amount
61. Wiles
62. Documents
63. Without

DOWN

1. Timetable, for short
2. Choir voices
3. Kettles
4. Weekend TV fare
5. Revolutionary name
6. Egg-shaped
7. Wind
8. Dutch city
9. Shelters
10. Racing
11. Slangy contraction
12. Wave: Fr.
13. Kind of battery: Abbr.
21. Ready
23. Grain seed
25. Plain of S.A.
26. Orchid tubers
27. Bud
28. Snake
29. Jeopardy
30. Running knot
31. Drone
32. Sing Sing accommodations
34. Eddas
37. Traded quips
41. Pinochle term
43. Away
44. Coins of Iraq
46. Surfeited
47. Nut
48. Declare
49. Kind of house
50. Ship's officer
51. Wind
52. Cant
53. Shade trees
56. Compass point

50

ACROSS

1. Wild guess
5. Byre tenants
9. Marked with ridges
14. Some lunch orders
15. Elliptical
16. Rousseau work
17. Exchange premium
18. P.I. tribesman
19. ___ à clef
20. Business acumen, U.S. style
23. Stir
24. Green: Fr.
25. Visit
28. Lacking harmony
30. Nymph
31. English river
32. Natch
36. A possible result of 48 Across
39. Abominate
40. Arab prince
41. "Sweet ___ O'Grady"
42. Drudge
43. July 4 event
44. Asian range
47. Satisfy
48. A talent of sorts
54. Truman's birthplace
55. Sugar source
56. City in Kansas
57. Bluenose
58. Bugs ___, humorist
59. Couple
60. Ran
61. Dilettante
62. Irish river

DOWN

1. Collar prop
2. ___ virilis
3. Opposed to: Colloq.
4. Volume's identification
5. Words of exhortation
6. Rounded
7. Admonish
8. Plod heavily
9. Film actor Oskar
10. Toujours l'___
11. Restrict
12. Gladden
13. Refuse
21. Wear with time
22. Maurice ___
25. Irish port
26. Region
27. Baltic native
28. Eschew
29. Day, in France
31. Arsenal contents, for short
32. Word for some sales
33. ___ Minor
34. Military blow
35. Fencing foil
37. Souvenir
38. Muse
42. Coupled
43. Place to keep goodies
44. City in Iraq
45. Madagascar mammal
46. Baseball deal
47. Trapshooting
48. Kubla Khan's river
49. Eastern church title
50. Approach
51. 3,600 seconds
52. Pearl Buck heroine
53. Proceed with difficulty

Answers

1

P	L	A	Y		A	R	A	B		R	E	S	T	
I	O	L	A		R	E	N	A		E	A	T	E	N
Q	U	I	Z	Z	I	C	A	L		Q	U	O	T	E
U	T	A		O	S	E		E	M	U		V	E	T
E	S	S	E	N	E	S		S	U	I	T	E		
			S	E	N	S	E		S	E	E	P	E	D
P	A	C	T	S		I	N	D	E	M	N	I	T	Y
O	R	O		D	O	T	E	S		P	R	E		
M	O	N	O	T	O	N	E	S		C	R	E	E	D
S	E	Q	U	I	N		R	E	F	I	T			
			U	T	T	E	R		R	E	V	E	R	S	E
A	P	E		T	E	A		V	I	E		O	A	R
S	E	R	G	E		S	C	I	N	T	I	L	L	A
S	P	O	O	R		P	I	N	T		A	L	E	S
O	R	T	S		S	A	G	S		N	O	S	E	

2

O	N	T	A	P		A	S	H	E		S	C	A	T
L	O	I	R	E		S	P	A	R		T	A	R	E
E	L	L	E	N		S	E	R	A		E	R	I	N
G	O	T	O	P	I	E	C	E	S		A	L	L	E
				A	N	T	I		U	T	M	O	S	T
S	C	H	U	L	E		A	R	R	A	S			
A	L	O	S	S		B	L	U	E	N	O	T	E	S
Y	A	L	U		J	A	D	E	S		P	A	T	H
A	P	E	R	T	U	R	E	S		D	E	L	T	A
				P	A	N	E	L		D	A	N	C	E	D
R	E	M	A	R	K		I	T	E	N				
A	M	A	T		M	O	V	I	N	G	M	A	I	L
M	C	I	I		A	F	E	R		L	E	T	G	O
O	E	N	O		I	N	R	E		E	S	T	O	P
S	E	E	N		L	O	Y	S		D	E	A	R	S

3

S	L	A	B		R	O	T	A	S		A	B	E	D
T	A	X	I		A	R	U	S	H		M	I	R	E
A	N	I	L		D	I	S	H	A	B	I	L	L	E
B	I	L	L	H	O	O	K		W	A	L	L	E	D
			F	I	N	L	E	Y		R	E	O		
R	O	B	O	T		E	R	A	S		A	W	N	S
E	V	I	L	L	Y		S	L	E	D		I	O	U
B	O	L	D	E	S	T		I	C	E	B	E	R	G
E	L	L		R	E	S	P		A	R	I	S	T	A
L	O	B	O		R	A	R	E		A	L	T	E	R
		A	R	E		R	E	M	A	I	L			
O	P	I	A	T	E		B	I	L	L	I	A	R	D
B	I	L	L	O	F	S	A	L	E		N	E	A	P
I	S	E	E		F	A	K	I	R		G	R	I	T
S	A	Y	S		S	W	E	E	T		S	O	N	S

4

P	L	A	S	T	E	R		P	O	S	T	M	A	N
E	A	R	L	O	B	E		E	X	T	R	E	M	E
A	T	E	A	P	O	T		D	E	R	I	D	E	S
T	E	A	M		N	U	T		N	A	T	A	N	T
				B	Y	R	O	N		F	E	L	T	S
R	O	D	E	O		N	I	E	C	E				
A	K	I	M	B	O		L	A	E		A	S	K	A
P	R	A	I	S	E	D		P	S	Y	C	H	I	C
S	A	L	T		I	R	K		T	U	M	U	L	T
			B	L	E	A	K		L	E	T	T	S	
S	P	I	C	Y		D	R	A	K	E				
P	A	R	O	L	E		L	I	E		A	L	G	A
U	R	A	N	I	A	S		S	T	I	B	I	A	L
D	E	T	E	N	T	E		E	C	L	I	P	S	E
S	E	E	R	E	S	S		R	H	O	D	O	P	E

5

6

7

8

5

```
B A L L   C R O   A R A B I C
I D E A   H O D   B O L E R O
D O M I C I L E   A B A T E D
  O R A T E       E R A S E
D O N   B O O K W O R M
E N J O I N   E A S T   S S E
C H U R N   S E N S A T I O N
R A I N   S E P T A   O D O R
E N C O M P A S S   S E E N O
E D E   A U T O   M U S S E L
    S T R O N G E R   A R S
A S P I C     E D G E D
C L O T H O   U N D E R D O G
T O R I E S   M I L   I L I A
S P E N D S   W E E   S E L L
```

6

```
R O A R S   J A V A   F R A P
A L L E E   A X I L   L E G O
J E O P A R D I Z E   Y E A R
A S P   F O E S   H E C K L E
    T I P S   K O L A
  S W O R E   F A U L T I N G
A T I M E   O R B S   C R O W
G A Z A   Q U E U E   H O N E
E V E N   U N A L   X E N O N
S E N D B A C K   M A R Y S
    J U N E   C O N S
T A G E N D   A L O T   T R Y
U X O R   A N T I T H E S I S
L E A R   R E I N   I C A M E
A L L Y   Y O K E   C U R E R
```

7

```
A B B A   S A M P   D U P E R
D E A N   C L I O   O S A K A
D A R T B O A R D   T U L E S
A M B I E N T   A S T R I D E
  L A C E D   A L E N
S V E L T E   E M B E R D A Y
T E N E S   T B A R S   R U E
O R C S   S A R R E   C O R A
I S A   R E L I C   S A M A R
C O M M E R C E   T U R E E N
  P E D I   F A R E D
R O M A N C E   M O D I S T E
A B E L E   C O M M E N T O N
D E N I S   H E A P   A L A N
A N T E S   O R N E   L O D E
```

8

```
  L A B   I C E R   F L U S H
T O D O   N A P U   R A N C E
A B R A   F R I S   E N T A L
F A I R C A T C H   E D I L E
T R A D U C E   E M P   L E N
  W E T S   S M O G
A L T A   S I E R R A N S
C A U L K   A I N   T A B O O
S I N K I A N G   S A R D
  S C A N   M O P S
S S E   K R A   E M I R A T E
C A L E B   B A R E P O L E S
O P E R A   E V I L   O L E S
T O N I C   R O D E   T I N E
T R A C K   G N A T   S N Y
```

9

```
S T R A T E G Y ░ B A K E R ░
T H E F I X E R ░ O L I V E R
R A T T L E R S ░ T A P A L O
A N I ░ T R Y ░ S T R ░ C A V
T A R E ░ T O M T O M ░ U T E
A G E N T ░ N O R M ░ P E E R
L E D G E S ░ R U S T L E R S
░ ░ ░ I M P O S T U R E ░ ░ ░
H O R N P I P E ░ P A N A D A
A L E E ░ N I L E ░ P U R E R
R D S ░ C E N S U S ░ M E N T
A S E ░ A L E ░ G E D ░ T I L
S T R I D E ░ D E P U T I Z E
S E V R E S ░ I N T E R N E S
░ R E S T S ░ S E A L I O N S
```

10

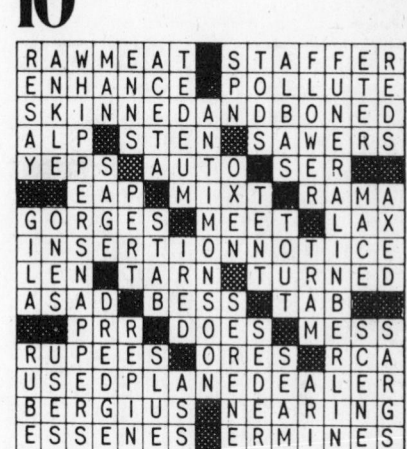

```
R A W M E A T ░ S T A F F E R
E N H A N C E ░ P O L L U T E
S K I N N E D A N D B O N E D
A L P ░ S T E N ░ S A W E R S
Y E P S ░ A U T O ░ S E R ░ ░
░ E A P ░ M I X T ░ R A M A ░
G O R G E S ░ M E E T ░ L A X
I N S E R T I O N N O T I C E
L E N ░ T A R N ░ T U R N E D
A S A D ░ B E S S ░ T A B ░ ░
░ P R R ░ D O E S ░ M E S S ░
R U P E E S ░ O R E S ░ R C A
U S E D P L A N E D E A L E R
B E R G I U S ░ N E A R I N G
E S S E N E S ░ E R M I N E S
```

11

```
M E S C A L ░ F L U ░ E A S T
O R I O L E ░ L A S ░ S T L O
W I L L I E M A Y S ░ T E I L
S A L L E ░ E M E R G E N C E
░ ░ A N T L E R ░ R E S E T ░
░ M O R S E L ░ B U M ░ ░ ░ ░
S A N D ░ L I N E O F ░ S K I
T H E S U L T A N O F S W A T
Y A R ░ D I E T E D ░ E A T S
░ H A T ░ ░ F L A N G E ░ ░ ░
A U R A L ░ D E F E R S ░ ░ ░
S M A L L T I M E ░ C A V A N
T I N S ░ S C O T C H T A P E
R A G E ░ A T T ░ H E E L E D
O K A Y ░ R Y E ░ A D D E R S
```

12

```
P A S T O ░ P R A Y ░ M A C E
A M A I N ░ R A R A ░ A L A N
R A N E E ░ E C U M E N I S T
C H A R W O M E N ░ A N G E R
░ ░ ░ A G E S ░ B R A N D Y ░
░ P R E Y E D ░ E E L ░ ░ ░ ░
C O A R S E ░ C L A Y F E E T
U N F I T ░ O A K ░ A L T A R
P E T E R P A N ░ S M I T T Y
░ ░ ░ E A R ░ T H E T A S ░ ░
S C A L E D ░ B E E R ░ ░ ░ ░
M A R A T ░ M A R R I A G E S
I N D I S P O S E ░ C R I M E
L O O T ░ A R I D ░ A T R I A
E E R Y ░ P O C O ░ N E L L S
```

13

```
S A L A   R A G E       A B C S
A G I N   I T E R   G L A R E
S U E D   B U R N S A L L E N
H E S S I A N S   E R O D E D
    H A L E   L E A F
A F I E L D   L A N G F O R D
R O T A L   L I S T E   M E R
E R I N   P A N T O   M E M O
A M O   R O B E S   V I G I L
D A N R O W A N   B E R A T E
    A M E N   A U S T
G R E T E L   S M O T H E R S
N I C H O L S M A Y   F L E E
A C H E S   T E T E   U B E R
T H O R   A W E D   L A F F
```

14

```
H O S E   S T A G E   N A T L
O K L A   A R R A Y   E C H O
E R A S   T O R T E   R T E S
S A V E D U P   O L I V I N E
      D E R   R E N O
O S C U L A T E   T A U R U S
R E A P   T A N K   P S A L M
T O P   S E N D O U T   D E I
H U R O N   G U L P   T I N T
O L I V E R   P A R T W I T H
      I L E D   O D E
R A F F L E R   N O S E G A Y
E B R O   F A G O T   Z O L A
F E A R   E M I L E   E Y E R
S T U M   R A B I D   R A C E
```

15

```
O W L S   M O R A L   D O R A
R I O T   E T U D E   E R I S
A F A R   A I D E D E C A M P
L E N I E N C E   G R A T E S
    S P E E   P E N N E D
U S H E R S   W O R S T
S P A   I T C H E S   E R S E
M A R I E   R O T   A D A P T
A R K S   P A S S E R   C A R
    L A R G E   R E V O T E
    S C A L E S   A N O N
A T O N A L   D E S A L T E D
G O O D N A T U R E   A E R O
E L S E   T A P I R   N U L L
D E A R   E D E N S   T R E E
```

16

```
C R E M E   E T N A   A D A R
H E X E D   A H E M   T O N E
O V A T E   R E D O U B L E D
R E M I N D E R S   S O T T O
E L S E   O D E   G E T
      R A G   B A S T I O N
O A K   T O S S E R   O C H O
M E N T I O N M Y N A M E I N
E R O S   D O U S E D   D O E
N O T A F E W   R O N
      R U R   S H E   E R I A
T U R I N   S H A D O W I N G
I N U N D A T E S   H E N N A
L I S A   D I E T   O S S E T
E T E S   A R T Y   S T E R E
```

17

```
J A P E   O F A R T   S H E A
I N O N   R O G U E   P I X Y
B A S T   B R O N X C H E E R
E X H I B I T   S T A I R S
      R A T E S   U R N
Q U E E N S   P A R O X Y S M
U N C L E   N O V E L   O T O
I D L Y   E T E     G N A T
T U A   A B E T S   B O G I E
S E T A S I D E   R E L E N T
      Z I G   D W A R F
  A S T A G E   H I T C H U P
Q U E E N A N N E S   L A C E
P R E C   M O I R E   U L L R
L A P S   E L L E S   B O A T
```

18

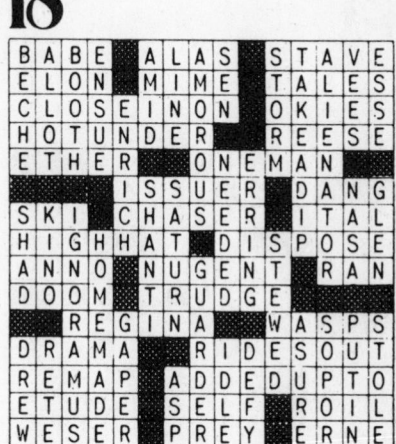

```
B A B E   A L A S   S T A V E
E L O N   M I M E   T A L E S
C L O S E I N O N   O K I E S
H O T U N D E R   R E E S E
E T H E R   O N E M A N
      I S S U E R   D A N G
S K I   C H A S E R   I T A L
H I G H H A T   D I S P O S E
A N N O   N U G E N T   R A N
D O O M   T R U D G E
    R E G I N A   W A S P S
D R A M A   R I D E S O U T
R E M A P   A D D E D U P T O
E T U D E   S E L F   R O I L
W E S E R   P R E Y   E R N E
```

19

```
F E L I N E   C A T S P A W
A D O R E S   A C R E A G E
D I R E C T   S T A N D I N S
E T A   K I T T E N S   L D R
    I S M Y   C O V E Y S
C A L M   A R R I E R E
A T O P   T A U T   S T A T S
T O P E   E N T E R   E R I C
O R E A D   T H R O   R A M A
  C R O S S A T   A B E T
  G A S H E S   T A R N
A H A   A C C R E T E   M A O
D E L A M A R E   O S T E N D
  A L L U R E S   R E A R E D
  D E E P S E T   S T R E W S
```

20

```
O L L A   S L E D S   S K I S
B I E N   T U L I A   E N N A
O F F T H E C U F F   S I G N
L E T   A R I L   E L A T E D
    H O U N D   S T E M
A P A R T   R A I S E S U P
D O N N E   B I N E S   I B A
M A D E   C O V E S   O D O R
I C E   A L G E R   C R E A M
T H R O W O U T   H A S T A
    R O S S   S C E N A
O N F I L E   G A O L   D Y E
P O R E   O P E N H A N D E D
A L A N   U I N T A   A L A D
L O U T   T E T O N   V E R Y
```

21

```
S Q U I B   T A F T   C H A P
C U R V E   O M A R   R A R E
R O B E D   S O D A J E R K S
A T A   R A C K   L U T I S T
P A N D O R A   G A G A
    A C E   I N L A N D E R
B L A C K A S C O A L   E V A
E A S E   A I M   A M E N
S I E   M A G N E T I Z I N G
S C A L A W A G   O N A
    I N K S   T U R N O F F
K O W T O W   T O R O   V I A
A T H A N A S I A   A L I B I
L I O N   R A N D   D I N E R
E S P Y   D O G Y   S T E R E
```

22

```
S Q U A B S   S I D E   D I M
A U G U R Y   P O I N C A R E
R E A S O N   A U G R A T I N
T U N   I G O R S   O B E S E
R E D O L E N T   A L E P H
E S A U   T A M P   R A S H
    S O D A   A R M   L E E
S W E E P E R   D O O R M A N
A I X   S U I   I N T O
L S T S   C O G S   M A S K
  H O P P E   R O S S E T T I
A B L E R   V A N C E   H O N
L O L L I P O P   A P P E N D
O N E T O U C H   L I O N E L
P E D   R T E S   D A T A R Y
```

23

```
  H O S S       F W D S
D A P H N E   B R O O K S
L E F T O U T   E A R R I N G
E B N   O F S T A T E   P A L
T U I S   F E R N S   J O K E
S T U M P   Q U E   P E L E E
S M A S H   C R E A S E S
    T H A N K Y O U S
C I T A D E L   S L I G O
S I N E W   T I L   S C E N A
A T O R   A W N E D   A N O N
G R R   F L O G G E D   E N D
Y O D E L E R   A L I A S E S
N E W A R K   L A N D I S
    R E N T   Y E A S
```

24

```
C A B I N   B A T S   A N E W
O R A T E   E P I C   L I D O
C A R E T   M E E R   U S E R
O B E R   B E A R I N M I N D
A S H   S O A K   P A N
  E O S I N   S T R A N G E
I S A B E L   L E W D   E A R
L O D I   E L D E R   B E T A
I L E   I D E S   I M A R E T
A D D E N D A   S T A N D
  M C I   T H E N   O P A
C O M M A N D E E R   S W A B
R H E E   N O P E   S E E D Y
A I N T   E M I T   T A L U S
M O D S   R E D S   A T L A S
```

25

```
TABU INTO ASSET
ATOP MOHR HOWTO
CARS POET ALINE
ELATIONS  ONAS
TEXANS  HIDING
  GETSONESGOAT
PATES AWFUL VIA
ERAS DIMES TENT
SIL LULUS AORTA
TAKEONESTIME
  ASSERT NADINE
LETT  GRENADES
ASHES SOAS NEWT
STORE PONS CASE
SENSE ANTE ELYS
```

26

```
APPMT ANGE EFFS
GRECO BOAR ELIA
NATIONALGALLERY
AME DIS ATTIMES
  ROLLER DEI
APPLE DEME SSDS
LEADON NOR THAW
TAU OOLONGS PRE
OLLA POI OPIATE
SERT EARS ODIST
  UTE  SPURON
SOBERED EST TRI
KRESSCOLLECTION
ISNT HULL ARNIE
TESS ODDS REGLE
```

27

```
SOFTSOAP SEDATE
CREATURE CREPES
ANABASIS ARMPIT
LASS ESTOPS ALE
ATT  TELE  ANTE
RESH HARE ALARM
  OMITS APOGEE
PROMISE ANISEED
REVERS PROSE
EVERY DARN ROSY
SERS LENO ITA
AIL VOLAGE BLOW
GLACER CARDAMON
ELIXIR ENSILAGE
SEDILE ATTAINED
```

28

```
SAWTO GAVE AIRS
OMAHA AMID DROP
LITER DATA MAGI
DEER MOZAMBIQUE
  REQUIEM ARIEL
INBOUND ILKA
NOONE KNEELING
SLY STRIKER NAE
POSITION ITSIN
  SIAM STERILE
OVOLO APPOSED
FARANDNEAR NEED
APIN ACAD STOLE
GOOD LESE ROUSE
ERNS IDES ONTAP
```

29

```
COLOR . . . LHASA
BENARES . DEADENS
ENTRANT . RAIMENT
ASA . LEADING . LEO
SORTS . PINT . HATS
TRIO . ILA . ORANTS
. SONGFEST . UNDE
. . SAAR . HANG .
. STUM . SLAPDASH
SHARER . EIR . RAAF
CONE . AGAL . ASTIR
RET . MILKAND . ILE
ABALONE . NOMINEE
PAROLEE . DEICERS
. GAPES . . . STATS
```

30

```
JAZZ . RAMON . BALD
OYEZ . EMOTE . ISEE
LINZ . NOTTINGHAM
IND . CANE . GAGES
ESSLING . HRE . .
. . ITS . FREESHIP
APACE . DOORSTOPS
RUSK . GORES . SPIT
CRESCENTS . PHILS
SEAPORTS . SRO .
. . INT . SHOWERS
. OTTER . LAUD . MEA
INSTRUMENT . OBER
ETAL . DANTE . BELG
SORE . ETTES . ERSE
```

31

```
MATH . GASPS . LIS
IDEA . OLPAE . DADA
AMEN . FOUNTAINOF
MANNERED . FONDLE
INSIDES . MORAS .
. . BEE . CARTHAGE
JAHAN . CARTA . KAT
ARAL . PARCH . HEBE
VAS . ARGOS . CASES
ANDSHELL . PAM .
. REUSE . CARIBOU
STUART . CHIPLESS
KUBLAIKHAN . CASH
ANAS . GRANT . ALIE
TAL . EASTS . REAR
```

32

```
. PEBBLE . OKAPI
SEVERAL . VIVANT
TUTELAGE . AVERSE
AGENTS . GETA . MUM
TART . PINE . HELP
ARS . MARAT . NASAL
. SOLACE . ABATE
BROWNLY . RAVINES
REMIT . SPINET .
OVENS . FINIS . MEL
MELE . BORG . MEMO
IRE . RARA . AMANDA
DETAIL . TALENTED
ENTICE . ITALIAN
. DELED . CENTAL
```

33

```
BAFFS  SHIP  ABAS
ATRIP  PINA  BRIO
THIRTEENTH  HERB
HED  SYNGE  MOAB
ONAS  EDEN  ARKOF
SAYTO  ESSAY  IRE
   ONER  ESP  NNE
STALES   TOGGED
THE  STP  TOLE
ARR  HARSH  ETHOS
SEATO  EPIC  SOAP
 ETAT  PICKS  OTO
COIL  WALKSUNDER
ANNE  ERLE  MOORE
TAGS  BEST  STOSS
```

34

```
AHAT  ARRAS  LALO
CORONAAUSTRALIS
TROUBLESHOOTERS
UNITES  SLOVENIA
PEDE   DIAPER
  RESOAR   ASIA
BOYSTOWN  PILLOW
ERA  TODDLED  UNA
TARTAN  ROSEGRAY
ANNA   BETTOR
  BEGASH   OGAM
LABORERS  ROWENA
ILLUSTRIOUSNESS
APARTMENTHOUSES
MESS  EDGER  PERE
```

35

```
BART  BAAS  STEAL
ALEE  RICE  PENNA
ROAN  IDEALISTIC
DEPENDED  ANTES
   MEED  ANNE
JADES  DICEDHAM
ANENT  TIMER  ALA
PINT  LINER  AVON
ELI  AIRED  SCENE
SEMESTER  PINES
   ACTS  ABED
 HOTEL  SPATTERS
DELINEATES  ERAT
ARENT  LORE  SITE
GROGS  PAYS  TSAR
```

36

```
ATES  QUOTH  JADE
NEXT  USURY  OVID
ACQUAINTED  HARD
SHUNTS  SERENITY
 ITALY   AMITY
PASS  IOU  SEI
ASI  SNUBS  NIZAM
CAT  AGROUND  IRA
KNEEL  SAGES  NON
  LIC  TAP  SFAX
 PIANO   REATA
CULPABLE  NIENTE
APOS  NIGHTRIDER
LIVE  URIAH  NELL
FLED  TASTE  SLEE
```

37

```
LADD  WOKE   ATTS
ITEA  HURLS  TROT
DOUBLETIME  WIRE
SIXBELLS  CHIPIN
    LAKE  ATALL
TOMES   THRILLER
INURES  AMOS  POI
PALS  PAGAN  ELAN
SIT  COLA  STMARK
 RIGHTARM  ABYSS
  FOILS  AGNI
ALLUDE  KNITTERS
ROOD  SINGLETREE
TORA  STEED  EINE
SPAS   SERA  REED
```

38

```
SELL   SAGS   CITE
OTOE   HEEP  GLARE
AURA   AINU  RAGER
RINGAROUNDAROSY
    URDU   ANE
BEGEMS   STUNTMAN
APERY  BEANY  UVA
SUNS   HEART  TROP
IRE  ZEALS  KYRIE
NETWORKS  PIPERS
    IRO   GUSH
PULLINONESHORNS
INALL  PATH  OHOH
CANIS  UNIE  NERO
KLEE   SAND  SAME
```

39

```
HATS  POSSE   MAME
ALBA  ESAUS   ABUT
LEAF  NOTRE   NEST
FERRO  RIN  TITHE
   AMANSAMAN
MANNEROFMAN  CPA
ITAINT  YEN  DAIS
TRANSIT  SAHARAS
RICE  SOB  COLONY
APP  MANUALLABOR
   MANSFIELD
CLEAN  UFT  YIELD
LOIN  BRAKE  EVER
ACRO  RELET  REDO
WIEN  ASONE  SNAP
```

40

```
 CORDAGE   ALERT
COVERLEY  CLOVER
OMELETTE  REVIVE
SPREE  HOE   EDEN
MESA  GLOVE  SENT
OLES   RILE  HENGE
 STEPOVER  ETTE
    EWE   SHE
SOSO   WATERGAP
LENIN  IMAM  ABEL
AMAD  PREYS  TINA
TIDE  EEL   CEDAR
ENAMEL  INCOMING
NATANT  TEADANCE
TREND   ARRANGE
```

41

```
ROME RABAT TOLL
ARIL ADELA ERIE
JACKOFALLTRADES
ALA ATIT ICONS
   USER MENU
STARER JACKPOT
HORNS MANUS RAG
AWES TOPES CAFE
YEN ARIAS PATIO
 LANTERN CEREAL
  ETTE IHRE
ABACA GRID ELS
JACKINTHEPULPIT
ANTE IRANI EIRE
READ PATEN ICAN
```

42

```
SOFAR GRAM DAIL
TRASH LINY ALSO
AERIE ENDS PLOT
GLEANING TAP
    INN GIRLISH
MORASS COQUETTE
IRISH SHOUT AIR
RAGS ATONE ELLE
AGO BLISS GRITS
GERBILLE QUEASY
ESSENCE BUS
   HEL FRESHETS
WISE ERIE EASEL
IBIS AONE TIARA
TORT RIND SLUNG
```

43

```
STRIA POSH SLAM
THING ALTO HALO
ROVER REAR AVID
ISERE AGGRAVATE
PESTERS SORE
   TAIL RATTAN
COMFORTER MAINE
OVAL AIDES IDES
BEGUM COVERLETS
BRETON NEMO
 TOAD REACHED
ADVERTISE DRIVE
BOAR IVAN HAVEN
ELSE VELD OVENS
DEED ERAS GESTE
```

44

```
CLAM SIGIL GMEN
RIGA AVISO HARE
AMAR MIAOW ARIA
MARKSMEN MARKER
  TOYS BASRA
SWIM MARKINGS
ICAME CONK TEA
MATE FLUES EONS
APE OARS JANIS
MARKDOWN ASYE
 MEATS LAZY
ALARUM SITZMARK
LARS ALIBI ARAL
TYKE RATEL RENE
ISSY KNELT KATE
```

45

```
CAVIL BROM SLEW
USAGE IOWASTATE
STINT PALOMINOS
SINISTER ANENT
  TOAD SARG
MATING BELT LOS
OLIO STARTEDOUT
LIMNS RIA NOISE
ANESTHETIC CREW
RED EONS HOTELS
 GAIT HILO
CREEL MANDRILL
EAGLEEYED MARIA
STAIRCASE ATEST
TEND UPAS NESTS
```

46

```
PERTH  TROT  ERST
ALARM  REVD  GETA
SIDESWIPES  ACES
SHAM  HOUR  ADEPT
EURODOLLARS  SPY
    RIDES  UKASE
VIA  LUTE  BETIDE
ENDRUNS  BEDEVIL
TAHITI  GOLF  ENS
  BEFIT  ARBOR
AIR  OSAGEORANGE
GLEAN  DRAW  GOUT
RINK  POURSFORTH
ETCH  HOLM  MUSTY
EYES  IRES  STEAL
```

47

```
HASH  AGAVE  TOTO
ALAI  VALID  AROW
PLUMMETING  GAOL
PEN  AREA  EVENT
YEARNS  SEWING
    EXEC  MIDDENS
LIRA  LAPSE  AYE
INAPPLEPIEORDER
ASI  RIVER  PETE
ROSEATE  ETYM
  INTERN  RESCUE
ANGER  IDEA  AND
OGGI  APPEARANCE
SHUN  TAUNT  NOUN
TAPE  EMPTY  NETS
```

48

```
JAZZ  POE  SHAD
ALEE  RUNG  SIRUP
MARBLEIZE  EJECT
SORAS  YRS  ANAS
  AXIOMATICAL
WEDS  DUE  ASK
AXE  SISSY  SEEM
CAMELOT  AMERCED
MINA  SEQUI  HAI
OVI  RUT  POND
EQUESTRIANS
STUN  MAA  TEARS
CHICO  STRIPLING
MITER  KIEV  MOUE
CEDE  COE  STGE
```

49

```
SAPS  ROGER  TAOS
KLOP  EVADE  HINT
ETTE  VALET  ENDO
DISCRETE  ROSTER
  TIRE  LEAP
SCRAPE  PLATONIC
ALATE  SEAT  RODE
LOCO  BARNS  TOLL
EVER  AGIO  MOSEL
PERSONAL  DEFERS
  PUTS  SILK
CAPOTE  MANDIBLE
OVER  REATA  NOEL
LENT  ENTER  GRAM
ARTS  DEEDS  SANS
```

50

```
STAB  COWS  WALED
TOGO  OVAL  EMILE
AGIO  MORO  ROMAN
YANKEEINGENUITY
  PROD  VERTE
CALLON  AJAR
OREAD  AVON  SURE
BETTERMOUSETRAP
HATE  EMIR  ROSIE
  PLOD  PARADE
  ALTAI  SATE
AMERICANKNOWHOW
LAMAR  BEET  IOLA
PRUDE  BAER  DUAD
HARED  ARTY  ERNE
```

VOLUME 3

1

ACROSS

1. Banner maker
5. The 29th
9. "The __ heard ..."
10. U.S. President
15. The 39th: Abbr.
16. Passport item
17. Permitted
18. Arnaz
19. Deficient
20. Mountain ridge
21. Poets' land
22. Canadian prov.
24. Weather abbr.
26. Name for a radioman
28. Sideshow rhetoric
31. City of Crete
32. Kind of boom
33. Kind of lot
34. Group organized in 1890
35. In need of practice
38. __ bagatelle
40. "One __ ..."
42. __ of well-being
43. Steak order
44. The 30th: Abbr.
45. Prefix with circle or colon
48. Credit of a kind
50. Ancient kingdom
54. __ grind
55. Call up
56. Andrews
57. Wife of Henry VIII
58. Confederate name
59. The 48th: Abbr.
60. The 34th: Abbr.
61. U.S. inventor

DOWN

1. Hostess's letters
2. The 17th
3. Passable
4. July 4 sight
5. Calendar time
6. River to the Baltic
7. "How __ to know?"
8. Similar
10. The 49th
11. Daggers
12. Golfer's thrill
13. Baseball gear
14. Declivities
23. Common verb
25. Mine: It.
26. Despise
27. Italian city
29. Contemptible ones
30. Pebble, in England
36. Aunt: Sp.
37. New __
38. "__ it"
39. __ amis
41. Frenchman's new
42. Roused
45. The 40th: Abbr.
46. Girl's name
47. The 32d: Abbr.
49. Monetary unit: Abbr.
51. Pasternak character
52. Dye shrub
53. Cloverleaf crossings, to some

2

ACROSS

1. Greek letter
5. Burned out
9. Intense zeal
14. Great
15. Up until
16. Geneva's lake
17. Elevator of a sort
20. Ladies' quarters
21. 0.3048 meter
22. Important exec.
23. "Life With Father" man
24. N. Y. subway line
25. Time units: Abbr.
26. Outcast
29. Properly pitched
31. Thoroughfares: Abbr.
32. Kind of wheel
33. Key figure in a child's game
37. Méditerranée, for one
38. Forest god
39. Charge
40. Gardening aid
41. Comparison shopper
43. Musical notes
44. Jargon
45. Matched
47. Feeling
48. Creole fried cake
51. ___ for apples
52. Game pieces
53. Suffix denoting action
54. Go bad
55. ___ y Gasset, Spanish writer
59. Certain fighters
62. Metric measure
63. Girl's name
64. Fighting equipment
65. Fished
66. Scout's good objective
67. For fear that

DOWN

1. One of the Little Women
2. Old Hebrew measure
3. Stratum
4. Agrees
5. Impudent
6. New York time: Abbr.
7. Shingles or tiles
8. Exertion
9. Dart
10. Third book of O.T.
11. Organic compound
12. Violent
13. Railroad men: Abbr.
18. Persian name
19. Water lilies
25. Grasp
26. Nightingale symbol
27. Continuously
28. Fairy
29. Noun suffix
30. Society page word
32. Large deer
34. Genghis or Aga
35. Ages
36. Network
38. Climbing plant
39. Transitory style
42. Auditing initials
43. Feverish
44. Pre-dialing phone girl
46. Set a travel course
47. Fluids
48. Hex
49. Narrow crest
50. Flat
52. Simple organism
54. Vehicle
56. Island country
57. Stones
58. Aide: Abbr.
60. State: Abbr.
61. Cheer

3

ACROSS

1. Try: Colloq.
5. Advantage
10. Pacific island group
14. Mariner's cry
15. House
16. Asian land
17. Spasm
18. Nautical term
19. Robes
20. Pink
23. Furnace
24. Accept eagerly
28. Agnew
31. West African region
33. Ping-__
34. Bubble
36. Indian weight
37. Swarm
38. Barkley
39. Punjab people
40. Inhabitant: Suffix
41. Records
42. Thought: Prefix
43. Ornaments
45. Bring together
46. Catch
47. Movie name
49. High climbers
55. Island
58. Tire pattern
59. Zenith
60. Incite
61. Resin
62. German three
63. Austrian city on Danube
64. Meal: Fr.
65. Sharp cry

DOWN

1. Undermines
2. Soften
3. Tops
4. Exclamation
5. Salads
6. Book of the Apocrypha
7. Noble: Ger.
8. Arab headband
9. Bottles of a kind
10. Blaze: Fr.
11. Adjective suffix
12. Duty
13. Edition: Abbr.
21. Road, in China
22. River of France
25. Spanish inn
26. Mountain crests
27. Museum pieces
28. Range
29. Venom
30. Endue
31. Kind of puzzle
32. Entry
34. Niter
35. Hamburg's river
39. Swell!
41. Rat-__
44. Artificial
45. Staff officer: Abbr.
47. Wool cloth
48. Form of Latin word for building
50. Gardner
51. A kind of show
52. Prepare, as fruit
53. Australian cuckoo
54. Small piece
55. State: Abbr.
56. Where: Lat.
57. Gentle or Big

4

5

ACROSS

1. "Salesman" star
5. __-cake
9. Fortification
14. Indigo
15. River to the Elbe
16. Ancient magistrate
17. Finding a spot for
19. Certain ball teams
20. Immutable
21. Aristotle's three __ of drama
23. France's Corse, for one
24. Female et al.
25. Stops up
29. Mendel's subject
32. Greek goddesses
33. Famous medical brothers
34. Border: Lat.
35. Assists
36. Baits
37. Monogram part: Abbr.
38. Danish coin
39. Despised
40. Schedule
41. Sneaky ones
43. 18 on most courses
44. Pair
45. Doctors' org.
47. Rescue
49. Kind of tribe
54. Mideasterner
55. Journey
57. Chop
58. Appoint
59. Louder: Music abbr.
60. Ridge of gravel
61. Dull color
62. Couturier's concern

DOWN

1. Condition
2. Step __
3. Snack
4. Smear
5. Corolla part
6. Nimble
7. Number
8. Keenly observant
9. Makes adjustments
10. Worked on papers
11. Departmental
12. Nautical term
13. Cape
18. Cordial flavoring
22. Tyrants
25. Confusion
26. River in France
27. Catalogue accompaniment
28. Road sign
29. Small animals
30. Stale
31. Constitutional Convention figure
33. Speaking indistinctly
36. Old weapon
37. Workers' group: Abbr.
39. __ than air
40. Chagrin
42. Monarch
45. Soul
46. Marks, reals, etc.
47. Coin
48. Goddess of discord
50. Chief
51. Presume
52. Thing
53. Luck: Irish
56. Seafarer

6

1	2	3	4		5	6	7	8	9		10	11	12	13

ACROSS

1. Kind of watch
5. Met head on
10. Birthplace of Eng and Chang
14. Prefix for mate or graph
15. Shun
16. Mediterranean island
17. Very little
20. Compass point
21. Gallery
22. Slope
23. Look in a way
24. Yarn
26. General in Michigan
29. Judge
32. Flower
33. Mona Lisa characteristic
34. Zodiac sign
36. Execute a ploy
40. Cape Verde island
41. Priestly vestment
42. Stake
43. Take away
45. Drinking spree: Slang
47. Girl's name
48. "Ah, me!"
49. Gladden
52. Harem rooms
53. Chinese pagoda
56. Unevenly
60. Type of muffin
61. Mature
62. Small spring
63. Mrs. Roosevelt
64. U.S. artist
65. Poultry

DOWN

1. Notorious marquis
2. Variety act
3. Indian
4. Kind of music
5. Withholds
6. Do a dressmaker's job
7. European region
8. Dutch town
9. Social gal
10. Something to keep
11. Miss Chase
12. Retired
13. South American beverage
18. Old road
19. More disagreeable
23. Keep informed
24. Pepper-pot ingredient
25. Grade of seaman
26. Russian planes
27. Nymph
28. Sir or dame
29. Enough
30. Antelope
31. French income
33. Polished
35. German river
37. Wasp
38. ___ go bragh
39. Brinker
44. Film produced by oxidation
45. Wild parties: Slang
46. Direction
48. Confuse
49. Dies down
50. Vega's constellation
51. Remote
52. Burden
53. Shoe preserver
54. Solar disk
55. Vipers
57. Spade
58. Fuss
59. Residue

7

¹	²	³	⁴	■	⁵	⁶	⁷	⁸	⁹	■	¹⁰	¹¹	¹²	¹³

ACROSS

1. Gem
5. Printer's signs
10. Embellishes an expense account
14. Port of Samoa
15. Wife's relative, for example
16. American writer
17. Clavicle
19. Korean of note
20. Not quite thigh-high
21. Render harmless
23. Wheel, in Berlin
24. Team
25. Bookmark of a sort
29. Missile part
33. Send out
34. Declaims
36. Photos, for short
37. Shelley's "The __"
39. Meet
40. Moment
42. Have __ at
43. Machine part
46. Distinctive person
47. On one's __
49. London's __ Hall
51. Ruining agent
52. One __ time
53. Strauss opera
56. Shiner
61. __ the air
62. Bullied
64. Temple of old
65. Not citified
66. Sign of tedium
67. Vexes
68. Part of the lex talionis
69. Maxwell

DOWN

1. Torquemada's persuader
2. Au courant
3. Black __
4. U. S. inventor
5. Weapon
6. Asleep
7. Spill
8. Healthy look
9. __ pancakes
10. Unit of astronomical distance
11. Turkish title
12. Game
13. Appear
18. Port in southern Spain
22. Relative of exempli gratita
24. __ voce
25. Sticker
26. End of a sequence
27. Italian names
28. Useful abbr.
29. Nights, in Paris
30. Believe, old style
31. More precise
32. Put into action
35. __ orange
38. Eastern religion
41. Roy
44. Darkness, in ancient Rome
45. Proportional
48. Steaks
50. Shoe part
52. Forever, long ago
53. Moslem mystic
54. Armadillo
55. Connection
56. Cause of 66 Across
57. Popular comedian
58. See 28 Down
59. Ornamental shrubs
60. Sicilian town
63. Seek office

8

ACROSS

1. Old riverboat figure
8. Word for agency such as Port Authority
15. Anthem by Samuel F. Smith
16. Pierced
17. Ostentatious
18. Girl's best friend
19. Condescend
21. Like some Britishers
22. Cuts in, at a dance
25. Jewish month
27. Mideasterners
29. Dupe
33. Pub
35. Have __ at it
36. Mild expletive
38. Barnstorms
40. Come to agreement
42. Tale
43. Churchill symbol
45. Medieval land tenure
46. Spreading machines
48. Allotted
49. Indignant
51. Regions: Abbr.
52. Fire-bomb ingredient
56. Swelling disease
59. U.S. space vehicles
61. Island country
65. Sky objects
66. Sounded, as a small bell
67. Ancient ascetics
68. Playground gear

DOWN

1. Tank contents
2. Elec. unit
3. Honey
4. Uncompromising
5. Roster
6. Nymph of myth
7. Dress material
8. One club, for example
9. Certain vaudevillians
10. Generates
11. Subdue
12. Lily plant
13. Mind
14. Current
20. 12-point type
22. Savory
23. Biblical mountain
24. Abundant
26. Old writing
28. Dunk
30. Post-armistice doings
31. Akin
32. Friendly dog
34. Poe word
37. Certain documents
39. Fluids
41. Gypsy male
44. Italian family
47. Matt
50. Revises
52. Single out
53. Zoo features
54. Containers
55. Nautical word
57. Indian
58. Biblical wall word
60. Draft abbr.
62. __ king
63. Unfamiliar
64. Dental degree: Abbr.

9

ACROSS

1. Furniture style
5. Famous publisher
9. Car adjuncts
14. Corrida protagonist
15. Partisan: Suffix
16. To any extent
17. Not __ (be calm)
19. Brouhaha
20. Colombian people
21. Reptiles
23. Prepared to drive
24. Franck
26. Provoked
28. A non-word, usually
31. "...end __ perfect day"
34. __ favor
37. Defense initials
38. Dairy product
40. Soft leather
42. Direct course
43. Occupant
44. City of Morocco
45. Beanery sign
46. Bearish time
47. King of Siam's song topic
50. Early Archbishop of Canterbury
52. Middle East capital
56. Dear: It.
58. Good sense
61. Idol, in Soho
62. Voiced
64. Shoe leather
66. Tailor's iron
67. Obscure
68. Noun ending
69. Assents
70. Catch sight
71. Mango or colima

DOWN

1. Athenian
2. Irma la __
3. Wall hanging
4. Day: Abbr.
5. Spanish numeral
6. Seafood dish
7. Sharp turn
8. Difficult position
9. Traffic situation
10. Tête-__
11. Scotland
12. Swiss painter
13. Luge
18. Realtor's unit
22. Compression
25. Honshu volcano
27. Motivate strongly
29. Defeatist
30. Sea-going initials
32. Printer's concern
33. Middle __
34. Book of Bible
35. Mets' home
36. Boomers
39. Flash
41. Pronoun
42. Ante
44. Certain voters
48. Adhere
49. Summoned, in a way
51. Futile
53. Measuring instrument
54. Rebelled
55. Certain Europeans
56. Shrewd
57. African lily plant
59. Faux pas
60. Ingratiating
63. __ Moines
65. Leaf cutter

10

ACROSS

1. L.A. footballers
5. Authorize
10. Exclamation
14. Soviet range
15. Abode
16. Disgrace
17. Matching tools of a sort
20. Mode of travel
21. Clamorous
22. Highway sign
23. Early Briton
25. Fire —
28. Precise persons
31. Part
32. Proofreading mark
33. Inlet
35. Treating, in a way
39. Compass point
40. Noblemen
41. Broadway playwright
42. Covers of a sort
44. "Gunsmoke" player
46. Associate
47. Eager
48. Pool-ball shot
51. School of philosophy
55. Togetherness, in a way
58. Umpire's cry
59. Beginning
60. Think, old style
61. Electric —
62. Abounds
63. New-math words

DOWN

1. Stadium sounds
2. Winglike parts
3. Family member
4. Acted fatuously
5. Weight units
6. Tends
7. Water bird
8. Foreign —
9. Thing, in law
10. Scarves
11. Norse god
12. Bothers
13. Weaver's reed
18. Ancient land
19. Abet
23. Eddies
24. Exacerbated
25. Spark streams
26. Kind of change
27. Passage
28. Newman and Pry
29. Threefold
30. Spills the beans
32. Threadlike
34. Periods
36. Hawker
37. Weather forecast
38. Hair style
43. Atelier equipment
44. Instruments
45. Tobacco, for one
47. Revoke, legally
48. Arouse resentment
49. Indonesian ox
50. Bewilder
51. — dixit
52. Concerning
53. Lauder, for one
54. Gulls
56. Dowry
57. Chemical suffix

11

ACROSS

1. Great Lakes fish
6. Sharpener
11. Have reliance in
12. Odious
15. Like Smokey
16. Chaotic place
17. Well-known tune
18. Impede
20. Manipulate
22. Early date
23. Ditty
24. Seine area
25. Toast
30. Small barracuda
31. Jacob's wife
32. French pronoun
33. Calendar abbrs.
34. Type of entertainment
37. Instigate
40. Olympian
41. Ma chère __
44. Famous seven
45. Property
48. Unit of length
49. Word in a wedding notice
50. Army man: Abbr.
51. Mold
52. Kind of bath
56. __ time
57. Do a photographer's job
59. Make a meal of
61. Mythical beings
62. Employ
63. Change
64. Acts

DOWN

1. Sweet
2. Encourage
3. Sporting equipment
4. Steer
5. Near-miss game for a pitcher
6. Leg part
7. Mind
8. Abundant
9. Expert
10. Spanish preposition
11. Boy's nickname
13. Green
14. Dirty
19. Natural resource
21. Wins
23. Tennis name
26. Former soprano
27. Sing, in a way
28. What "they're playing"
29. NATO member: Abbr.
30. Pundit
35. Guinea pigs' home
36. Conjuror, old style
37. Kind of car
38. Bas- __
39. Lead ore
42. Alternatively
43. Beverages
46. Essential
47. Pit
52. Garment
53. Precise
54. Architectural curve
55. Headland
56. Heavenly being: Fr.
58. Top
60. Like: Suffix

12

ACROSS

1. Fiction's vis-à-vis
6. Soul seller
11. Explanatory designs
14. Old trial device
16. Sensibility
17. Thomas More's country
18. Club
19. Rascality
21. School subj.
22. Single
24. Dupes
25. Outrigger
26. Purport
28. Resourcefulness
29. Ascertain
30. "... __ too late ..."
32. __-face
33. Middle East city
35. Word in a thoroughbred's lineage
36. Center of worship
37. __ de cacao
38. Descendant
39. Common verb
40. Leather band
44. Attention-getter
45. Paradise
47. Peeved: Colloq.
48. Big casino
49. Annuls
51. Digit
52. Warning, old style
54. Esteemed position
56. Square
57. Small sturgeons
58. Slender
59. __ Oro

DOWN

1. Extract of dried leaves
2. Chair material
3. Sound of disgust
4. Journey
5. Common contraction
6. Bridge groups
7. Dilettante
8. Japanese herb
9. Autonomous
10. Custom-made
11. Society event
12. Cried, in a way
13. __-faire
15. Goods thrown into sea for recovery later
20. Knead, old style
23. Large gun
25. Small shots
27. Defensive structure
29. Soils
31. Diversity: Abbr.
32. Inlet, in England
33. College degree
34. Make unfriendly
35. Overflowing stream
37. Ripples
38. Soul buyer
39. __ mode
41. Based
42. Florid
43. Oven shovels
45. Jolty
46. Jewish service
49. Britisher's sovereign
50. Sonoran people
53. Fluidity unit
55. Traffic-sign word

13

	1	2	3	4	5	6	7		8	9	10	11	12	
13									14					15
16									17					
18					19		20		21					
22				23			24		25					
26			27					28		29				
		30				31		32						
33	34	35					36							
37				38	39									
40		41		42					43	44	45			
46	47		48					49						
50		51		52			53							
54			55		56	57								
58					59									
	60				61									

ACROSS

1. Major city problem
8. Seafood
13. Bizet character
14. Consequence
16. Shoe job
17. Gauzy paper
18. Inclined
19. U.S. agency
21. __ Coeur
22. Folding money
23. Emotions
25. Thread of a sort
26. Poker word
27. 1945 conference site
29. Prefix for tribe or thermy
30. Man in Genesis
31. Chewing scenery
33. Vivid events
36. Immerse
37. Takes to task
39. Blind part
40. Suffix denoting an art
41. Amble
43. Pronoun
46. Cliff edge
48. One kind of mill
49. Medical unit
50. Down
52. Prosperous
53. Perfume
54. Celebrated
56. Small, light vehicle
58. Puts in appearance
59. Backtracking of a sort
60. Doctrine
61. Disputed

DOWN

1. Beard
2. Girl's name
3. Involuntary responses: Abbr.
4. Hemp fiber
5. "Much __ About ..."
6. Philistine ex-champ
7. Raises
8. Appeals or Supreme: Abbr.
9. Garlands
10. Put to trial
11. French revolutionary fop
12. Slighting
13. "__ all"
15. Bobby-sox set
20. Transfer
23. Difficult position
24. Tested
27. Alps
28. Incisor's neighbor
30. Dallas school
32. Exclamation
33. Basketball maneuver
34. Apostate
35. Outright
38. Beach sight
39. Level of achievement
42. Narrowed the gap
43. Balzac
44. Printed
45. Confronts
47. Anglo-Saxon god
49. Come out
51. Lived
53. Acapulco residence
55. Summer time
57. Seize

14

ACROSS

1. Numerical prefix
5. Soviet sea
9. Over
13. Pertinent: Lat.
14. A kind of dive
15. Gary Cooper word
16. Fun in Soho
19. Mouthful, of sorts
20. __ the mark
21. River in Argentina
22. Hard hitters
24. Unmixed
25. Sound, usually dull
26. Landing field
30. Ornamentation
32. Hornless cow
33. Mideast initials
34. A caliph
35. Fully satisfied
36. Site of W. W. II battle
37. Me, in Munich
38. Goads
39. Persian sprites
40. Unmodern
42. Olive genus
43. Uses crooked dice
44. Nemesis
47. Beset
50. Eye section
51. __ Claire
52. Weather words
55. Make money
56. Bird of ballet
57. Rejoice
58. Nervous
59. Subdued
60. Slope

DOWN

1. Old music hall
2. Modern money
3. Sloping lawn: Abbr.
4. Dilettante
5. Home of the Incas
6. Antarctic sea
7. First man, in Nordic myth
8. Unhurried
9. Horn
10. Weight of India
11. Unclosed, to poets
12. Philippine money
13. Fundamentals
17. French direction
18. Dilatory
23. U. S. missile
24. Oodles
26. Other: Fr.
27. "Arrows of __ fortune"
28. African republic
29. Cupid
30. Major __
31. Man's name
32. Uses roughly
35. Lookout's instrument
36. Understood
38. Impassive
39. Anyone who advocates
41. Meager
42. Kitchen item
44. Before, in Paris
45. Golf score
46. Color
47. French weapon
48. Aforementioned
49. Confess: Slang
50. Defense unit: Abbr.
53. "__ if by sea"
54. Sixth-century date

15

ACROSS

1. Preparing peaches
8. Gracious
15. Upset
16. Army food packet
17. Exalt
18. Fine wine
19. Showed an old movie
20. Algonquian Indian
22. Takes advantage of
23. Pitching statistics: Abbr.
24. Inlets
26. Weight units
28. Threshold
33. Sense of superiority
36. Occupied
37. Station, in Paris
38. Western bean
39. New York theater
40. Much ado
44. Fix a pillow
45. Veterans; of a sort
46. Look upon favorably
48. Sheik, for one
52. City near Leghorn
56. Footless animal
57. Mink piece
58. Arouse
60. Tallinn's country
62. Betrayer
63. Request more goods
64. Constellation on equator
65. Spring and fall

DOWN

1. Metric measure
2. Lodge doorkeeper
3. __ buffa
4. Modern Acadia
5. Grand duke of Muscovy
6. See-through material
7. Urn of verse
8. Opposite
9. Cooked, in a way
10. Cooling device
11. Largest of Near Islands
12. Leaning
13. Booth
14. Chemical suffixes
21. Military group: Abbr.
24. Church title
25. Kind of sweater
27. Things to be done
29. Avant-garde people
30. Memorable actor
31. __ perpetua, motto of Idaho
32. Gaseous element
33. On __ with
34. Characterization
35. Invitation request: Abbr.
40. Mobile homes
41. Hodgepodge
42. Bases for whodunits
43. __ Curie
47. Legendary friend
49. Musical work
50. Strange
51. Tolerates
52. Places in competition
53. Concerning
54. Port in Tunisia
55. Came to rest
57. Greek colonnade
59. __ glance
61. Ascertain

16

ACROSS

1. ___ Ababa
6. Hope: Lat.
10. Baseball team
14. French battle site
15. Dance
16. Settled
17. Yesterday's child
18. Young's destination
19. New Guinea river
20. Affluent men
22. Unreal
24. ___ hand
26. Peter out
27. Free
30. Constellation
31. Greek letter
32. Renown
34. Papal name
38. Distant, in a way
40. Brazilian people
42. ___ -da-fé
43. Wine and dine
45. Cereal plant disease
47. I do
48. Bark
50. Kohl
52. Awkward step
55. This: Fr.
56. Weather condition
58. Dismissed
62. Horse
63. Muse
65. Song and movie title
66. Volcano
67. Conveyance
68. Biblical father
69. Fume
70. Montand
71. Winchester

DOWN

1. Make ___ of
2. Art style
3. Cudgel
4. ___ parentis
5. Delay
6. Son of Ra
7. Utilize
8. Bible country
9. Wasteland
10. Kind of sauce
11. Antelope
12. Culinary aid
13. House area
21. Declaim, informally
23. Hindu pundit
25. Owing
27. Ledger entry: Abbr.
28. Nike's cousin
29. Green shade
33. Hasso
35. Betel leaf
36. Sun disk
37. Inquisitive
39. Early time
41. Under, in Italy
44. Soft mineral
46. Nominal
49. Excellent: Slang
51. Ore range
52. Baseball thrill
53. Shaped, in a way
54. City on the Aar
57. European
59. Sward
60. Epochal
61. Baronet's wife
64. Approves

17

ACROSS

1. Expert on dog reflexes
7. Marked with a sweeping stroke
14. "Do __ Waltz?"
15. Printed chintzes
17. Open footwear
18. Asian people
19. German composer
20. Word before bolt or clap
22. Game pieces
23. Tend
24. Finally
26. Former diva
29. French explorer
32. Sky sight
33. Dear: Ger.
34. Early sword
38. Guinness
39. Tally
41. Only
42. Movie marquee word
44. Lighten
45. Soviet city
46. U. S. humorist
48. Trim
49. Site of 23 Down
52. Costae
54. Uncle, in Scotland
55. Translucent opal
58. Not talking
61. Pioneer reformers
63. People of Africa
65. Habitués
66. Peaceful
67. Not now
68. Color

DOWN

1. Tourist city
2. Ishmael's skipper
3. Orifice
4. "That's a good __"
5. Sound forth
6. Odin's home
7. Encompass
8. Swedish Nightingale
9. Toughen
10. Frighten
11. Emoter
12. Swelling
13. Rx. directions
16. Directed
21. Independently
23. Italian landmark
25. Classwork
26. Amo, amas, __
27. French composer
28. Scott
30. City on the Meuse
31. Vituperative ones
35. Sped
36. Olive genus
37. Certain European
40. From time to time
43. River from Tibet to Shanghai
47. Irritating one
49. Western lake
50. Actuate
51. Girl's name
53. Proclaim loudly
56. Neighbor of Virginia City
57. Relative of an org.
58. Peanut: Sp.
59. Modern author
60. Spice
62. Meet
64. Debussy's "La __"

18

ACROSS

1. Fish-drying frame
6. Salk's place
9. Word for a quick exit
13. Postpone
14. Mountain in Asia Minor
15. Old Antwerp coin
16. Loos
17. Mrs. Gump
18. Kind of soup
19. Famous first words
22. Napoleon's marshal
23. Old French coin
24. Oriental prince
25. Double is one
27. Psychiatric concern
28. Mountain pass
31. Modern material
34. Horses of a dark reddish color
37. Furrows
38. Possess, in Scotland
39. Displayed temper
40. Convicts' work spots
42. People who take advantage
43. Certain vote
44. Result
45. Prussian town
46. "__ One"
47. Forest Hills move
49. Of a calling: Abbr.
52. Sporadically
57. Transmit, in a way
58. Busy fellow
59. Site of Tokyo
61. Point of __
62. Western Indian
63. Word in "Wanted" circular
64. Word in Einstein's equation
65. Beetle
66. Peter and others

DOWN

1. Religious title
2. Noted Russian
3. Chemical compound
4. Famous aviation locale
5. Greenland base
6. Place of confinement
7. Farewell
8. Loud sound
9. Medicinal plant
10. 152
11. Conflict, in literature
12. Chinese dynasty
15. Caribbean noisemaker
20. Time zone: Abbr.
21. Shakespearean character
26. Mystery story character
27. Eternities
28. U. S. composer
29. __ and terminer
30. W. W. II vessels
31. Nimble
32. Bitter drug
33. Mythical creatures
34. __eagle
35. Golfer's concern
36. Musical instruments
41. Inca sun god
45. Central American tree
46. Parisian friends
47. Musical instruction
48. Aquatic animal
50. "__ vincit amor"
51. Tree
52. Word used in subtraction
53. __ avis
54. Bettor's concern
55. Scottish plaid
56. For all __
60. Wartime agency

19

ACROSS

1. Crossing sign
5. Type of lift for a winter sport
10. French miss: Abbr.
14. Throw
15. Out
16. Certain votes
17. "Cogito, ___ sum"
18. Strongholds
20. No special place
22. Kind of kick in football
23. Modify
25. ___ Plaines
26. Imitator
30. Sharp pain
32. Old word for a post
35. Newsroom man
37. Spatial infinity
39. Repent
40. Certain transactions
42. Prevailing outlook
44. Abbr. on a business letter
45. Treas. or Agric.
47. Wood louse
48. Suffix for thermo
50. Durocher and others
52. Armadillos
53. Certain carriers: Abbr.
55. Character in "Ring" operas
57. "Perils of Pauline," for instance
60. Protein in egg white
65. Leading figures
67. Eye: Fr.
68. Arrow poison
69. "Coffee ___?"
70. Maiden
71. Russian press agency
72. Wanting
73. Commedia dell' ___

DOWN

1. Stadium
2. Left or U
3. Carousal
4. Move strongly, with "through"
5. Hungry
6. ___ a church mouse
7. Prefix for mycin
8. Carson
9. Japanese case
10. The common people
11. Aristophanes heroine
12. Tune, in Scotland
13. Essential being
19. Goal
21. Stassen
24. Mineral
26. Pools
27. A kind of card, for short
28. Goes wrong
29. Greek letter
31. French dances
33. Exterior
34. Drinks
36. Dance
38. City in Italia
41. Gush forth
43. Driver's help
46. Tardy
49. Sets of three
51. Designed
54. Military group: Abbr.
56. Analyze
57. Barbecue item
58. Girl's name
59. Pride member
61. Dreyfus defender
62. Leap ___
63. Become blurred
64. In addition
66. Nova Scotia's Grand ___

20

ACROSS

1. Game piece
5. Aside
10. Plagiarize: Colloq.
14. Ymir's slayer
15. Roadside spot
16. Meadow creature
17. Peel
18. Ignorant
20. Kind of dancer
21. Puffed
22. Started
23. Main and Mott
25. Salt
26. __ gestae
27. Common prefix
29. Inferior
33. Rampart area
36. Biblical pronoun
37. Robert E., for one
38. Russian name
39. Embarks
40. Freshwater fish
41. Wine
42. Spanish relatives
43. Pub orders
44. Biblical name
45. "__ Alone"
46. Midwest college
47. Sea bird
49. Presidential first name
53. Like some summer days
55. Done for, informally
56. Primate
57. Leader of a musical group
59. Certain addresses
60. Type of milk
61. Aspect
62. Lie at anchor
63. Coteries
64. Terms of address
65. Guitar part

DOWN

1. Wrongful acts
2. Blithering one
3. Baseball hit
4. Football position
5. Voters
6. Longs
7. Over
8. Roulette bet
9. Board men
10. Sorority meeting V.I.P.'s
11. Score
12. Out of sorts
13. Ocean area
19. Chinese tea
21. Indian clarinet
24. Perennial shrubs
27. Small bottle
28. Uncles, etc.: Abbr.
30. Vigor
31. Religious division
32. Espies
33. Tears
34. Cry
35. Seam
36. Follow
39. Frames for sample displays
43. Ginsberg, for one
46. Duties
48. Clear
49. Opted
50. Swinelike animal
51. Lyric poem
52. Fix again
53. Cod's cousin
54. Military body
55. Julie Andrews movie
57. Documents: Abbr.
58. State Street's city, for short
59. Sandy's word

21

ACROSS

1. European basin
5. Cucumber
9. Biblical kingdom
13. Plankton
14. Shortening
15. River of Africa
16. Stumped
18. Straight: Prefix
19. Before
20. Bronze and golden
21. Evangelist
22. Sweep of a scythe
24. Not dense
26. Bloke
28. Rolls up
31. Balanced
35. Apply
36. Savvy remark
37. Black bird
38. Rail bird
39. Allen or Brooks
40. Blooey
44. Lavish
46. Old name for Tokyo
47. Foolish
49. Produce
52. State in India
54. Italian river
56. Man's name
58. Cremona name
59. Member of the wedding
61. Covered with hoarfrost
62. Mine tunnel
63. Latin abbr.
64. Carry burdens
65. Famous Ernie
66. "Riding on a ___"

DOWN

1. Sensible
2. Then: Fr.
3. Nixon V.P.
4. Whack
5. Stovepipe
6. Quiet
7. One of the media
8. Bizarre
9. Bog
10. Immediately
11. Eastern title
12. Lush period
15. Part of a ranch
17. Machine tool
21. Portuguese navigator
23. Pinnacle
25. Still
27. Babbles
29. River to the Seine
30. Luminary
31. Short for a boob
32. Belgian river
33. TV rerun
34. Wife of Athamas
38. Wild plum
40. Excelled
41. Government agency: Abbr.
42. Ruling principle
43. Tongue
45. Six-___
48. Thomas or Oliver
50. Place for worthless things
51. Channel
52. Carping remark
53. Chère ___
55. Vex
57. Griffith
59. Passage
60. Taste

22

ACROSS

1. Thick fog
8. First on the list
15. Man in white
16. Work of fiction
17. Loggerheads
18. Word on some parcels
19. Where Cnossus is
20. Literary name
22. Wartime group
23. Sock-knitter's problem
24. Round-table meetings, of a kind
26. __ de corps
28. Treatise on trees
32. Eyebrow shape
35. Prepare, as potatoes
36. Movie director's order
37. Former Belgian king
39. Grapple with
40. Beset
41. Cart, old style
42. Govt. dept.
43. Tranquil
44. "The Green __"
46. Archipelago
48. Chief
52. Good times
55. Bearcat
56. Delusion's partner
57. Bolivia's lack
59. Harder up
61. Blow up
62. Wrinkled
63. Person of powerful voice
64. Perpetual

DOWN

1. Curve, for one
2. Accrue to
3. "On __ by a river ..."
4. Decide
5. Heraldic bearing
6. French pronoun
7. Annoyed
8. Pram passenger
9. Kind of lens
10. Fleeting
11. March girl
12. Hodgepodge
13. Norse name
14. French verb form
21. Nursery sound effect
24. Relieve
25. Rests (on)
27. Wet blanket's cousin
29. Stone: Suffix
30. Meadow mouse
31. What "de novo" means
32. Word of regret
33. Caesura
34. Thus: It.
36. Astrological sign
38. Buddhist language
39. Tribal ceremonial
41. Proceed on (one's way)
44. Raillery
45. Footwear
47. Piece of music
49. More pay
50. Ojibwas' cousins
51. Crowds together
52. Wields
53. Shut in
54. Advertised event
56. Canary food
58. Rotate, as a TV camera
60. Man's nickname

23

ACROSS

1. Music sign
5. Young fellow
10. Strip
14. Floor covering, to the British
15. Contract
16. Uses
17. Lose __ cool
18. One of high rank
20. U.S. composer
22. Necessities
23. Routing word
24. Stupid people
27. Plays for time
30. Japanese herb
31. Does archeological work
35. Grain market
36. Strong, in phonetics
38. Hungary's Nagy
39. Surveyor's device
41. Postal worker
43. City in Hoover Dam's state
44. Repeat marks
46. Kimono part
47. Move gradually
48. Environment: Prefix
49. Tasks
51. Creator of Lefty
53. Can. province
54. Loos
58. Some sportsmen
62. Certain reference works
65. Over
66. Cards
67. Good show!
68. Tissue
69. Lively
70. Distinction
71. Helper: Abbr.

DOWN

1. Obstruct
2. Cable
3. Devitalizing
4. Outdated person
5. Cole __
6. Risk
7. Ball game halted by weather
8. Publication: Abbr.
9. Procure
10. Portuguese coin
11. Gain
12. State: Fr.
13. W. W. II vessels
19. Crys of pain
21. __ loaf
25. Poet
26. Genus of alga
27. Lean
28. Like some roofs
29. Fixed the lawn
31. Kind of view
32. Solicits
33. Diving bird
34. Mexican Indians
37. Chill again
40. Forest creature
42. __ in the dark
45. In all
50. __ time
51. Cereal
52. Scent
54. Malay palm
55. Mediterranean resort
56. One of a Caucasus people
57. Exam.
59. "__ sow, so . . ."
60. Units in electricity
61. Overcome a fly
63. College degrees
64. Word of exception

24

ACROSS

1. Uninteresting
5. Tree of laurel family
14. Black tea
15. Fine
16. Vegetable liquid
17. Musician of a special talent
18. Heliotrope
20. Cutting instrument: Suffix
21. Pacific sea
22. Marseilles relative
24. Family member
25. Anti-Prohibitionist
27. Rulers: Abbr.
29. Localities
31. Home of Wilson Dam
33. Word: Prefix
35. Fortress
36. Plastic used for film
40. Shelf along a bank
41. Twists
42. Willow tree
45. King of Israel
46. Invite
47. Post-season basketball tourney: Abbr.
48. Easy
51. __-ce pas?
53. Asian shrubs
55. Raise funds
59. Disturbing
61. Utility
62. Contrition
63. Outcome
64. Disaffected
65. Relax

DOWN

1. Puppet
2. Electrical circuit resistor
3. The vowels
4. Sousa and others
5. After Aug.
6. Truths
7. Locality
8. Religious feast
9. Mountain
10. Dart
11. Calmness
12. Lack of vigor
13. Emphasize
14. Hairdo
19. Season
23. Diligent one
25. Army member
26. Wallach
28. Tree
30. Ecclesiastical court
32. Ruth
33. Tie
34. Part of a circle
37. Director Litvak and others
38. Gridiron plays: Abbr.
39. Northern native: Abbr.
42. Recorded
43. Prolonged troubles
44. "__ Necessarily So"
45. Now
49. Repeatedly
50. Carefree time
52. Drudge
54. Disturb
56. Up in years
57. Family member
58. Part of the court scene
60. One __ time

25

26

DOWN

1. Wake-robin
5. Light carriages
10. Furrow
14. Comedian Bob
15. Man of easy life
16. Wrinkle
17. Biblical king
18. Inventors' fortes
19. Foretoken
20. First-aid item
22. Desisted
24. Work unit
25. Look after
26. Most bushed
30. Handle badly
34. 30, to some
35. Talk foolishly
37. Waterway
38. "Come into the garden, __"
40. Marsh birds
42. Feel inclined
43. Attorney-__
45. Call for a flip
47. Sleuth, for short
48. Totted up a profit
50. "He's the __"
52. Sidestep
54. Prefix for corn
55. Foster parent, at times
58. Workshop
62. Spanish painter
63. Of course: Slang
65. "... volume of forgotten __"
66. Russian city
67. Love, in Livorno
68. Volcano
69. Virus's cousin
70. Did carpentry
71. Wood file

ACROSS

1. Melville character
2. European capital
3. Fairy-tale word
4. Seamstress, at times
5. Initiates
6. Revere took one
7. Drink
8. Nursery-rhyme vegetables
9. Network
10. Knee-on-handkerchief routine
11. Piece of sugar
12. S-shaped curve
13. Fairy equipment
21. Dull
23. Producing: Suffix
25. Place for unneeded furniture
26. Eve was the first
27. Make proud
28. Movie classification
29. Chimney lining
31. Weld
32. Ends
33. Opt
36. Criminals' hangout
39. Oasis scenery
41. Did detective work
44. Part of a shoe
46. Sound
49. Spanish landladies
51. Helmsman's charge
53. Soap opera, e.g.
55. Eager
56. French illustrator
57. Hearing of a deed in court
58. State in Brazil
59. Greek letter
60. Sea birds
61. Garner
64. Kind of head or boat

27

ACROSS

1. Cartoonist Al
5. Cavity: Suffix
9. Take __
14. Money for Loren
15. Biblical name
16. Columbus's birthplace
17. Source of indigo
18. Hard word to say
20. Advice for a lady
22. Talbot
23. Silent movie fare
24. Liver: Fr.
26. Ball or biscuit
28. Undecided
33. Place in position
37. Time for night's dream
39. Part of A.E.S.
40. Front: Prefix
41. Greenish blue
42. Poet
44. Upbeat, in music
45. More peevish
46. Perched
48. Waste allowance
50. __ - pas?
55. Snakes
59. Advantage
61. Yukon capital
63. Brightly colored fish
64. Red dye
65. U.N. member
66. Split
67. Precious ones
68. Colors
69. River to North Sea

DOWN

1. Hammer parts
2. Eldest daughter, in France
3. Inquisitive one
4. Feelers
5. Coax
6. Red-coated cheese
7. __ Moses
8. Does needlework
9. Mature
10. Reconcile
11. Black
12. Seasonal time
13. Biblical weed
19. Guidelines, of a sort
21. Most smart
25. Trains
27. Electrical quantity
29. Bradley
30. Refs' cousins
31. Half a disease
32. Speaker of baseball
33. Gender: Abbr.
34. Perfume
35. Of a bone: Prefix
36. Girls' names
38. Pique
43. Abraham's father
47. One of the astronauts
49. Succinct
51. Yarn
52. Floor or table cover
53. Ask earnestly
54. Heavens
55. Impressed
56. Oxford
57. Province in Tuscany
58. Calaboose
60. Rated, as property: Abbr.
62. Abstract being

28

ACROSS

1. Weather word
5. Kind of tiger
10. Morse symbol
13. Japanese seaport
14. Sprout, as a tree
15. Allotted
16. Brookings, for one: Abbr.
17. Estate
18. Common Latin abbreviation
19. Deals with
21. Spellbind
23. Unobtrusive
25. Appear
26. Like a hot rod
29. Stage fare
33. Assent, in Paris
34. Nile region
36. __ sides
37. Thine: Fr.
39. British coin
41. Lackawanna's partner
42. Cut down
44. Unearthed
46. Draw from
47. Polite agreement
49. Fighter
51. One: Lat.
53. Lawgiver
54. Trends
58. Marsh plants
61. English painter
62. Bumpkin
64. Station, in Paris
65. Intellect
66. Stage fare
67. If not
68. Culmination
69. Mideast desert
70. Exploit

DOWN

1. Auto mishap
2. An infection, for short
3. Fawning
4. Arises
5. Accentuated
6. Gov't agency
7. Shave off
8. Roulette bets
9. Completed a court argument
10. Computer input
11. Relative of a circle
12. Archer
15. Pertinent
20. Très __
22. Role
24. Packaged, in a way
26. Like unrinsed clothes
27. Bizarre
28. Kind of lamp
30. Tack item
31. Another name
32. Wooed Morpheus
35. Cattle breed
38. Made certain
40. Man of Zagreb
43. German article
45. Rug feature
48. Historian of the Broadway scene
50. Came to rest
52. Mine excavation
54. Get along
55. __ arms
56. Marmalade ingredient
57. Keel part
59. Gaelic
60. Progeny
63. Present, in Soho

29

ACROSS

1. Javanese tree
5. Grandma's pillow covers
10. Milady's concern
14. Superlative
15. Oriental gateway
16. Letter, of a kind: Abbr.
17. Peruvian tribesman
18. Addition
19. The sun
20. Golfers' mecca
23. Scott
24. Affirmative
25. Apple
28. Twittering
33. Tapestry
34. Cultivate
35. Standard: Abbr.
36. Straight
37. Scottish port
38. Chide
39. Butt
40. Sheets
41. Outstanding figure skater
42. Da Vinci
44. __ scouts
45. Gershwin
46. African musical instrument
47. Tearing
54. Eagle
55. Items of interest
56. Pakistan's neighbor
58. Social asset
59. Between: Fr.
60. Captain of fiction
61. Weaver's reed
62. Stratum
63. Exploit

DOWN

1. Where: Lat.
2. Author of "No Cross, No Crown"
3. Fungus spore sacs
4. Remain firm
5. Island off Jersey
6. Sharpened
7. English composer
8. Bearing
9. Of indefinite age
10. Stocking run, for one
11. Wise
12. Call a number
13. Raison d'__
21. Sister of Ares
22. Present
25. Dress adornment
26. Castle
27. Spanish museum
28. Monte __
29. Long-run shows
30. Fatuous
31. Out
32. Receive
34. Designer of U.S. flag
37. Map marking
38. Enjoying a hammock
40. Marionette creator
41. Mata __
43. Victor Hugo's "__ - Three"
44. Restless sleeper
46. Category
47. Comprehends, informally
48. Of the mouth
49. Silent movie director
50. Hebrides island
51. Girl's nickname
52. Actor Beerbohm __
53. Edible tubers
57. Common word

30

ACROSS

1. Praise
5. "And while ye may, go —"
10. Proceed
14. Mountain in Thessaly
15. Pyrenees peak
16. Overlook
17. Capital of the Ukraine
18. Agitator
20. Badge
22. Rich altar hanging: Var.
23. Dried orchid tubers
24. Beau —
25. Long way
28. Entries
31. Oriental name
32. Small aperture, in botany
33. Myrna
36. Tumult
40. Pitching statistics: Abbr.
41. Relieve
42. Look, in a way
43. — Flow
44. Examiner
46. Game of chance
49. City in Chile
51. Beached
53. "And — when I saw him..."
57. Unit of infantry soldiers
59. Leak
60. "What have — to show for it?"
61. Namesakes of a queen
62. Teutonic deity
63. TV feature
64. Impertinent
65. Ending with gyro or thermo

DOWN

1. Norse god
2. Hindu month
3. Purposes
4. Goal in a certain game
5. For the most part
6. Orphan girl
7. Summaries
8. Road map abbreviation
9. Over there, to poets
10. Balances
11. Pile up
12. River to the Danube
13. Distinction
19. Tenets
21. Civil War initials
25. Clotho
26. But: Ger.
27. City on the Tevere
29. Utensil
30. Nonflying bird
32. Word with one or two
33. Dietrich feature
34. Capital city
35. Belgian river
37. Armed guard
38. Bath, for one
39. Plane figures
43. Ermines
44. Posh
45. Medieval shield
46. Coat trimming
47. Siouan language
48. Coverlet
50. Mountains in France
52. Time periods
54. Stadium sound
55. Old Testament book
56. Depression
58. — shoestring

31

¹	²	³	⁴		⁵	⁶	⁷	⁸		⁹	¹⁰	¹¹	¹²	¹³

ACROSS

1. Organization: Abbr.
5. Exclamation
9. Some iron
14. Actress Janice
15. Impose
16. Woolly beast
17. Night sound
18. Obscure
19. Rowed
20. Scents
22. Machine tool
24. Second performance
26. Iranian river
27. Adheres, in British dialect
29. Pet: Abbr.
32. Without deflection
35. Length unit
36. Assume
37. Importers' concerns
39. Grafted, in heraldry
40. Moneyed man
42. Gov't. agency
43. Part of a space vehicle
44. Midwest Indian
45. Relax
49. Certain hospital workers
53. Russian stockade
54. Mideasterner
55. Racetrack staple
57. Wine pitcher
58. Winds, in Spain
59. Member of a church group: Abbr.
60. __ -do-well
61. Not the __ bit
62. Evening in Naples
63. Goes wrong

DOWN

1. Suit of sorts
2. Shoe material
3. Sailboat
4. Quest of a cooking buff
5. "__ Man and the Sea"
6. Notice
7. Emote
8. Assumed
9. Ski routes
10. Companion to Lewis
11. Like whooping cranes
12. Singing brothers
13. Space-age platforms
21. Burst of fire
23. Carnivore
25. Possible hockey outcome
28. Showing perfidy
29. Popular name for a French poodle
30. Landon and others
31. Weskit
32. "Sweet are the __ of . . ."
33. Sisters
34. Gov't. units
35. Significant event
38. Eastern title
41. Petroleum derivative
43. Certain camp dweller
44. Pianist Earl
46. Old German coin
47. __ Peninsula
48. Noblemen
49. Coin of Iran
50. Pennsylvania city
51. Feminine name
52. To-do
56. Railway stop: Abbr.

32

ACROSS

1. Hebrew measure
5. Certain talk
10. Analyze poetry
14. Info
15. Estate
16. Sea bird
17. Of a verse form
18. Long-distance riders
20. Access
22. Triangular insert
23. Signify
25. Child
26. One kind of seat
29. A job of sorts
31. Reputation
34. Bowsprit angle
36. Bedouin
38. Presidential nickname
39. Wood-smoothing machines
41. Church stipend
43. Wing
44. Night: Prefix
46. Gratify
47. Legend
49. Loose garment
51. ___sanctum
52. Boat accessory
54. Port on Firth of Tay
56. Warren's successor
59. Traffic court problem
63. Part of the throat
65. Greek letter
66. Relative of etc.
67. Mountain crest
68. Waste allowance
69. Thespian's goal
70. Amusement park attractions
71. Delighted: Slang

DOWN

1. Hint
2. Fashion
3. Impressively great
4. Shrank back
5. Fashionable
6. Young ones
7. Rabbit ears
8. Direction: Abbr.
9. Rum and water
10. Spring
11. Shrimp or crab
12. Stake
13. Retreat
19. Printer's measure
21. Erose
24. Hamlet
26. Shillong's state
27. NATO member
28. ___ courtesy
30. Twist
32. Minister's residence
33. Churchman
35. Greek god
37. Persuasion
40. Tropical fish
42. Charity functions
45. Confided in
48. Wrangle
50. Stir up
53. Bro. or sis.
55. Certain allotments
56. Beverage
57. Until
58. Zoo sound
60. Knowledge
61. Solar disk
62. Scottish inventor
64. Numerical prefix

33

34

ACROSS

1. Tijuana —
6. River of China
9. After: Fr.
14. — lunch
15. Fleming
16. Ranch rope
17. Obtain relief
20. Attacked
21. Adorn
22. Pronoun
24. City of Texas
27. Tops
28. Nit-picking scholar
30. British Navy girl
32. Book leaves: Abbr.
33. Nobleman
34. Stage in cell division
36. Flag
38. Doer: Suffix
39. Bread ends
42. Certain court
44. A year
45. Nigerian people
47. Lake in Ireland
48. Run out on
50. Ring arbiters: Abbr.
52. Cold-weather gear
54. Ship initials
55. Girl's name
57. Have, in Paris
59. Somehow
64. — say
65. Grande or Rita
66. Kentucky's Chandler
67. Whales
68. Keep out
69. Golfing name

DOWN

1. Become sunk in
2. Wish one hadn't
3. Pronto
4. Columned walk
5. French Legion locale
6. Heel layers
7. One of a pair
8. Daughter of Cadmus
9. In —
10. Historic ship
11. Cold-war weapon
12. Forever, in Rome
13. Raiment for ranees
18. High-strung
19. Features of horses
22. Expedited
23. Take evidence
25. Tornado
26. Upset
29. Indonesian island
31. Degree
34. Moon goddess
35. Fish
37. U.S. writer
40. Porsena
41. Certain cities: Abbr.
43. Crack
45. Language used in Jordan
46. — Gourmont, French writer
48. Jones
49. Noteworthy times
51. Noise of a kind
53. — of love
56. Performs
58. Shah's land
60. Globe
61. Inlet
62. W. W. II agency
63. 16th-century English dramatist

35

ACROSS

1. Shea players
5. Sampling implement
10. Feudal land
14. Big-league name
15. Precipitateness
16. Spanish pot
17. Tale
18. Issues
19. What's left
20. Emulates a bloodhound
22. Indian chief
24. Money getters: Abbr.
26. __ bene
27. French boîtes
31. Engage, as a lawyer
35. Glassy silicas
36. Sticks
38. Army man: Abbr.
39. French direction
40. Fountain items, in Rome
41. Genesis name
42. Sea bird
43. Desk for Picasso
44. Soil
45. __ -eyed
47. People on pension
49. Kind of school: Abbr.
51. Poon tree
52. Former Mexican President
56. Parking place
60. Ludwig
61. Weeping Greek mother
63. Hurried home, in baseball
64. Daily grind
65. Bitter __
66. Today: It.
67. Western state: Abbr.
68. Establishes
69. Firmly fixed

DOWN

1. Ex-Giant star
2. Ardor
3. Convex moldings
4. Baseball playing area
5. "__ Also Rises"
6. Zodiac sign
7. "What __?"
8. Nick __, one-time Yankee
9. Revises, as music
10. Book dimensions
11. Islands, in France
12. Other
13. Name in fashion
21. Pros
23. Western Indians
25. Lilies
27. Sounds
28. Captain's word
29. Black Sea resort
30. More furtive
32. Orphan
33. "Here __"
34. Margins of some victories
37. Lacking guidance
40. Peppers
41. __ judgment
43. Whodunit name
44. Colorado tributary
46. Cincinnati player
48. Detroiters
50. Lobster source
52. Game fish
53. Love: Lat.
54. Liturgy
55. Pop
57. Seaweed
58. Light carriages
59. Work on papers
62. Pari-mutuel item

36

ACROSS

1. Undermines
5. Let
10. With "dead," certain faces
14. Eskimo town
15. First President of Guinea
16. Latin abbreviation
17. Girl's name
18. Companion of 3 Down
20. Small bird
22. City in County Kerry
23. Marie Antoinette
24. Leaf detail
25. Kind of path
27. Cap
28. Scarlet
29. Lawn tools
31. __ jure
35. Avid
37. Objective
38. Hurt
39. St. Paul's architect
40. Granitelike rock
42. Common verb
43. Flintlike rock
45. More unbelievable
47. Bill Russell, for one
50. Dry gully, in India
51. Marine hazards
52. Ducks
55. Relative of 52 Across
57. Mrs. Helmer
58. Indian
59. Tidal bore
60. Annual golf match
61. Smears
62. True's companion
63. Bastes

DOWN

1. Part: Abbr.
2. Thine: Fr.
3. Pear-tree present
4. Humiliated
5. Harmonized
6. Spoil, with "up"
7. Spoon or spinner
8. Crumb
9. Some fighters
10. Schoolmasterish
11. Kwajalein
12. H.M.S. Pinafore's fleet
13. Weather term
19. Cleveland sight
21. Ship
24. Composer of "Ernani"
25. Concoction
26. Grade of admiral
27. Name in U.S. poetry
30. Kind
32. Bird in a Paton title
33. Like the Sahara
34. River to the Baltic
36. Surrounded lands
38. Ugly __ sin
40. Prepares
41. Pursued
44. Loki's daughter
46. Plains of southwest
47. Tie
48. "He went __ way"
49. Bridge card
50. Pearl-shell substance
52. Wise men
53. Pulled
54. Without: Fr.
56. Kind of bell

37

ACROSS

1. Delectable fish
8. Reflection
15. Small pits
16. Noisy-tailed snake
17. Evergreens
18. Deprive of dignity
19. Between ifs and buts
20. Place of refuge
22. Old English letters
23. Particularly: Abbr.
25. Lend __
27. Seizing
31. Intended
35. Sheets on a schooner
36. British word for an adder
37. Hall of Fame athlete
38. Doctor's soft hammer
40. Native: Suffix
41. Of irregular quality
43. Poker Flat people
45. Hilo greeting
46. Alabama Indians
47. Fish garnish
49. Rite words
50. Horse's predecessor, in saying
53. Wading birds
55. Western wine valley
59. In __ (disturbed)
61. Hoped
63. Stein words
64. Place of misery
65. Lower in value
66. Heavy betting favorites

DOWN

1. Initials for an amino acid
2. Algerian port
3. Pinochle term
4. Spiced drinks
5. __ carte
6. Love of the forest
7. Hellenic mountain
8. Making exact
9. Guild
10. Military study unit: Abbr.
11. Said
12. Content
13. Biblical ancestor of Hittites
14. Very, in France
21. Popular name for a summer cottage
24. Ear depressions
26. Punished
27. A face to __ clock
28. Of an insect's back
29. Inclined
30. Seine area
32. __ of one's own medicine
33. Clean, in France
34. Hair
36. Words for a sweet 16 girl
39. Wild boar genus
42. Talk
44. Pains
46. Crowns
48. Newspapers
50. Life of the party
51. Bitter drug
52. Tool
54. Como, for one
56. Peter
57. Friend William
58. Feminine names
60. Hurry
62. Degree

38

ACROSS

1. Screen
5. Moslem priest
9. The 7-10 is a tough one
14. Olaf's capital
15. Half of N.B.
16. Comb in a way
17. Take a trip of sorts
20. "Must'a been somethin' —"
21. Wish one hadn't
22. Get in good graces
23. Palest
25. Word with Shoppe
26. Ending meaning small
27. Le dernier —
28. Fragment
32. Quechuan Indians
34. Kind of anesthetic
36. I, in Latin
37. Self-possessed
40. Old name for Tokyo
41. Flirts' ploys
42. Track events
43. Old World lizard
45. Phone book abbreviation
46. Flavoring
47. Echoes
49. Intimate dining décor
52. Clean- —
55. Writer Wolfert
56. Banking abbreviation
57. Fall short, socially
61. Then: Fr.
62. Modern painter
63. Piece of hardware
64. Use a certain stick
65. Town on the Thames
66. Chemical suffixes

DOWN

1. Balkan capital
2. Holms
3. Take it on the lam
4. Superfluously
5. Steep
6. Church song
7. Belgian town
8. West
9. Taboret
10. Hung fire
11. Put on cargo
12. Island, in Spain
13. Golfer preparing to drive
18. Woodcutter for pattern work
19. Near the sun: Astron.
24. Typesetting instruction
25. Roman Hades
27. Tilts
29. Boxer and others
30. "— a kick out of..."
31. Lancelot's uncle
32. Chills
33. Joint of a stem
34. Bowlers' milieu
35. Of a light unit
38. Loreleis
39. Pinochle play
44. Some relief pitchers
46. Evolutionist
48. Nursery-rhyme porridge
49. Venetian sky
50. Result
51. Proofreaders' words
52. Food fish
53. Nimbus
54. Confess
58. After A B
59. Slum problem
60. Siouan Indian

39

ACROSS

1. Mail
6. Prefix for potent
10. Elm
14. Sycophant
15. Picnic spoiler
16. Sounded
17. Inclines, as a mast
18. Alms box
19. Preposition
20. Scottish uncles
21. Stimulates to activity
23. Letter
24. U.S. playwright
25. __ soldier
26. Relatives
28. Hairdressers, at times
32. Modify
34. Covenant
35. River islet
36. Part of et al.
37. Japanese port
39. Goddess in Wagner's "Ring"
40. Wool: Prefix
41. Verify
42. Recent
44. Recited, in a way
46. Equal
47. Oslo resident: Abbr.
48. Speck
49. How: Lat.
52. Morning shout at camp
56. Scoreboard statistics
57. Settled
58. Bit
59. Thumbs through a book
60. Voice
61. Undid, poetically
62. Former actor Jack
63. Common verb
64. Elliot
65. Small barracudas

DOWN

1. Up __
2. Ranges
3. Hits the jackpot
4. Literary works
5. Certain carriers: Abbr.
6. Zoo animals
7. River in France
8. Precise
9. Tongue-tied
10. School problem
11. Declaim
12. Grafted, in heraldry
13. Selves
21. Withdrawal into oneself
22. Card game like bridge
24. Chemical ending
27. News service initials
28. Pitch
29. Upheaval
30. Take a bus
31. __ pupil
32. Anklebones
33. Enthusiasm
34. Equality
38. Man's nickname
39. Common abbreviation
41. After a while
43. Used up
45. Capacity of some trucks
46. Simple organisms
48. Tiny creatures
50. Improper
51. African foxes
52. Austrian statesman
53. That: Lat.
54. Locale
55. Confidence
56. Garner
59. The: Sp.

40

ACROSS

1. Like a Dali watch
5. Emulates a glutton
10. "Spartacus" author
14. Jewish month
15. Kind of theater, for short
16. Pale
17. Call to Fido
18. "Bombs bursting __"
19. Writer of light verse
20. Newscasting name
22. Wine left after leakage
24. Muscle
25. Sequel to "Typee"
26. Mind
29. Sino-Soviet trouble site of late '60's
33. A Beatle
34. Dealt
35. Scotsman's to
36. Old man, in Berlin
37. Like some excuses
38. Dear, in Roma
39. Neckline
40. Famous Athenian
41. Crosscut saw
42. Cores
44. Nobles
45. Korean troops
46. Dance
47. Headpieces
50. Modern folk singer
54. Trials
55. Metroliner
57. Miner's prize
58. Boleyn
59. Girl's name
60. Sicilian town
61. Does a field job
62. North and South
63. Fasten

DOWN

1. Famed lion
2. Notion, in Nimes
3. South American rodent
4. Importance
5. Gradual changes, in biology
6. Freshen
7. Pulitzer historian (1934)
8. Roman 1002
9. Lute player
10. Attack
11. On the briny
12. Field flies, in batting practice
13. Spare, in London
21. "__, not again!"
23. Burden
25. Of a certain grain
26. Atlanta man
27. Gets one's goat
28. Contributes in a way
29. Populace
30. Sully
31. Gold unit
32. Lean and leap
34. Some people
37. A type of march
38. Disintegrates
40. TV ailment
41. Godsend
43. Removes
44. Birds
46. Composure
47. Bash
48. Mood
49. Rip
50. A kind of bird
51. Tops
52. Millay
53. Passion
56. Postal abbreviation

41

ACROSS

1. Tourist site in '70
6. Musical note
11. Composer Rorem
14. Arrested
15. __ better
16. Eggs: Lat.
17. Cliff-hanger's vacation spot
19. Namely: Abbr.
20. Start of a letter to Mr. Boone
21. Measure
22. Ordinary: Abbr.
25. Chip
26. Agreements
27. Protective cover, for short
29. Long time
30. Vamp
31. Fish
33. Guarantee
37. Tester
39. Kind of lot
40. Japanese symbol
42. Former Premier of Japan
43. Thought: Prefix
44. Compass reading
46. Brief moments: Abbr.
47. Flat sections
49. In a tricky way
51. Haggard title
52. Abbreviation for incoming mail
53. Leader
55. Loot on the Spanish Main
56. Picturesque Eastern city
60. Headlight word
61. Streaked
62. Spa
63. Poker word
64. Nails
65. Showing edges

DOWN

1. Group: Abbr.
2. Island off Italy: Abbr.
3. Prefix for gram
4. Sort
5. South American sight
6. Seaweed products
7. Handles gently
8. Like Nathan Hale
9. Shortly
10. A scholar's arrival time
11. Motel sign
12. Throw out
13. Confuses
18. __-pie
21. Stops, in Madrid
22. Essence
23. Actress Diane
24. Figure on a tax report
26. Trims
28. Clad like a Scot
30. Street sight
32. Author of "The Tastemakers"
34. Vacation boons
35. Snare
36. Uneven
38. Vanity
41. Loosened, as a shoe
45. New England sights
47. Incites
48. Nest
49. Medicinal plant
50. Contemporary of Thackeray
53. Broadway show
54. Crystallized snow
56. Law degree
57. Inlet
58. Girl's nickname
59. __ day now

42

ACROSS

1. Hibernated
6. Thomas
10. Lump
14. Electrician
15. Miscellany
16. Abbreviation in a date book
17. Mideasterner
18. Like some skiers' feet
19. Undeniable
20. Cactus
22. Extended
24. Branch of physics: Abbr.
26. At least as much
27. Watercraft
31. Ingot
32. Seagoing initials
33. Part of Vietnam
35. Nature
38. Delicacy, to some
42. Miss
43. Long time
44. Audience
45. Surpass
47. Minor
49. L. P., for one
52. Personal: Prefix
53. Time of day
55. Bespatter
59. Heavenly spirit: Fr.
60. Row
62. Western horse
63. "This __ me"
64. Lioness
65. Common suffixes
66. Camera part
67. Kind of story
68. Irritates

DOWN

1. Brave the Channel
2. Money in Genoa
3. Times
4. Narrow flag
5. Feeler
6. Heir
7. Jewish month
8. Master of Flavius
9. Pal around with
10. __ fact
11. "__ moi le ..."
12. Cowboy gear
13. Check
21. Sierra __
23. Quest for a prince
25. Penuche
27. Eat
28. Supposedly
29. Quechua
30. Condensed files
34. Florida city
36. Shorten, as a sail
37. A kind of drop
39. Cuisines
40. Alumni
41. Afflict
46. For the nonce
48. Nabokov heroine
49. Washer cycle
50. Incite
51. Mat
53. "__ Columbia"
54. Group of fitted objects
56. Insects
57. Short distance
58. Bronc
61. Cheer

43

ACROSS

1. Jejune
5. Times of day: Abbr.
9. Figure in Hindu myth
13. Like George Apley
14. Ralph: Fr.
16. __ a dream
17. __, 1 vote
18. Algonquian Indian
19. Pierce slightly
20. Wire measure
21. Secondary
22. Hair style for yesterday's girl
24. Baudouin's offspring
27. Born
28. Figured out
29. W. W. I initials
31. Rushed
34. Fresh
35. U.S. poet
38. __ sixpence
40. Made of certain wood
41. Clotheshorses, in a way
42. "Le Coq __"
44. Cote mothers
45. View
46. Modern serais
48. Following: Abbr.
50. Plymouth Rock in Dublin
55. The "Angelic Doctor"
57. Tip
58. Coin of Norway
59. Division of a Gaelic poem
60. Passé
62. Half a prison
63. Give ear
64. "__ Angels"
65. Inter __
66. Rubber trees
67. Urban problem
68. Strip

DOWN

1. Out on __
2. Fiber
3. "Darn __!"
4. Scout unit
5. Kin in the WAC's
6. Highly colored pottery
7. __ tee
8. Dug out a drain
9. Engrossed
10. Mao took a jet
11. Early type of bullet
12. Joint
15. Year of Nero's first marriage
21. Bridge call
23. Chalice
25. Bangtail
26. Cut
30. Dean of a group
31. Man's nickname
32. Egg: Prefix
33. Conventional Muscovite
35. Hoax
36. Common verb
37. Japanese money: Abbr.
39. Liquid fat
42. Spanish numeral
43. Shakespearean dupe
46. Title
47. Went first
48. Hindu holy man
49. On a par
51. Outbreak
52. Fiber cloth
53. Ford
54. Princely
56. Fluids
61. Eastern name
62. Fall guy

44

ACROSS

1. Cordage material
5. Cabals
10. Does schoolwork
14. Adjective ending
15. Porch of Oahu
16. Fume
17. Departed
18. Mediterranean land
19. Jai __
20. Tobacco containers
22. Cribs
23. Brew
24. Worthless trifle
25. Humane org.
27. Sits on
33. Xanthippe
34. Expedite
35. Musical syllable
36. Olympian
37. River in upstate New York
38. Tunisian seaport
39. Part of the street scene
40. Pâtisserie item
41. Hesitate
42. Missing ones
44. Have sway
45. Carney
46. Tittle
47. Wheedles
49. Equivocating
56. Field
57. Oarsman
58. Become fixed
59. Fuzz
60. Dagger's predecessor
61. Italian numeral
62. City on the Moselle
63. Wines and dines
64. __ out

DOWN

1. Embraces
2. North Carolina college
3. By hand: Prefix
4. Introduces
5. U.S.M.A. figure
6. Rupanco or Puyehue
7. Gem stone
8. Record
9. Presides
10. __ numeral
11. Enjoyable
12. Dizzy or Daffy
13. Sun Valley gear
21. Weak point
24. Outfield chance
25. Garden plant
26. Salesman, of a sort
27. Cambridge or Devon
28. Cite
29. Presses strongly
30. Pitching statistic: Abbr.
31. Wipe out
32. __ -Gotha
33. West Indies island
37. Add
38. Table wine
40. Explosive
41. Campus man
43. Synthetic
46. Yanks
47. Emollient
48. Buffalo's waterfront
49. Musical group: Abbr.
50. __ contendere
51. Braces
52. Calor
53. Recess
54. Inlet
55. Vous __

45

46

ACROSS

1. Himalayan goats
6. Captain of the Pequod
10. Ancient Syria
14. City on the Missouri
15. St. Philip —
16. Sun hat
17. — the mill
18. South American
20. California fort
21. Instigates
23. Function
24. S. A. Indian
26. Gardeners' implements
28. Yellowish-pink
30. Cuchulainn's wife
31. U. S. spacecraft
32. Ones versed in law
36. Italian city
37. Brake part
38. Birds
42. End of the ball game
45. Performing group
46. Curls
47. Cruet item
50. Marsh bird
51. Exclamation
52. Veteran
54. Lose no time
57. Middle-Easterner
59. Beginnings
61. Celt
62. "—, you noblest English!"
63. Strip off
64. "— virumque cano..."
65. Implants
66. Heartsease

DOWN

1. Arena figure
2. Border river of Asia
3. Vendors' wagons
4. Greek letter
5. Crocus
6. "The world is so full of — of things..."
7. "— goes!"
8. Novel by Kenneth Roberts
9. Top banana's milieu
10. Suffix in zoology
11. A kind of welcome
12. Swiftly
13. Makes money
19. Turkic people: Var.
22. River to the Seine
25. Short song
27. English port
28. U. S. agents
29. Naturalness
33. English breed of cattle
34. All, in Paris
35. Stage designs
39. Unit of work
40. Marts
41. In music, a mute
42. Attends
43. — meridiem
44. Nautical rope
47. River to the Caspian Sea
48. "— you calling me"
49. Nine: Lat.
53. English novelist and scientist
55. Like —
56. Discover
58. Wing
60. People of Tierra del Fuego

47

Crossword grid puzzle 47

ACROSS

1. Slip
6. Draped garment
10. Genitive or ablative
14. Florida city
15. Consumer
16. West of Sask.
17. Tyrants
18. Robt. E. Lee, for one
20. Odds and ends
22. Gladden
23. Equitable
24. Frank
25. Cocktail
28. Devotee
29. Happened
30. Casino game
35. Opening lines, for short
36. No point, in tennis
37. Greeting
38. Evening sight
40. Long-missing jurist
41. Assent
42. Transportation for Holmes
43. Wrench
47. Drink flavor
48. Adjust
49. Munchausen's forte
54. Circus area
56. Incongruity
57. Woody fiber
58. French husband
59. Dress material
60. Fits to __
61. Between once and a
62. __ pros

DOWN

1. Word for a Ranger
2. Prefix for an acid
3. Paris area
4. Blackthorn
5. Time to put on finery
6. Carriage
7. Type of flu
8. Accelerates, for short
9. Choler
10. Mooring line
11. Float __
12. Assert
13. Peter or Jack Sprat
19. An encore, of sorts
21. Cry of revelry
24. World War II corps
25. Nevada city
26. Eight: Lat.
27. Storage place
28. Superfluity
29. Barbados native
30. Occasional bonnet occupant
31. Too bad!
32. Prefix for gravure
33. Attention-getting word
34. Seafarer
36. Psychedelic drug
39. Noun suffix
40. Summon
42. __ one
43. Card game
44. Fold
45. Hair tint
46. Type size
47. African city
49. Snare
50. Gaelic exclamation
51. Take it easy
52. Chemical compound
53. Since, in Scotland
55. Large bird

48

ACROSS

1. After Cicero's "O"
8. Kind of bridge
15. Thinks productively
16. Crumbly
17. Walks
19. Plant disease
20. Disappeared
21. Foch and others
22. Be speedy
24. Rood
26. Exultant song
29. Old swimming hole
30. Small shark
34. As a friend: Fr.
35. Ours, in Paris
37. Bean
38. Electronic brain
41. Games in a sweep
42. Novelist Glasgow
43. Flavorsome herb
44. Look of sorts
46. Uppity habits
47. Critical military times
48. American geologic period
50. View
51. Take to the ice
54. Distant: Prefix
56. Cold, cold sea
60. Thoughtlessness
63. Undrinkable cocktail
64. City in Cyprus
65. Had a midnight snack
66. Diamond city

DOWN

1. Nervous movements
2. Esau
3. Waiter's offering
4. Deli treat
5. Giant among Giants
6. Rule
7. Concerning
8. Hot times in summer
9. Swiss canton
10. Twigs for grafting
11. Celtic lord
12. Borneo sea Dyak
13. Spanish jar
14. Monster loch
18. Insouciant
23. Weld together
25. African timber tree
26. Piano part
27. Like an old crone
28. Nester on crags
29. Giving temporary relief
31. Port of old Rome
32. Lyric expression
33. Journeys in court circuit
36. Digging tool
39. Kirghiz range
40. Menace for surfbathers
45. Adapt for new devices
49. __ car
50. Canarylike bird
51. Igneous rock
52. Granny or square
53. Philippine hardwood
55. Siberian river
57. Compiegne's river
58. Evening: Fr.
59. Sudden break
61. Drunkard
62. Behave

49

ACROSS

1. More skilled
6. Antiaircraft fire
10. Safeguard: Abbr.
13. Pass a rope through
14. Outing spoiler
15. Asian palm
17. Two-sided
19. State of irritation
20. Whodunit weapon
21. Of a star: Prefix
23. Caroline island
24. Heating apparatus
26. Chairman's concern
29. Medicinal quantity
30. Be sociable
31. Pet name
33. ___ hand
36. Grampuses
38. Get busy
40. Terminals: Abbr.
41. Pivots
43. Moving throng
45. Elevations: Abbr.
46. Asian plain
48. Sponsor's child
50. Fruit plant
52. Go amiss
53. Blunt
54. Food in the field
59. Ancient Greek coin
60. Pet name
62. Present
63. Look after
64. Raw
65. Bad: Prefix
66. Rockingham ratios
67. German city

DOWN

1. Incoming trains: Abbr.
2. Borsch item
3. Son of Jacob
4. Girl's name
5. Checks one's prose
6. Material formed by fusion
7. Swan song, of a sort
8. Trouble
9. Massages
10. Gradually
11. Fraction
12. Ex-V.P. Agnew
16. Suffix for a doer
18. City in Minnesota
22. Rock formation
25. Artery
26. Andy's associate
27. ___ scout
28. Apologetic
32. Peninsula for tourists
34. Malay chief
35. Organization: Abbr.
37. Firm regulations
39. Almond-flavored syrup
42. Theater scenery
44. Tenon's partner: Var.
47. Companion of chango
49. Hairdressing equipment
50. Exclamation of disdain
51. Fell gradually
55. Cherry and ruby
56. Musical piece
57. Group of pheasants
58. Pictured
61. United

50

ACROSS

1. __ -evident
5. Raiment
9. Frozen
13. Unique individual
14. Frenziedly
15. Join
16. A type of star
17. New York signer of Declaration of Independence
19. Rarest signature
21. Outsiders
22. Neighbor of Col.
23. Paris friends
24. Bright
27. Precipitating
31. Follow
32. Low point
33. Deer
34. Greek contest
35. Hymn sung a cappella
36. Holbrook and March
37. Ruby
38. More balanced
39. Sea writer and others
40. Forensics
42. Sheep
43. Hearty's companion
44. Hunted animal
45. Rabbit-sized rodent
48. Connecticut signatory
52. Connecticut signatory
54. Great number, informally
55. Antisubmarine device
56. Ionian Sea gulf
57. Fabled mountain
58. British ordnance
59. Peter I, for example
60. Opposite of 32 Across

DOWN

1. Lay
2. Sufficient, poetically
3. Biblical tribe
4. Pennsylvania signatory
5. Ability
6. Skips
7. Leg. and exec. are parts of it
8. Footwear of a sort
9. Demand
10. Summon
11. Jacket
12. Sancta
15. Less charming
18. "Just __"
20. Unguis
23. Northern tree
24. Put on
25. One seeking to persuade
26. Ruth's mother-in-law
27. Gluts
28. Mideasterner
29. Man without a country
30. Plaster of paris
32. Time being
35. Use a postbox
36. Virginia signatory
38. Radio nuisance
39. Start a card game
41. Invalid
42. Hungarian dramatist
44. Flora and fauna
45. Exclamations
46. Outburst
47. Wave: Fr.
48. Restaurant employees: Abbr.
49. __ - ran
50. Middle: Prefix
51. Cygnus
53. Pistol: Slang

Answers

1

```
ROSS        IOWA
SHOT ADAMS NDAK
VISA LICIT DESI
POOR ARETE ERIN
 SASK  TEMP
SPARKS SPIELS
CANEA  SONIC
ODD     DARE
RUSTY  AMERE
NATION ASENSE.
 RARE  WISC
SEMI KUDOS ELAM
DRIP EVOKE DANA
ANNE RELEE ARIZ
KANS       YALE
```

2

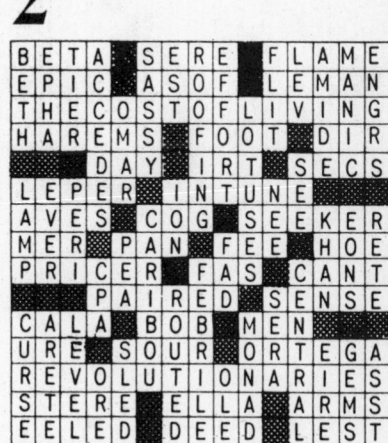

```
BETA SERE  FLAME
EPIC ASOF LEMAN
THECOSTOFLIVING
HAREMS FOOT DIR
 DAY IRT SECS
LEPER INTUNE
AVES COG SEEKER
MER PAN FEE HOE
PRICER FAS CANT
 PAIRED SENSE
CALA BOB MEN
URE SOUR ORTEGA
REVOLUTIONARIES
STERE ELLA ARMS
EELED DEED LEST
```

3

```
STAB STEAD FIJI
AHOY LODGE LAOS
PANG ABEAM ALBS
SWEETWILLIAM
 OAST  JUMPAT
SPIRO RIODEORO
PONG SEETHE SER
HIVE ALBEN JATS
ESE ALBUMS IDEO
ROSETTES AMASS
ENTRAP LADD
 STEEPLEJACKS
CUBA TREAD NOON
ABET ELEMI DREI
LINZ REPAS YELP
```

4

```
BAND ARBOR SPED
ALII TAUPE PERU
LIES HINTERLAND
SECEDED SLUICES
ANEMONE   STE
 BEAR NOTOPEN
DATA ASININE
ALARMED RECEPTS
TANKARD   SEES
ENGAGES ATIT
 ITY MELISSA
LABIATE ENACTED
OFLORRAINE KIND
BEEN AVERT ELSE
SESS MESAS TEED
```

5

```
COBB  PATA  REDAN
ANIL  EGER  EDILE
SITUATING  FIVES
ETERNAL  UNITIES
     ILE  SEXES
CLOGS  HEREDITY
HORAE  MAYOS  ORA
AIDS  LURES  INIT
ORE  HATED  SLATE
SERPENTS  HOLES
   BRACE  AMA
DELIVER  NOMADIC
IRANI  ITINERATE
MINCE  NAME  CRES
ESKER  GRAY  HEMS
```

6

```
STOP  DARED  SIAM
AUTO  ELUDE  ELBA
DROPINTHEBUCKET
ENE  TIER  GRADE
     PEER  TALE
MOTORS  ARBITER
IRIS  SMILE  LEO
GETTHEUPPERHAND
SAL  ORALE  ANTE
DEPRIVE  BENDER
   ANNE  ALAS
ELATE  ODAS  TAA
BYFITSANDSTARTS
BRAN  ADULT  SEEP
SARA  MOSES  HENS
```

7

```
RUBY  FISTS  PADS
APIA  INLAW  AGEE
COLLARBONE  RHEE
KNEEDEEP  DISARM
   RAD  SIDE  E
DOGEAR  NOSECONE
EMIT  MOUTHS  PIX
CENCI  SIT  TRICE
AGO  STATOR  ONER
LASTLEGS  ALBERT
   BANE  ATA
SALOME  BLACKEYE
UPIN  BROWBEATEN
FANE  RURAL  YAWN
IRKS  ANEYE  ELSA
```

8

```
GAMBLER  BISTATE
AMERICA  IMPALED
SPLASHY  DIAMOND
   STOOP  TWEEDY
TAGS  NISAN
ARABS  CATSPAW
SALOON  AGO  EGAD
TROUPES  ARRANGE
YARN  VEE  SOCAGE
TEDDERS  METED
   IRATE  TERS
NAPALM  EDEMA
APOLLOS  IRELAND
METEORS  TINKLED
ESSENES  SEESAWS
```

9

```
ADAM OCHS  JACKS
TORO CRAT  ATALL
TURNAHAIR  MELEE
ICA  COBRAS TEED
CESAR  PIQUED
  SEQUITUR OFA
ASKA USN  EGGNOG
CHAMOIS  BEELINE
TENANT FEZ  EATS
SAG  ETCETERA
  ANSELM  AMMAN
CARO REASON  ERO
ALOUD ALLIGATOR
GOOSE VEIL  NESS
YESES ESPY  TREE
```

10

```
RAMS  CLEAR  ALAS
ALAI  AERIE  SOIL
HAMMERANDSICKLE
SEAPLANE  NOISY
   EATS  PICT
ALARMS  PURISTS
ROLE  CARET  RIA
COLDSHOULDERING
SSE  EARLS  INGE
 EYELIDS  ARNESS
   ALLY  AGOG
MASSE  IDEALISM
INTERDEPENDENCE
FOUL  ONSET  TROW
FANS  TEEMS  SETS
```

11

```
 CISCO  STROP
BANKON  HEINOUS
URSINE  INFERNO
TAPS HINDER  RIG
CMI  AIR   ILE
HERESTOYOU  SPET
 LEAH NOUS  WEDS
  MELODRAMA
URGE  ARES  AMIE
SEAS  BELONGINGS
ELL   NEE   SGT
DIE  SPONGE ATNO
 ENLARGE DINEON
 FAIRIES ENGAGE
 DIMES  DEEDS
```

12

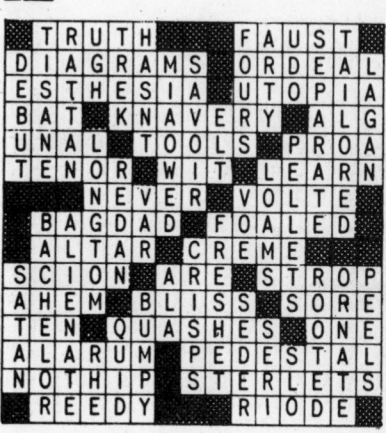

```
 TRUTH   FAUST
DIAGRAMS ORDEAL
ESTHESIA UTOPIA
BAT KNAVERY  ALG
UNAL TOOLS  PROA
TENOR  WIT  LEARN
  NEVER  VOLTE
 BAGDAD  FOALED
 ALTAR   CREME
SCION  ARE  STROP
AHEM  BLISS  SORE
TEN  QUASHES  ONE
ALARUM  PEDESTAL
NOTHIP  STERLETS
 REEDY   RIODE
```

13

G	A	R	B	A	G	E		C	L	A	M	S
T	O	R	E	A	D	O	R		R	E	S	U	L	T
H	A	L	F	S	O	L	E		T	I	S	S	U	E
A	T	I	L	T		I	C	C		S	A	C	R	E
T	E	N	S		H	A	T	E	S		Y	A	R	N
S	E	E		P	O	T	S	D	A	M		D	I	A
		S	E	T	H		E	M	O	T	I	N	G
D	R	A	M	A	S			P	L	U	N	G	E
R	E	B	U	K	E	S		S	L	A	T
I	C	S		S	A	U	N	T	E	R		H	I	M
B	R	O	W		T	R	E	A	D		D	O	S	E
B	E	L	O	W		F	A	T		C	E	N	S	E
L	A	U	D	E	D		R	U	N	A	B	O	U	T
E	N	T	E	R	S		E	R	A	S	U	R	E	S
	T	E	N	E	T		D	E	B	A	T	E	D

14

O	C	T	A		A	R	A	L		A	T	O	P
A	D	R	E	M		N	O	S	E		N	O	P	E
B	E	E	R	A	N	D	S	K	I	T	T	L	E	S
C	U	D		T	O	E	S		S	A	L	A	D	O
S	M	I	T	E	R	S		P	U	R	E
		T	H	U	D		A	I	R	D	R	O	M	E
D	E	C	O	R		M	U	L	E	Y		U	A	R
O	M	A	R		S	A	T	E	D		S	T	L	O
M	I	R		S	P	U	R	S		P	E	R	I	S
O	L	D	S	T	Y	L	E		O	L	E	A
			C	O	G	S		A	V	E	N	G	E	R
A	S	S	A	I	L		U	V	E	A		E	A	U
R	A	I	N	C	A	T	S	A	N	D	D	O	G	S
M	I	N	T		S	W	A	N		E	X	U	L	T
E	D	G	Y		S	O	F	T		R	I	S	E

15

S	T	O	N	I	N	G		A	F	F	A	B	L	E
T	I	P	O	V	E	R		D	R	A	T	I	O	N
E	L	E	V	A	T	E		V	I	N	T	A	G	E
R	E	R	A	N		C	R	E	E		U	S	E	S
E	R	A	S		F	I	O	R	D	S
		C	A	R	A	T	S		L	I	M	E	N
A	R	R	O	G	A	N	C	E		I	N	U	S	E
P	O	S	T	E			P	I	N	T	O
A	L	V	I	N		C	O	M	M	O	T	I	O	N
R	E	P	A	D		A	L	U	M	N	I
		A	D	M	I	R	E		A	R	A	B
P	I	S	A		A	P	O	D		S	T	O	L	E
I	N	F	L	A	M	E		E	S	T	O	N	I	A
T	R	A	I	T	O	R		R	E	O	R	D	E	R
S	E	X	T	A	N	S		S	E	A	S	O	N	S

16

A	D	D	I	S		S	P	E	S		M	E	T	S
M	A	R	N	E		H	U	L	A		A	L	I	T
A	D	U	L	T		U	T	A	H		R	A	M	U
N	A	B	O	B	S		I	M	A	G	I	N	E	D
			C	A	P	I	N		R	U	N	D	R	Y
A	T	N	O	C	O	S	T		A	R	A
C	H	I		K	U	D	O	S		U	R	B	A	N
C	O	L	D		T	U	P	I	S		A	U	T	O
T	R	E	A	T		E	R	G	O	T		Y	E	S
		Y	A	P		A	N	T	I	M	O	N	Y
H	O	B	B	L	E		C	E	T	T	E
O	V	E	R	C	A	S	T		O	U	S	T	E	D
M	A	R	E		C	L	I	O		L	A	U	R	A
E	T	N	A		H	A	C	K		A	B	R	A	M
R	E	E	K		Y	V	E	S		R	I	F	L	E

17

```
PAVLOV   SLASHED
LHEARA   PINTADOS
SANDAL   ANNAMESE
ABT  THUNDER  MEN
   LEAN   ATLAST
ALDA   LASALLE
MARS  LIEB  ESTOC
ALEC  ADDUP  SOLE
TODAY  EASE  OREL
   LARDNER  NEAT
MILANO   RIBS
EME  GIRASOL  MUM
APOSTLES  DAMARA
DENIZENS  IRENIC
LATERON  CERISE
```

18

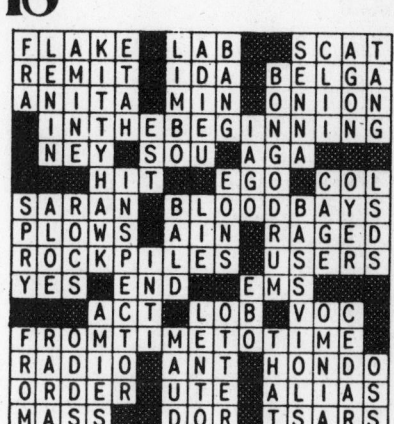

```
FLAKE  LAB   SCAT
REMIT  IDA  BELGA
ANITA  MIN  ONION
INTHEBEGINNING
NEY  SOU  AGA
   HIT   EGO  COL
SARAN  BLOODBAYS
PLOWS  AIN  RAGED
ROCKPILES  USERS
YES  END   EMS
   ACT  LOB  VOC
FROMTIMETOTIME
RADIO  ANT  HONDO
ORDER  UTE  ALIAS
MASS   DOR  TSARS
```

19

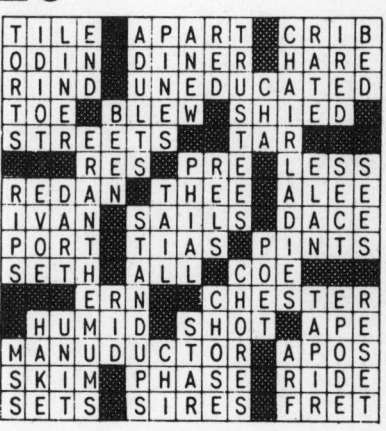

```
STOP  UPSKI  MLLE
HURL  NOTIN  AYES
ERGO  FORTRESSES
ANYWHERE  ONSIDE
    ADAPT  DES
MIMER  STAB  STOB
EDITOR  OLAM  RUE
RESALES  CLIMATE
ENC  DEPT  SLATER
STAT  LEOS  APARS
   RRS  WOTAN
SERIAL  LYSOZYME
PRINCIPALS  OEIL
INEE  ORTEA  LASS
TASS  NEEDY  ARTE
```

20

```
TILE  APART  CRIB
ODIN  DINER  HARE
RIND  UNEDUCATED
TOE  BLEW  SHIED
STREETS   TAR
   RES  PRE  LESS
REDAN  THEE  ALEE
IVAN  SAILS  DACE
PORT  TIAS  PINTS
SETH  ALL  COE
   ERN  CHESTER
HUMID  SHOT  APE
MANUDUCTOR  APOS
SKIM  PHASE  RIDE
SETS  SIRES  FRET
```

21

```
SAAR PEPO  MOAB
ALGA LARD CONGO
NONPLUSED ORTHO
ERE AGES GRAHAM
 SWATH SPARSE
  CHAP AMASSES
SYMMETRICAL PUT
ISEE ANI SORA
MEL OUTOFKILTER
PROFUSE YEDO
 DOTISH YIELD
BARODA ARNO IRA
AMATI GROOMSMAN
RIMED ADIT IBID
BEAR PYLE PONY
```

22

```
PEASOUP ITEMONE
INTERNE NOVELET
TURTLES FRAGILE
CRETE TWAIN OSS
HEEL SEANCES
 ESPRIT SILVA
ARC PEEL ACTION
LEOPOLD WRESTLE
ASSAIL WAIN HEW
STILL BERETS
 ISLANDS ARCH
UPS PANDA SNARE
SEAPORT NEEDIER
ENLARGE CREASED
STENTOR ENDLESS
```

23

```
CLEF SPRIG PEEL
LINO LEASE EATS
ONES ARISTOCRAT
GERSHWIN WANTS
 VIA LOONS
STALLS UDO DIGS
PIT FORTIS IMRE
ALIDADE STAMPER
RENO DITTOS OBI
EDGE ECO CHORES
 ODETS ONT
ANITA AMATEURS
TIMETABLES ANEW
ACES BULLY TELA
PERT STYLE ASST
```

24

```
 DRAB SASSAFRAS
BOHEA EXCELLENT
OLEIN PIEDPIPER
BLOODSTONE TOME
 SULU MERE SIS
WET EMPS AREAS
ALABAMA LOGO
CITADEL ACETATE
 BERM STRANDS
OSIER AHAB ASK
NIT SOFT NEST
TEAS FLOATALOAN
AGITATING VALUE
PENITENCE EVENT
ESTRANGED REST
```

25

```
GOSH  WEFT  JAILS
ACTE  ROAR  ENSUE
FEAR  INDIANSIGN
FAROUT ETRE  SET
ENGINE  OUSE
  ACQUAINTANCES
PAZ UPTO  INONE
ALTKE ADO  SALVE
WINOS  IRAQ  DYS
LIGHTNINGBUGS
   LION   YOUTHS
STA ORNO  SIRREE
HAMANDEGGS  GENE
OXIDE  ELEE  LARD
WISED  DEMS  EMYS
```

26

```
ARUM  TRAPS  PLOW
HOPE  RILEY  RUGA
AMON  IDEAS  OMEN
BANDAGE  STOPPED
   ERG  SEETO
WEARIEST  MISUSE
OLD  DROOL  CANAL
MAUD  SORAS  LIKE
ATLAW  TAILS  TEC
NETTED  GREATEST
   ELUDE  UNI
ADOPTER  ATELIER
GOYA  NATCH  LORE
OREL  AMORE  ETNA
GERM  SAWED  RASP
```

27

```
CAPP  CELE  AHINT
LIRA  ADAM  GENOA
ANIL  JAWBREAKER
WEEPNOMORE  LYLE
SERIAL  FOIE
   TEA  INDOUBT
MOUNT  MIDSUMMER
ADLAI  PRE  CAPRI
SONNETEER  ARSIS
CROSSER  SAT
   TRET  NESTCE
ASPS  AHEADSTART
WHITEHORSE  OPAH
EOSIN  USSR  RIVE
DEARS  REDS  YSER
```

28

```
SMOG  PAPER  DOT
KOBE  LEAVE  GAVE
INST  ACRES  ETAL
DOESBY  ENTHRALL
   QUIET  SEEM
SOUPEDUP  DRAMAS
OUI  NUBIA  ONALL
ATOI  PENNY  ERIE
PRUNE  DUGUP  TAP
YESSIR  PUGILIST
   UNUS  SOLON
CURRENTS  SEDGES
OPIE  YOKEL  GARE
MIND  OPERA  ELSE
END  NEGEV  DEED
```

29

```
U P A S   S H A M S   M O D E
B E S T   T O R I I   I N I T
I N C A   A N N E X   S T A R
  N I N E T E E N T H H O L E
    D R E D       Y E A
P I P P I N   C H I R P I N G
A R R A S   R A I S E   N O R
N E A T   P E R T H   R A T E
E N D   S A I L S   H E N I E
L E O N A R D O   T A L E N T
      I R A       G O R A
G O I N G L I K E S I X T Y
E R N E   L O A N S   I R A N
T A C T   E N T R E   N E M O
S L E Y   L A Y E R   G E S T
```

30

```
L A U D   M A R R Y   P A S S
O S S A   A N E T O   O M I T
K I E V   I N C E N D I A R Y
I N S I G N I A   D O S S E L
      S A L E P   G E S T E
F A R C R Y   I T E M S
A B O U   S T O M A   L O Y
T E M P E S T U O U S N E S S
E R A   S P E L L   O G L E
      S C A P A   C E N S O R
L O T T O   T A L C A
A S H O R E   I L A U G H E D
P A R A T R O O P S   O O Z E
I G O T   A N N E S   N O R N
N E W S   S A S S Y   S T A T
```

31

```
A S S N   O H O H   S C R A P
R U L E   L E V Y   L L A M A
M E O W   D E E P   O A R E D
O D O R S   D R O P P R E S S
R E P E A T   A T R E K
      C L I T C H E S   F A V
U N D I V E R T E D   M I L E
S U P P O S E   T A R I F F S
E N T E   C A P I T A L I S T
S S S   N O S E C O N E
      H U R O N   R E S T U P
R E S I D E N T S   E T A P E
I R A N I   O A T S   O L P E
A I R E S   U N I T   N E E R
L E A S T   S E R A   E R R S
```

32

```
O M E R   S L A N G   S C A N
D O P E   M A N O R   E R N E
O D I C   A S T R O N A U T S
R E C O U R S E   G U S S E T
      I N T E N D   T O T
A I S L E   S N O W   N A M E
S T E E V E   A R A B   C A L
S A N D E R S   P R E B E N D
A L A   N O C T   P L E A S E
M Y T H   S A R I   I N N E R
      O A R   D U N D E E
B U R G E R   S C O F F L A W
E P I G L O T T I S   I O T A
E T A L   A R E T E   T R E T
R O L E   R I D E S   S E N T
```

33

```
HASH   NAMES   LOCH
ALTO   ECLAT   ABLE
STALAGMITE   ROUE
PARABLE   SNARLED
    SEE     CRY
GAB  SCI  EIN  HAT
AGER   TROGLODYTE
URGE    ORG   UPON
DEADCENTER   NONE
YET  ANY  ROE  SET
    ARC     URE
LYCIDAS   GLINTED
EGAD   STALACTITE
NUDE   EASED   ELAN
ENID   SYCEE   REST
```

34

```
BRASS   LEI   APRES
OUTTO   IAN   RIATA
GETOUTFROMUNDER
   HADAT    ATTIRE
SHE   AUSTIN   AONE
PEDANT   WREN   FOS
EARL   DIASTER
DROOP   IST   HEELS
 PROBATE     LEAP
ARO   ERNE   DESERT
REFS   EARLAP   USS
AMANDA    AVOIR
BYHOOKORBYCROOK
IDARE   RIO   HAPPY
CETES   BAR   SNEAD
```

35

```
METS   TRIER   FIEF
ALOU   HASTE   OLLA
YARN   EMITS   REST
SNIFFS   TECUMSEH
   IOUS   NOTA
TAVERNES   RETAIN
OPALS   GLUES   NCO
NORD   COINS   ENOS
ERN   EASEL   GRIME
STARRY   RETIREES
   ELEM   DILO
CARDENAS   GARAGE
EMIL   NIOBE   SLID
ROTE   ENDER   OGGI
OREG   SEATS   FAST
```

36

```
SAPS   ALLOW   PANS
ETAH   TOURE   ETAL
CORA   TURTLEDOVE
TITMOUSE   TRALEE
   REINE   VEINLET
BRIDLE   BERET
RED   EDGERS   IPSO
EAGER   END   ACHED
WREN   GNEISS   ARE
  CHERT   TALLER
ATHLETE   NALLA
SHOALS   MALLARDS
CANVASBACK   NORA
OTOE   EAGRE   OPEN
TARS   TRIED   SEWS
```

37

```
POMPANO  THOUGHT
AREOLES  RATTLER
BALSAMS  UNSTATE
ANDS  OASIS  EDHS
     ESP  ANEAR
SNATCHING  MEANT
TOPSAILS  NEDDER
OTT  PLESSOR  OTE
PATCHY  OUTCASTS
ALOHA  TUSKEGEES
     ASPIC  IDO
CART  RAILS  NAPA
ALATHER  ASPIRED
ROSEISA  GEHENNA
DEPRESS  ODDSONS
```

38

```
SIFT  IMAM  SPLIT
OSLO  NOTA  TEASE
FLYOFFTHEHANDLE
IET  RUE  ENDEAR
ASHIEST  OLDE
   ETTE  CRI  DRIB
INCAS  LOCAL  EGO
COOLASACUCUMBER
EDO  WINKS  MEETS
SEPS  RES  DILL
   APES  CANDLES
SHAVEN  IRA  INT
HAVEASCREWLOOSE
ALORS  DALI  TNUT
DOWSE  ETON  OSES
```

39

```
ARMOR  OMNI  TREE
TOADY  RAIN  RANG
RAKES  ARCA  UNTO
EMES  INNERVATES
ESS  INGE  TIN
   AUNTS  TINTERS
TEMPER  PACT  AIT
ALII  OTARU  ERDA
LAN  AVER  LATTER
INTONED  MATCH
   NOR  MOTE  QUA
RISENSHINE  RUNS
ALIT  IOTA  LEAFS
ALTO  OPED  OAKIE
BEEN  NESS  SPETS
```

40

```
LIMP  CRAMS  FAST
ADAR  LEGIT  ASHY
HERE  INAIR  LEAR
REASONER  ULLAGE
   THEW  OMOO
BRAINS  DAMANSKY
RINGO  METED  TAE
ALTE  LAMER  CARA
VEE  SOLON  BRIAR
ESSENCES  COUNTS
   ROKS  PROM
STRAWS  JOANBAEZ
WOES  TRAIN  LODE
ANNE  ELISE  ENNA
TEDS  POLES  SEAL
```

41

```
OSAKA   AFLAT  NED
RANIN   GOONE  OVA
GRANDCANYON    VIZ
   DEARDAN    PACE
AVG  SPALL   PACTS
TARP  AGE   BARA
TROLL  ASSURANCE
ASSAYER   USEDCAR
RISINGSUN   SAITO
   IDEO  NNE  SECS
PANES   SLYLY  SHE
RECD   HEADMAN
ORO  LANCASTERPA
DIM  LINEY  EVIAN
SEE   BRADS  SEAMY
```

42

```
SLEPT   SETH   MASS
WIRER   OLIO   APPT
IRANI   NUMB   TRUE
MESCAL  LONGTERM
   ELEC   NOLESS
SAILBOAT    BAR
USN  ANNAM   SORT
PICKLEDPIGSFEET
FAIL   YEARS   EAR
   TOP  SMALLFRY
RECORD   IDIO
HIGHNOON  SPLASH
ANGE  TIER  PINTO
ISON  ELSA  ETTES
LENS  MYTH  RASPS
```

43

```
ARID   AFTS   RAMA
LATE  RAOUL   ASIN
IMAN  MIAMI   PINK
MIL  BYE   PIGTAIL
BELGIANHEIR   NEE
   EDUCED   AEF
TORE  NEW  MILLAY
IVEGOT    ALDERN
MODELS  DOR  EWES
   SEE  MOTELS
SEQ  IRISHSETTER
AQUINAS  END  ORE
DUAN  STALE  SING
HARK  HELLS  ALIA
ULES   RIOT   PEEL
```

44

```
HEMP   PLOTS   ADDS
ULAR   LANAI   REEK
GONE   EGYPT   ALAI
SNUFFBOXES    BINS
   ALE     FIG
SPCA   SQUELCHES
SHREW  HURRY  TRA
ARES   TIOGA  SFAX
BUS  TORTE   PAUSE
ABSENTEES    RULE
   ART     JOT
BEGS  ONTHEFENCE
AREA  ROWER  ROOT
LINT  CLOAK  NOVE
METZ  HOSTS  EKES
```

45

```
SPAR   SCOOP   ISON
ALLA   PARLE   NONO
LADYFINGER    TUTU
ATE  INT   ACHERON
DOREN   ANTHEM
   SETTEE   APPAL
LAPS  EAU   ETERNE
ASHE  ASTIR  RANT
STONES  RNS  AYES
TONTO   LATENT
   INSOLE   OESEL
BELASCO  REP   EVA
EMIL   OPENLETTER
GIRL  PERES  RUNE
STAY  ERASE  APTS
```

46

```
T A H R S   A H A B   A R A M
O M A H A   N E R I   T O P I
R U N O F   U R U G U A Y A N
O R D   F O M E N T S   A C T
      C A R I B   D I B B L E S
T E A R O S E   E M E R
M A R I N E R   L E G I S T S
E S T E         S H O E
N E S T E R S   L A S T O U T
      T R I O   I N T O R T S
V I N E G A R   S T I L T
O H O   O L D S T E R   H I E
L E V A N T I N E   R O O T S
G A E L   O N O N   U N R I P
A R M A   S O W S   P A N S Y
```

47

```
L A P S E   S A R I   C A S E
O C A L A   U S E R   A L T A
N E R O S   R I V E R B O A T
E T C E T E R A S   E L A T E
        E V E N   W I E N E R
  R O B R O Y   F A N
B E C A M E   B A C C A R A T
I N T R O   L E T   A L O H A
M O O N R I S E   C R A T E R
        N O D   H A N S O M
S P R A I N   C O L A
A L I G N   T A L L T A L E S
M E N A G E R I E   I R O N Y
B A S T   M A R I   O R L O N
A T E E   U P O N   N O L L E
```

48

```
T E M P O R A   A U C T I O N
I D E A T E S   F R I A B L E
C O N S T I T U T I O N A L S
S M U T   G O N E   N I N A S
    R U N   C R O S S
P A E A N   P O N D   T O P E
E N A M I   A N O U S   S O Y
D I G I T A L C O M P U T E R
A L L   E L L E N   A N I S E
L E E R   A I R S   D D A Y S
      E R I A N   S E E
S K A T E   T E L E   R O S S
I N C O N S I D E R A T I O N
M O L O T O V   N I C O S I A
A T E L A T E   A N T W E R P
```

49

```
A B L E R   F L A K   I N S
R E E V E   R A I N   N I P A
R E V E R S I B L E   S N I T
S T I L E T T O   A S T E R O
      Y A P   R A D I A T O R
A G E N D A   D O S A G E
M I X   S U G A R   L E N D A
O R C S   L A Y T O   S T A S
S L U E S   S W A R M   H T S
      S T E P P E   G O D S O N
P E A R T R E E   E R R
O B T U S E   K R A T I O N S
O B O L   S W E E T I E P I E
H E R E   T E N D   C R U D E
      D Y S   O D D S   E S S E N
```

50

```
S E L F   T O G S   I C E D
O N E R   A M O K   U N I T E
N O V A   L I V I N G S T O N
G W I N N E T T   A L I E N S
      K A N S   A M I S
S U N L I T   S L E E T I N G
T R A I L   N A D I R   R O E
A G O N   M O T E T   H A L S
G E M   S A N E R   D A N A S
E R I S T I C S   M E R I N O
      H A L E   B O A R
A G O U T I   W I L L I A M S
H U N T I N G T O N   S L E W
A S D I C   A R T A   O S S A
S T E N   T S A R   N O O N
```

VOLUME 4

1

ACROSS

1. North Atlantic fish
6. Spanish relatives
10. Swindles
14. Goddesses of the seasons
15. Heraldic band
16. Mohammedan priest
17. Semblance
18. Goad
19. Be "in"
20. Hawaiian island
22. Take it all back
24. Musical direction
26. Greek letter
27. Smear
30. Sitting in for
35. Roman spirit
36. __-frutti
38. Light craft
39. State
41. Pools
43. French dream
44. Verne character and others
46. Passover rite
48. Legal thing
49. "La __"
51. Lie close
53. Newt
54. Cup, in France
56. American novelist
60. Go over
64. Sharpen
65. Sinister glance
67. Overgrown, in a way
68. "__ the fence is out"
69. Fluid rock
70. Cape __ Islands
71. Gulls
72. Tarry
73. Eat, in Berlin

DOWN

1. Wedge of wood or metal
2. Lake or Perry
3. Russian range
4. Bangkok sight
5. Try to reach
6. Theme
7. Type of verb: Abbr.
8. African plant
9. Dignified
10. Type of staircase
11. Persian name
12. International org.
13. Diving duck
21. Collector's book
23. Soft mineral
25. Legal copy
27. Like a used pencil
28. Chewer
29. Albee's field
31. Mixed up, as type
32. Indolent
33. Unusual
34. Silly creatures
37. Exam
40. Birds, at times
42. One of five
45. Study, as clues
47. Fidgety
50. Bikini and Eniwetok
52. Answers a purpose
55. Adorn
56. Pronoun
57. Stopped a ship's motion, with "to"
58. Over again
59. Undiluted
61. Tunes
62. Give up
63. Garden
66. Girl's name

ACROSS

1. Without variations
8. Gasconader
15. Area in an arsenal
16. Raised on high
17. Arranges the pool balls
18. Examines
19. Inner: Prefix
20. "Origin of __"
22. Counterpart of ASCAP
23. Avoid
25. Committed a faux pas
26. Rack's partner
27. Arrangement
29. Poetic contraction
30. Glass slabs
31. Inhabitants of communes, ideally
33. City slickers
34. Zeros
35. W.W. I spy
36. Beverage
38. Rainy day scarcity
41. Economical one
42. Prohibit
43. "Dear Sir or __"
45. Infuriates
46. One of the Keys
48. "Zhivago" heroine
49. Disfigure
50. Letter
52. Brit. medical degrees
53. Draw a mental picture
55. Often-nice girls
57. Table vegetables
58. Cartilage
59. Rudimentary principle
60. Imposing

DOWN

1. Exit for Barnum
2. Puts down
3. Ill-mannered
4. __ of the covenant
5. Tweed, for one
6. Jeweler's glass
7. Monarchs
8. More occupied
9. Made a choice
10. Catch __
11. Sward
12. Defender of the people
13. Belligerents
14. Varnish ingredients
21. Louder, in music: Abbr.
24. Shades
26. Extremist
28. Monastery man
30. Jewish festival
32. Highest note
33. French spa
35. Wall decorations
36. Candy-counter item
37. Amount in excess
38. Nicotines' partners
39. Nudist
40. Item for a gymnast
41. Poetic device
42. Of the lowest kind
44. Former film actor Raymond
46. Fabric
47. Manifest
50. Imitator
51. Kazan
54. Sticky substance
56. Naval vessel: Abbr.

3

ACROSS

1. Social insect
5. Port of Spain
10. Where Tabriz is
14. Resound
15. Market place
16. Isinglass
17. Cupid
18. Diamond coup
20. Utensil ware
22. Councils in Europe
23. Hesitates
26. Recent: Prefix
27. Limber
29. Audience
31. Oxidizes
35. Hair style
36. Florida resort town
39. Pack
40. First __
41. Garden frame
43. Wonder
44. Boor
46. Customer
47. Exclamation
48. Lumberman
50. Ten rin
51. Awake
53. Tiny __
55. Unchanging
57. Thankful
61. Enhance
64. Playwriting
67. Post
68. Coin
69. Oakley
70. West Coast campus
71. Spots
72. Minimal
73. Passé dance

DOWN

1. Drip
2. Israeli port
3. Where the mannequins are
4. Kind of zone
5. Chaplain
6. In the past
7. Lady in a poem
8. Spheres
9. Art gallery
10. Profane
11. Vex
12. ". . . to skin __"
13. Some votes
19. Hardly __
21. Happening
24. Drives off
25. Quips
27. Disconcert
28. Duplicity
30. Yield
32. John Wayne oldie
33. Stand high
34. Fragrant
37. Curved line
38. Err
42. U.S. department
45. In good season
49. Latvian gulf
52. Acid indicator
54. Gold, for instance
56. Up till now
57. Race-track term
58. Cheese
59. Cloth
60. Sandhill
62. Threadlike structures
63. Ensign
65. Basic cell substance
66. U.S. troops

4

ACROSS

1. Bird call
4. Prepares apples
9. Venus's island
13. Italian port on Adriatic
14. Wagnerian work
15. First letter: Abbr.
16. Thoroughfares: Abbr.
17. __ base
18. Siva's wife
19. Spots for statues
21. Avails oneself of
23. Birds, of a sort
25. Knowing
26. Fuel gas
31. Blood substances
36. Suppressed
37. Congers
38. Urban blight
40. Direction, in Paris
41. Indian maids
43. Eskimo's wherewithal
45. Ante
47. Washington
48. Condiment
54. Clearance, of a sort
58. Ancient city-state
59. Surrounded by
60. Kind of fund
62. Pigeon breeds
63. Occasion
64. San __, Calif.
65. Hill crest, in England
66. Laurel
67. "All wool and __ wide"
68. Word of agreement

DOWN

1. Find fault
2. Asian palm
3. Weak
4. Is made up of
5. W.W. II agency
6. Musical show
7. Muse
8. Like the ocean
9. Skirt
10. Girl's name
11. Like some TV
12. Early patriot
13. Judge's seat
20. "Iliad," for one
22. Vessels at Anzio landing
24. Earth scientists: Abbr.
27. Devious activity
28. Thine: Fr.
29. Goddess of destiny
30. Things to make meet
31. Harvest
32. Blood: Prefix
33. Custard pastry
34. Herb of grace
35. Fishing vessel
39. Careless
42. U-boats
44. ". . . a giant __ for mankind"
46. Transfusion material
49. Put to rest
50. Port opposite Gibraltar
51. Tidy the hedge
52. Lab items
53. File
54. Butter, oleo, etc.
55. Copy: Abbr.
56. Terza __
57. Anthony
61. Religious discourse: Abbr.

5

ACROSS

1. Detroit players
6. "__ small world"
10. Merry sound
14. Leading
15. Cruise
16. Bovines
17. Silly talk
18. Sooner
20. Mark in curling
21. Key Biscayne, for one
23. Poison for arrow tips
24. "And __ grow on"
25. Hot iron
26. Roman 1970
29. Have-nots
31. Egg-shaped
32. Capek of "R.U.R." fame
33. Pastured
36. Rare
40. Stain
41. Promenades
42. Egyptian singing girl
43. Voodoo
44. Cash keeper
46. Plods through mire
48. Scented
50. Deposit
51. Arctic canoe
52. Through: Prefix
55. Span
57. "Of thee __"
59. Tributary of Seine
60. Olympian goddess
61. Neighbor of Sverige
62. Asian weight
63. Large quantity
64. Sights in Holland

DOWN

1. Choir's place
2. Regarding
3. Western Indian
4. "__ as a Stranger"
5. Enigmatic one
6. Lady of Arthurian romance
7. Act like a champ
8. Muddy deposit
9. Term in cookery
10. Cheer
11. Logger
12. Got wind of
13. Bancroft
19. Obstacle
22. Latin 6
24. Word for a shoppe
25. Charqui
26. Humor
27. Rabbit
28. Small game for tabby
30. Discord goddess
32. Persian carpet
33. Coins of Iraq and Jordan
34. Madame Bovary
35. Wild game
37. Counterparts
38. Cheap platers
39. Pastry item
43. Small amount
44. Girl's nickname
45. Harsh
46. Narrow groove
47. Kind of change
49. Cash in Turin
50. Glengarry man
51. Layer of the iris
52. Dagger
53. American dramatist
54. Dark __
56. Electrical unit
58. Self, in France

6

ACROSS

1. Moonlighting group
5. Awry
10. Basic principles
14. Acknowledges
15. Stock, in cards
16. Child lacking manners
17. Authentic
18. Webfooted animal
19. Movie dog
20. Speech sound
22. Book of Bible
24. Girl's nickname
25. Replay medium
26. Primps
29. Quit
33. Ex-Yankee pitcher
34. Peg for Hillary
35. New Havenite
36. Mil. addresses
37. Guinevere
38. Short rail extension
39. Gumshoe
40. Bacharach and Lancaster
41. Scold
42. Sources of baseball bats
44. Do-___
45. Slacken
46. Coalition
47. Alive
50. More posh
54. Sustain
55. Hawkeye
57. Pale color
58. Villain of drama
59. Player of Chan role
60. Becloud
61. Animal sac
62. Eelworms
63. Ko-Ko's weapon

DOWN

1. Ibsen role
2. Frightens
3. Easy job
4. ___ not (in all probability)
5. Ermines
6. Soigné
7. Word for Adenauer
8. Adversary
9. Irrationality
10. Marbles
11. Baloney!
12. Shelter
13. Yard
21. Rave's pal
23. Weave
25. French heads
26. S.A. river
27. Things to know
28. Period in history
29. Skips second helpings
30. Not so hot
31. Slip away from
32. More desperate
34. Soup
37. Wonder about
38. Horror movies
40. Light brown
41. Animal, for short
43. Drink-maker
44. Endocrines
46. Master, in Africa
47. "Odyssey," for one
48. Lab picture
49. Clothing
50. Enjoyed the surf
51. Image
52. Canal
53. ___ of thumb
56. Cheer in Madrid

7

ACROSS

1. Mother of Isaac
6. Word for a young person
12. Famous shrine
13. Meandered
15. Tremble
16. Relinquish
17. Instrument: Suffix
18. Roman dictator
20. "___ one's life depended on it"
21. Soviet sea
22. Grafted, in heraldry
23. Feat of skill
24. Keep ___ on
25. You: Ger.
26. Football throw
27. Spanish queen
28. Expensive
29. Vivacious
30. Jargon
31. Members of blind trio
32. Goes for a spin
35. Yawn
36. Certain voter: Abbr.
39. Show
40. Irving's sleeper
41. Lustrous cloth
42. Like meshed fabric
43. Stun
44. Rara ___
45. Sandarac tree
46. Foreshadowed
47. Sleep uneasily
48. Form a passage
50. Excessively
52. Drew out
53. Dealer in hot goods
54. Recent
55. Honored

DOWN

1. Of a desert
2. "Arabian Nights" character
3. Becomes frayed
4. Soul: Fr.
5. Prudent judgment
6. Casino furniture
7. Sicilian city
8. Nigerian town
9. Debating side
10. Obliteration
11. Of part of the eye
13. Reuther or Scott
14. With dexterity
15. Roofing material
19. Eastern-rite Christian
23. Ingredient of a girl
26. Decamped
28. "Pride and Prejudice" hero
30. Kind of bridge
31. Corn color
32. Threat
33. Generally
34. Oberon's better half
35. Worked on a road
36. Reno specialty
37. Isolated
38. Having great bulk
41. Evident
43. Tractor-driven machine
46. Morsel
49. Illuminated
51. Churchill sign

8

ACROSS

1. Inky sea creature
6. Impossible dream
13. Treeless plain
15. Balloon rider
17. Food share
18. Revives
19. Freshen, as linens
20. __ fide
21. Poker round
22. Like a nervous stomach
24. Conduit
25. One-time editor's wear
26. Metric unit
27. Living-room sets
28. Beluga's gift to man
29. Electrical units
34. Stirs up
35. Hitchcock subject
36. Word with chicken or small
37. Regarding
38. Olympics contestant
44. __ majesty
45. Historic Utah rail site
46. Chemical endings
47. French milk
48. Grisly
49. Table wine
51. Martyred Armenian saint
52. Washington, Adams and Jefferson
53. Kind of pitch
54. Harden, as glue
55. British guns

DOWN

1. Rake with fire
2. Plover of Canada
3. Fallacious
4. Know-nothings
5. Farmer's fear
6. Taxi men
7. Water birds
8. Enraging
9. First name in Louvre
10. School course: Abbr.
11. Noted Russian
12. "__ of the Breakfast Table"
14. Aardvark
16. Walks off balance
23. Meets by arrangement: Abbr.
24. Disreputable place
26. Take it on the __
28. Pretentious fops
29. Dumbfounded
30. Husband of Helen of Troy
31. Sales tactic
32. Sea bird
33. Spoil
34. Kind of rubber
36. Remonstrate
38. Threesomes
39. Mounds
40. Difficulty
41. __ one's time
42. Up
43. U.S. painter and family
45. Cleveland suburb
47. Page
50. Explosive

9

ACROSS

1. One kind of race
6. Jenny Lind or Greta Garbo
11. Room in a harem
14. Part of a Virginia Woolf title
15. Grew ashen
16. Girl's nickname
17. Water activity
19. Language: Abbr.
20. Reward for a good horse
21. Distinction
22. Press agent's concern
24. Bowling alley
25. Hymn of praise
27. Have reference
30. Mineral suitable for jewelry
33. Incensed
34. Harass
35. Word with brass or banana
36. Tabletop décor
37. Gentleman of Acapulco
38. Emphatic negative
39. Superlative ending
40. Havelock
41. Let go
42. Light again
44. Conveyance of sorts
45. Wants
46. Vote count
47. Port of Brazil
49. Giants' old grounds
50. Certain G.I.
53. Nickname for a Greek
54. Having sway
58. Rubbing fluid: Abbr.
59. Fisherman
60. Nerve networks
61. Traveler's rider
62. Beans
63. Long

DOWN

1. Door fastener
2. Killer whale
3. Debacle
4. Sound of sorrow
5. Flow out
6. Malice
7. Beauty-parlor job
8. Hebrew priest
9. __ of thieves
10. Most nervous
11. Reciprocal pronoun
12. Rural oath
13. Heavenly creature: Fr.
18. "Thy will be __"
23. Launching pad for an acrobat
24. Recent
25. Mexican money
26. New World resident: Abbr.
27. Housatonic
28. Remove
29. Bringing up the rear
30. Aladdin's friend
31. Canonical hour
32. Lyric poem
34. Haberdashery items
37. Coasted
38. Not written
40. Ill-wishers
41. Convict population
43. Direction to a horse
44. __ in one
46. Presides at tea
47. Event for Cinderella
48. Canal finished in 1825
49. Legal action
50. Cordage fiber
51. "My __ Lady"
52. Social group
55. Prefix with classic or mycin
56. Texas leaguer
57. Launching pad on the links

10

ACROSS

1. Kind of hist.
4. Southern city
9. Savvy
12. Pastures
14. U.S.S.R. mountains
15. Put aside
16. Soaking
18. Unvaried
19. Great Lake
20. Safari redcaps
22. Signs
23. Pennsylvania city
24. __ de Boulogne
25. Sheep-counter's ailment
29. Arithmetic word
30. Favoring
31. "When day __"
33. Mild expletive
34. Bridge call
36. Roman dates
37. Remove by erosion
39. Religious group: Abbr.
40. North or South
41. Medicine injectors
43. Citrus fruit
44. Allot
45. Appetizer spread
46. Crusaders' foe
49. Shallow baking dish
52. Urge
53. Envelope contents
55. "__ Karenina"
56. Cordage fiber
57. Sediment
58. Jane __
59. Hebrew letter
60. Alphabet letter

DOWN

1. Likewise
2. Kind of sign
3. In a faultfinding way
4. North African city
5. Jason's ship
6. Cavernous opening
7. Military freshmen
8. Minor planets
9. __ a heart
10. Always
11. Submarine docks
13. Medina-Sidonia's fleet
15. Able to make lucky discoveries
17. Irritates
21. Objectives
24. Unshaped masses
25. Anger
26. Aristocrat
27. Of an antiseptic test
28. Anoint, old style
29. Snead's org.
30. Most attractive
32. Compass point
35. Suppliers of the ego
38. Started off a game
42. Kind of elbow
43. Varnish ingredients
45. Pulitzer novelist of 1918
46. Mining nail
47. Italian river
48. Certain ranger
49. Dressed
50. Prefix with meter and printer
51. Punta del __
54. Civil War initials

11

ACROSS

1. Large moth
5. Owns
8. Desert in northeast Sudan
14. Short saying
16. Lack of muscle coordination
17. Hemingway's "A __ Feast"
18. Tedious
19. Collection of items
20. Park features
22. Pieces of fuel turf
23. Hone
24. What a Manx lacks
26. __ escape
29. Inhabitants of southern Asia
33. Willow
34. Couch
35. Pol. party
36. Draw
37. Member of the electorate
38. Comet's head
39. Beverage
40. Dotted patterns, in heraldry
41. Weight unit
42. Chemical warfare weapon
44. Procession
45. Jai __
46. Chalcedony
47. Lewis Carroll animal
50. Artless
52. Dante's gal
55. City of Crete
57. Infant garments
59. William Waldorf and John Jacob
60. Civil War vessel
61. Word of appreciation
62. Feminine suffix
63. Deep cut

DOWN

1. Tibetan priest
2. Atop
3. Kind of star
4. Consumed
5. Mideast language
6. Shoelace tip
7. U.S. duck
8. Seize
9. Visionary
10. Just about
11. South African iris
12. Common contraction of sorts
13. Some horses
15. Egyptian goddess of mirth
21. Verses
23. Small bird
25. Winged
26. Man without a country
27. Sotto voce
28. Versifier: Var.
29. Small sums
30. Ancient assembly
31. Rover
32. Sudden outburst
34. Sphere of activity
37. Bright star
38. Droll fellow, familiarly
40. Original Robinson Crusoe
41. Course
43. Golf star of past
44. Roadbuilders
46. Fathers
47. Go away!
48. Old auto
49. Broadway group: Abbr.
51. Culmination
52. Part of an Eastern church
53. Epochs
54. Sholem __, novelist
56. Blockhead
58. Iron mold

12

ACROSS

1. Navy trials aboard ship
6. Sultan of __
10. Accepted: Abbr.
14. Honolulu greeting
15. Old ale jug
16. Past
17. Noted sculptor
18. Colonizer of Greenland
19. Directed
20. Coldstream men
22. Spartan king
24. Manual-training system
26. Slips
27. Old Spanish coins
30. Conveyance
31. Greek nickname
32. Library contents
34. Famed Swede
38. St. Andrews sport
40. Ice pinnacle
42. Hit it on the __
43. Organic compounds
45. Scandinavian wind god
47. Spanish article
48. Exclamation
50. Gargantuan
52. Ceramist
55. Brown print
56. Underwater apparatus
58. Latin gentlemen
62. Indonesian islands: Var.
63. Seaweed product
65. Soda adjunct
66. Camera part
67. Alaskan port
68. Extreme
69. Cattle feed
70. Waste allowance
71. Manchurian city

DOWN

1. Page edge: Abbr.
2. Matty of baseball
3. Scotch's companion
4. Craving
5. Ballfield of sorts
6. Sault __ Marie
7. October event
8. Name in long-run play
9. Famous Tiger
10. Dodger's Jackie
11. Sidestep
12. Kind of closet
13. Mini or midi
21. Arias
23. Certain word
25. Arab republic
27. Senate employee
28. Golf club
29. Missile housing
33. French river
35. Machete
36. Jacob's brother
37. Subtraction word
39. Dodgers' old home
41. Harvests
44. Queens landmark
46. Parches
49. Unmitigated
51. Mickey of the Yankees
52. Work of David
53. Botanical sheath
54. Changes color, as a leaf
57. Stravinsky
59. Straight: Prefix
60. __ avis
61. Graceful bird
64. Inactive: Abbr.

13

ACROSS

1. Prefix for physics
5. Small type
10. Spaniard's cloak
14. Encourage
15. Aromatic seeds
16. Elliptical
17. Bonbon
19. Dickens heroine
20. Whole
21. Consoles
23. Diameter parts
26. Franklin
27. Make a new judgment on
30. News hot off the press
34. Overlook
35. Adores
37. Army man: Abbr.
38. Relative, for short
39. Down-to-earth person
41. Stock-market quotation
42. Wing of a building
43. La Douce et al.
44. Hock
45. Equivalent of believing
47. Loams
50. Long __
51. Explode
52. Advance
56. Armed merchant ship
60. Melville hero
61. Colorful
64. S. A. country
65. Congo-Sudanese people
66. Abhor
67. Impertinence
68. Feminine suffixes
69. Greek god

DOWN

1. Spice
2. Black
3. Loose dress
4. ". . . loved not __ sight?"
5. Consent
6. Violin-string material
7. Friend, in France
8. Spanish uncles
9. Elevates
10. U.S. educator
11. With: Fr.
12. Enclosure
13. "__ well"
18. Periods
22. Minimal
24. Religion of East
25. Set apart
27. Flowers
28. Rousseau's fictional pupil
29. Two on the __
31. Chou __
32. Angry look
33. Localities
36. Shade
39. Starr
40. Argue logically
44. Covered vase
46. Metrical foot
48. Soups
49. Resorts
52. Soft foods
53. Big bird
54. Paddles
55. Common Latin verb
57. First word of a letter
58. Within: Prefix
59. U.S. 1 and others: Abbr.
62. Savings-bank word: Abbr.
63. Presidential initials

14

ACROSS

1. Cast out
6. Alps or Andes: Abbr.
10. Color
14. ___ will (testate)
15. Paducah river
16. Piped
17. Auto rider's insurance
19. ___-cake
20. Roulade
21. Shelter, in Soho
22. Lawful
23. Hoist
27. Slough
28. Performs
29. Daisy
31. Egg cells
32. Wash. agency
36. Physicist's concern
40. Superlative endings
41. Morsel
42. Perch
43. Native of Zanzibar
46. Sgt., e.g.
47. Hawk, so to speak
52. Wing-shaped
53. Wool: Prefix
54. Tennis score
55. Plant of pea family
56. Catcher's equipment
60. Hardwood
61. First-rate
62. Seething
63. Present-day netman
64. Hear ye!
65. Confab à la hippie

DOWN

1. Loop sights
2. Auto components
3. Shining
4. Office employee
5. Make lace
6. Capone, for one
7. Last stop
8. Naught
9. Inebriate
10. Garnish
11. Medicaster
12. Before
13. Playing marble
18. Couple, as oxen
22. ___ Cruces
24. Indian of Canada
25. Hindu goddess
26. Subway, busses, etc.: Abbr.
27. European fish
30. Metallic elements: Abbr.
32. Tail: Prefix
33. Evergreen of Europe
34. Refuse to believe
35. Renowned Roman
37. Front seats in a theater
38. Algerian port
39. The Red
43. Furtive
44. Blasco-___, author of "Four Horsemen"
45. Auld ___ syne
47. ___ mañana
48. Agalloch
49. Indian leader
50. English admiral
51. Mecca shrine
56. ___ Paulo
57. Heavy barge
58. Mideast initials
59. Road sign

15

ACROSS

1. Hawaiian gifts
5. Walk nervously
9. Ancient region of Asia Minor
14. Part of an auto
15. Blunders
16. Old Greek coins
17. River to the Colorado
18. Moderately priced
20. Thoroughly excellent
22. Ceremonies
23. Kind of nut
24. Bourbon St. feature
25. Oriental nurses
28. Servicing a dinner party
32. Levee sights of old
33. One past recovery
34. Tumultuous sound
35. Book holders
36. Raise livestock
37. Bristlelike part
38. Donkey, in France
39. Pointed instruments
40. Set in operation
41. Officious meddlers
43. Borders, in heraldry
44. Garden implement
45. Portico
47. One of a Tolstoi pair
49. TV divisions
53. Name in detective fiction
55. Courage
56. Kind of sanctum
57. Hunter's cry to hounds
58. Existence: Lat.
59. Exploits
60. Sweetsop
61. Nurture

DOWN

1. Falls behind
2. Stage direction
3. That, to Cicero
4. Explores
5. Jeopardy
6. Amphitheater
7. Jutting rock
8. Sigmoidal figure
9. Pine or spruce
10. Subtracter
11. Vestment
12. Misfortunes
13. Peer Gynt's mother
19. Made a formal speech
21. Minus-yardage in football
24. Certain candy shapes
25. Nautical word
26. Divine food
27. Northern tree
28. Some college students
29. Standard of perfection
30. Saltpeter
31. Annoying insects
33. British historian
36. Wall Street man
37. "__ in Paradise"
39. Surface mineral deposits
40. Promptly
42. Babbled
45. Portion
46. Armored vehicles
47. Yearn
48. Old slave
49. Talk, in a way
50. Gaelic
51. Mona __
52. Silver: Abbr.
53. Word with day or night
54. Rolled tea

16

ACROSS

1. Economize
7. After this, twilight
13. Eternally
14. Boone was one
16. Rival
17. King Arthur's mother
18. In medias __
19. Cuddled up
21. Open a barrel
22. Spatiate
24. Rumbullions
25. __ Raton
26. Be philanthropic
28. "__ Rheingold"
29. Handles, as a shrew
30. Jiggled
32. Up-to-the-minute
33. Skedaddled
34. Indian of Colombia

35. Declare
38. Withers
42. Baseball's hot corner
43. Companion of cry
44. Last straw
45. Participants in 24 Across
46. Met basso
48. Eldest: Fr.
49. Be beholden to
50. Tossed to and fro
52. Educ. group
53. Domestic
55. Giants or Jets
57. Territory on Adriatic
58. Surrounds
59. Pulled quickly
60. Out-of-studio TV show

DOWN

1. Unidentified person
2. Zealot's enterprise
3. Electrical unit
4. Abdul the Bulbul's rival
5. Gasman's reading matter
6. Was chairman
7. Long-legged birds
8. Yens
9. Aromatic ointment
10. Saint-Tropez is one
11. Abstract
12. A-Q and K-J
13. Polecat's cousin
15. Meal
20. Natterjack
23. Carey and Shipton
25. City in New York
27. Mysterious

29. Language of Ceylon
31. Steep
32. Small ape
34. Tune-caller's creditor
35. Maximally
36. Raining off and on
37. Asian area
38. Brought to court
39. Noteworthy
40. Ancestry
41. Gets hot under the collar
43. Insinuated
46. French toast
47. Old name for Ireland
50. Soak up sunshine
51. Campus building
54. City on 118 islands: Abbr.
56. Spanish relative

17

ACROSS

1. Applaud
5. Moves
10. Thuringian city
14. Laugh
15. Sacred book
16. Assert
17. Caterpillar
20. Calif. time
21. Irish islands
22. Place of pleasant aromas
23. Disagreeable person: Slang
24. Broadway role
25. Abilities
28. Suffer from heat
31. Held and others
32. Swine
33. Pile
35. Pleasant
36. Nebs
37. Roman 1502
38. Overwhelm
39. Perry Mason's detective
40. Provide quarters
41. Gazing people
43. Made a breach in
44. Scarves
45. Byway
46. Expose
49. Saarinen
50. U.S. agency: Abbr.
53. Man who sees the dull side
56. "Pompeii" girl
57. Friction match
58. Spanish jar
59. Queries
60. Sumptuous meal
61. Slang for money

DOWN

1. Fellow
2. Moos
3. "There'll be __ time in . . ."
4. By: Sp.
5. Plays a bagpipe
6. Musical term
7. Persia, today
8. Brit. fliers
9. Shock absorbers
10. Book part
11. Bacchanal's cry
12. Close
13. Affected, in a way
18. Posts
19. Barriers
23. Frolic
24. Rouse
25. Mrs. Roosevelt
26. "Sees all, __ all"
27. Map addition
28. Penetrates, with "in"
29. Conclude
30. Lift
32. Trio of children's story
34. Jumbled, as type
36. Discontinue
37. Brood
39. Waste product
40. Asian capital
42. Degrades
43. Poet's traditional milieu
45. Laws: Lat.
46. Gov't. news agency
47. Army men: Abbr.
48. Fur
49. It, in Italy
50. Groundless
51. Amoeba
52. Suffix for demo or auto
54. Regret
55. Drink

18

ACROSS

1. Sphere of influence
7. Genus of African herb
13. In a wicked manner
14. Pop the question
16. Barren
17. Italian mush delicacy
18. Brother of Moses
19. Annual bank giveaway
20. Lily: Fr.
21. In the least
23. Fishing-fly barb
24. Syrian city, to French
26. Umpire's call
27. Oscar film of 1955
28. Mailer's "The __"
30. Declare verboten
31. Least interesting
32. Narcotics-squad man at times
35. O. T. book
36. Curse on an ocean cruise
38. Earthen pot
41. Basin
42. Swan or gainer
43. Run swiftly
44. Tear-sopping device
45. Fiber knot
46. Making use of
48. Good buy: Colloq.
50. Chanting
51. Feminine
53. Glut
54. Instanter
55. More hair-raising
56. Teased

DOWN

1. Gave chapter and verse
2. Supervisor
3. Spanish painter
4. Icelandic measure
5. Badly
6. U.S. humorist
7. Dismay
8. Fish, in a way
9. Part in a play
10. Munificent
11. Mull over
12. Suddenly
15. Betimes
16. Dieter's lunch
19. Part of a horseshoe
21. Embarrass
22. Biting
25. Borodin opera
27. Bit part in a play
29. Fast look
30. Recalcitrant
32. Downright
33. Natural elevation
34. Uncovered
36. Fine vase
37. Answer
38. Pursue
39. Small valley
40. City in New Jersey
41. Family-planning pioneer
44. Turning point
47. River of central Italy
48. Air-pollution factor
49. Pungent flavor
51. Civil or Crimean
52. Japanese river

19

ACROSS

1. Rotating machine part
4. Highway stops
10. Greek letters
14. Caucasian language
15. Turkish inn
16. "__ Britannia"
17. Excessive thirst
19. Initiate
20. Gay
21. Farming: Abbr.
22. Father: Prefix
23. Borscht topping
29. Gasket
30. Vistas
31. Restraint
32. Black: Prefix
33. Map lines: Abbr.
34. Misery
37. Pier, in architecture
41. Angers
42. Skyborne
47. Victim, of a sort
49. Button source
50. Porringers
51. Dutch __
52. Civil War soldier
53. Heathen
54. Issue
56. Portliness
61. Princess of India
62. Mosaic gold
63. Screw pines of Pacific
64. Restrained eating
65. Forest paths
66. Snake

DOWN

1. Trophy
2. Worship: Lat.
3. Home reserve
4. Snack time for some
5. Leave out
6. Faucet
7. Hesitant sounds
8. Garland
9. Depot: Abbr.
10. Usher's offering
11. Sherbet glass
12. __ de France
13. Japanese coin
18. Tales
21. Summit: Prefix
22. Warsaw's land: Abbr.
23. Undersized person
24. Breakfast dish
25. States of turmoil
26. Circular: Scot.
27. Swiss river
28. Future books: Abbr.
35. I hear, in Spain
36. Son of Zeus doomed to frustration
37. "The jawbone of an __"
38. Cpl. or sgt.
39. Resembling a bull
40. "Bon __!"
43. Kind of order
44. Pacific island area
45. Langford or Perkins
46. Vietnamese holiday
48. Decline
53. Influence
54. European shrew
55. French month
56. Camper's item
57. British peace Nobelist
58. British West Point: Abbr.
59. Oahu fare
60. Form of precognition: Abbr.

20

ACROSS

1. Oceanic tunicate
5. Bum __
8. Pointed tool
12. Hebrew month
13. Historic periods
15. City on the Seyhan
17. Returns
19. French sculptor
20. Okefenokee feature
21. Small cask
23. Plagiarize
24. Ad lib
27. Embrace
30. Menlo Park monogram
31. La __
32. Where the Shannon flows: Abbr.
33. Mild expletives
35. Soda __
38. Camping gear
40. Puts an end to
43. Mother of the Titans
44. Stripling
46. Spanish article
47. Oriental name
49. Weeks in the year: Lat.
50. With reference
51. Musician
55. Norse god
56. Ordinal ending
57. Castle or Dunne
60. Consternate
62. East African
65. Norwegian playwright
66. Formerly
67. Words for a bit more
68. Meeting: Abbr.
69. Back, in France
70. Does fancy work

DOWN

1. Bearish time
2. Star in Draco
3. Certain debris
4. Made raids on
5. Debater's second round
6. The Altar
7. Peddlers
8. Normal quality
9. Reveres
10. Seaport of Spain
11. Bolo, for one
14. Beehive
16. Hill dweller
18. Red or White
22. Certain party: Abbr.
25. Kind of bird
26. Oriental V.I.P.
27. White lie
28. Neighbor of Nev.
29. Mother of Helen of Troy
33. Factotum
34. Seafood
36. Poison ivy genus
37. English county
39. Gains
41. Employs
42. __ Paulo
45. Veteran
48. African hemp
50. ". . . things __ what they seem"
51. Aerosol devices
52. Edict
53. "Tell __ the marines"
54. Period
55. Chou En-__
58. Act of 1930s: Abbr.
59. "__ of Eden"
61. Letters
63. Army man: Abbr.
64. Some votes

21

ACROSS

1. Miss Marple
5. Never-lose lawyer
10. Family members
14. The __ Duke (Wellington)
15. Bone: Prefix
16. Broadway hero
17. Conrad's "__ Jim"
18. Twenty: Prefix
19. Civil wrong
20. Procrastinator's time
22. Sam Spade or Philo Vance
24. Horse color
25. Brew, in Munich
26. Comprehends
29. Urgent
33. Rajah's wife
34. Unrefined
35. Chaney
36. Retired
37. Move aside
38. Hindu deity
39. Luzon town
40. Stretches over
41. Type of berth
42. Old clerical scarf
44. Nuremberg events of 1945-6
45. Storm
46. Small talk
47. Spread open
50. Strangles: Var.
54. Nick Charles's wife
55. Battery part
57. Jot
58. Greek ruler of Syracuse
59. Extort from
60. Hebrew letters
61. Russian queen
62. Western park
63. Pâté de foie __

DOWN

1. Cast aside
2. Irish exclamation
3. Standard
4. Approved
5. Shearer and others
6. Type of sponge
7. Pack
8. Alphabet letters
9. Most raucous
10. Office stamps
11. __ ben Adhem
12. Soil
13. Thomas of clock fame
21. Cheap cigar
23. Minus
25. Seed coats
26. Galahad's quest
27. Amateur sleuth who slept late
28. Close by, in poems
29. Make concise
30. Ancient Spanish town
31. Out of the ordinary
32. Growls
34. Scabbard trim
37. Lost liquid
38. One kind of image
40. Boom
41. Mineral
43. Lizard
44. "Bad things come in __"
46. Put the bite on
47. Release
48. Short fiber
49. Amphibian
50. Foot ailment
51. Duty turn
52. Volcano
53. Talk back
56. Digits: Abbr.

22

ACROSS

1. Show
5. Pickpockets: Slang
9. Monopolized, with "up"
14. Nautical direction
15. "The very __!"
16. Famed fountain
17. Register
18. Dickens heroine
19. Free
20. Air-conditioning, so to speak
23. Sandwich, for short
24. __ Alamos
25. Floral leaf
27. Milieu for cop on the beat
32. List
35. Timetable abbreviation
36. Litigants
38. Shampoo cycle
39. One-time Turkish governors
41. Cheers
43. Swerve
44. Actress Stevens
46. Anaconda
48. Poet's word
49. Gender
51. Shakes
53. Stowed
55. Cover
56. One of D.D.E.'s titles
58. Impetuous
64. Peppery sound
66. Galway country
67. Noted marsupial
68. "__ evil . . ."
69. Mailbox part
70. Mine car
71. Annexed
72. Disseminates
73. Deal

DOWN

1. Tuileries Gardens, e.g.
2. Spread
3. Collation
4. Hawk
5. Alley Oop's mount
6. Common footnote
7. Lucre
8. Name for Shropshire
9. Speak haltingly
10. Sea bird
11. Killjoy
12. Corrupt
13. Regimen
21. Browbeats
22. Holzman or Grange
26. Monkshood
27. Developer of polio vaccine
28. Greek goddess
29. Killed from ambush
30. People born in July and August
31. Swedish coin
33. River in France
34. Delaware resort city
37. Dance extra
40. Bristle
42. Pans
45. California sight
47. Cause: Prefix
50. Pacific herb
52. Embraces
54. Gown
56. House, in Spain
57. Kind of tea
59. Wheeler-dealer of "Catch-22"
60. Edge of a hill
61. Dumb one
62. Equal: Fr.
63. Vault
65. Pronoun

23

ACROSS

1. Kashmir people
6. U.S. jurist
9. Feigns
13. On the other hand
14. Pronoun
16. Sound of thunder
17. Sublease
18. Hypocritical
20. Get new bearings
22. Ventilate
23. Soot
24. Modified
25. "Dear __"
28. Certain felons
30. Invent
32. Spanish hero
33. Printing style: Abbr.
36. Equivalent of a miss
37. Divinity degrees
38. Money: Slang
39. Carry on
40. Ruby or Sandra
41. Author of "Almayer's Folly"
42. Toothlike formation
45. Affirmative
46. New Netherland landholder
48. Mine car
50. African antelopes
51. Learned society of France
55. Other than indicated
57. Numbskull
58. Huntley
59. Maneuverable, as a ship
60. Tuscan city
61. Assuage
62. ". . . ring I thee __"
63. Rational faculty in Buddhism

DOWN

1. English lawyer: Abbr.
2. American author
3. French composer
4. Stadium sections
5. Hint
6. Cheap dives
7. Polly, to Tom Sawyer
8. Parts of cens.
9. Process of growth
10. High area of a cathedral: Var.
11. Item in a Paris bakery
12. Momentum
15. Alderfly
19. Meshed fabrics
21. River to the Seine
24. Black cuckoos
25. Cicatrix
26. Girl's name
27. Puts back
29. Music group
31. Take turns
34. Wings
35. Boys
37. Green or snap
38. Doctrine expounded by Leibnitz
40. Full of impurities
41. Girl's name
43. McKuen and Serling
44. Suffered from mosquito bites
46. Shilling components
47. Greeting
49. Press, radio, etc.
51. Farm unit
52. Carriage
53. Scottish island
54. Greek letters
56. Detroit-based union: Abbr.

24

ACROSS

1. North Dakota city
6. Normandy beach
10. Repose
14. Suppose
15. Have trust in
16. Perceive
17. Forks
19. Fratricide
20. Compass point
21. Transaction
22. Three in one
24. Ocean vessels: Abbr.
25. Auto-horn sound
26. Crowns
28. Radiant
32. Looked the place over
33. Leslie Caron role
34. __ account
35. Steel area
36. Brazilian dance
37. Rome's Censor
38. Sheltered, at sea
39. Equals
40. Church plate
41. Labyrinth monster
43. Mentions
44. Hodges and Blas
45. Be fatuous
46. Plow's trail
49. Paint medium
50. Common verb
53. Scope
54. Miner's disease
57. Speak falteringly
58. Uproar
59. Hunter of the sky
60. Arthritis aid
61. Very: Fr.
62. __ porridge

DOWN

1. Pendants
2. Sacred bull
3. Prevalent
4. African antelope
5. Unit of magnetic intensity
6. Russian great divide
7. Head: Fr.
8. Stout's relative
9. Emotional state
10. Give as good as one gets
11. Biblical brother
12. Gyrate
13. English river
18. U.A.W. output
23. Early auto
24. Three-D picture
25. Fall-planting items
26. Nobel physicist of 1945
27. Made of a wood
28. One taking a sight
29. Growing out
30. Ponies up
31. Ten o'clock scholar's hour
32. Last-minute study
33. Oedipus's father
36. True-blue
40. Pause in the Indy 500
42. Spanish relative
43. Mountain passes
45. Legislative assemblies
46. F.D.R.'s pet
47. __ acid
48. Remainder
49. Wind instrument
50. One of a world seven
51. Rivers: Sp.
52. Domestic slave
55. Title
56. Western state: Abbr.

25

ACROSS

1. Unit of magnetic induction
6. Iranian king
10. __ out (made do)
14. Concert hall
15. Renovate
16. Prefix meaning dry
17. Item on a spice rack
19. Acclaim
20. Event at the pass
21. Small compensation
23. Do a farm chore
25. Suitor
26. Mastodon feature
30. Secret nationalist org.
32. Blot
36. Word heard in the back room
37. Liquid container
39. Perplexed
40. Hospital employees
43. Certain potatoes
44. Enthusiastic
45. S-shaped molding
46. Author of "The Flies"
48. Pitiful
49. Information
50. O'Neill
52. Gillespie, for short
54. Hoarded
58. Of bodily motions
63. Musical instrument
64. Douglas fir
66. Grow hazy
67. Place
68. Obsolete
69. Understands
70. Lunar vehicles
71. Came into play

DOWN

1. Garment for a quaestor
2. Cheese
3. Balkan native
4. Whopper
5. Off the mark
6. Classmen: Abbr.
7. Jumbled mass
8. Comic's specialty
9. Cold remedy of yore
10. Total consumption
11. Shakespearean actor
12. Father of Leif
13. Disburse
18. Grade of meat
22. French smoker's item
24. Destruction
26. Hacks
27. U.N. agency
28. Part of a building
29. Pennsylvanians
31. Timber trees
33. American Indian
34. Breathe life into
35. Foundations
38. Work, as clay
41. Sharp spasm
42. Color
47. Sign up
51. Mountain stronghold
53. "The Prisoner of __"
54. Loads
55. Competent
56. Debauchee
57. Adjudge
59. Mast
60. European head of state
61. Feminine suffixes
62. Relinquish
65. Augie's other nickname

26

ACROSS

1. Maxwell
4. Rank above maj.
9. Guide
13. Stead
15. Redolence
16. Suffix with din or pal
17. Churchill's successor
18. Powers: Lat.
19. Fish
20. Denture bite, so to speak
23. __ good advantage
24. Fabulous bird
25. "__ down his throat"
28. Old English money
30. City south of Portland
34. Hams it up
36. "__ aboard!"
38. Mother of Pollux
39. Drag strip
42. Worn to __
43. Metric measure
44. Brand
45. Surveys
47. "__ were king"
49. Ermine
50. Approximate flight hour: Abbr.
52. Type of ink
54. Tokyo lifeguard, in a way
61. Smart one
62. Playwright Padraic
63. Prefix with space or naut
64. Four-handed exercise
65. Confuse
66. Tubers
67. Sovereigns: Abbr.
68. Wears
69. Sodium hydroxide

DOWN

1. Bar figure
2. Radames's beloved
3. Film part
4. "__ en Rose"
5. __ size (cut down)
6. Bare midriffs, in a way
7. Hebrew measure
8. Beam
9. Possible last words for "Life With Father"
10. Small case
11. __ extra cost
12. Dizzy
14. Turns for burlesque performers
21. Chemical compound
22. Mayday
25. Summary
26. Acid
27. Powerful person
29. Bar order
31. Release
32. Swelling disease
33. He took a bath
35. Main
37. Baseball positions: Abbr.
40. Numerical prefix
41. "__ the bag"
46. Penn, for one: Abbr.
48. Scurrility
51. Design transfer
53. Knights' wives
54. Weary
55. Styptic
56. Kind of show
57. Beverage
58. Type of ticket
59. Host
60. Pry

27

ACROSS

1. Loyal
5. Vote to accept
10. Swimmers' milieu
14. Khayyám
15. Roman dictator
16. Jai __
17. Lizard
18. Cross as __
19. German nyet
20. Cede
22. Pea soup
24. H.H. Munro
26. Ago: Scot.
27. Ointment ingredient
31. Australian, for one
35. Of the ear
36. Actor Howard
39. __ Veneto
40. Common contraction
41. Part of a wedding gown
42. Part of S. A. R.
43. Direction: Abbr.
44. Undertake
45. Sheep
46. Meaning
48. Gulfweed
50. Macaws
53. Heat units: Abbr.
54. W.W. II propagandist
58. Present
62. Words of understanding
63. Collect
65. "__ But the Lonely Heart"
66. Biblical name
67. Like 45 Across
68. Sicilian peak
69. Without: Fr.
70. Present or past
71. Beloved

DOWN

1. Verne hero
2. Eastern prince
3. Spanish room
4. Negotiate
5. __ rule
6. Work by Joyce
7. Spread
8. Blueprints
9. Dilatory
10. Hide worker
11. Hebrew letter
12. Hawaiian tree
13. Honor card
21. Headwear
23. Formerly
25. Caber-tosser's wear
27. Morse and area
28. In agreement
29. Fabric
30. Namesakes of Isaac's son
32. Confesses
33. Grape products
34. Rope
37. Vegetables
38. Powerless
42. Experienced
44. Flying prefix
47. Writer Dorothy
49. Kind of string
51. Slang
52. Unravel
54. Spanish relatives
55. Greek peak
56. Sharp
57. German possessive
59. Show fondness
60. King Mongkut's teacher
61. Leap, for one
64. Wedding-account word

28

ACROSS

1. Behold: Lat
5. Baseball's Manny
9. Severe
14. Conversation
15. Cupid
16. Speak pompously
17. Covered with scales
19. Poem by Keats
20. Burning
21. Of the kidneys
23. Kind of verb: Abbr.
24. Two fins
26. "Call Me __"
28. Horse opera
30. Kind of street
34. German reformer
38. "Macbeth," for one
39. Spanish exclamation
40. Pours forth
42. Title
43. Tiniest
46. Drove recklessly
49. Money handler
51. Queen of Thebes
52. Bumpkin
55. Boring tool
58. Puts __ (delays)
61. Dried coconut
63. Cheer
64. Trees of a region
66. American writer
68. __ thief
69. Famous Knick
70. Sunder
71. Make rotten
72. Greek god
73. Squirrel's nest

DOWN

1. Fanfare
2. Rub
3. Williams play
4. Endless
5. __ de tête
6. Moslem leader
7. Animal image
8. Game place
9. City in Michigan
10. Constellation
11. Branches
12. Agitate
13. Learn
18. British courts
22. Fuss
25. Steeps
27. "La __"
29. In ecstasy
31. Trash
32. French friend
33. Measure
34. Foal
35. Away from the wind
36. Goddess: Lat.
37. Minnesota player
41. Cut
44. Roguish
45. British sweet
47. Bull, at times
48. French scholar and lover
50. Greek letter
53. Donizetti work
54. Gavel-wielder's word
56. Make amends
57. Indigent
58. Bones
59. Determine in court
60. Decamped
62. U.S. author
65. Lace
67. Newspaper items

29

ACROSS

1. Hindu title
4. Hardwood trees
9. All: Lat.
14. Haw's partner
15. Book of the Bible
16. Marine hazards
17. Itinerant Johnny
19. "What's It All About, __?"
20. Movie maker's light
21. Moderately slow, in music
23. Spat
25. Police officer: Abbr.
26. Abbreviation in a rental ad
29. Chose
31. Wedding-notice word
32. Digit
33. Manhattan garnishes
37. Game __ and seek
39. "You're pulling __"
40. Civil War initials
42. Was "in"
43. "Easy __"
45. Happily
47. Watercourse: Abbr.
48. Buchwald
50. Used credit
51. Religious group: Abbr.
52. Tarts
54. Bible book
58. Subjects of a discourse
61. Linen
62. "__ far, far better thing . . ."
64. Hand grenade
66. Impassive
67. Illusory paintings
68. Footlike part
69. Talking bird
70. Home, of sorts
71. Person

DOWN

1. Military cap
2. Answer
3. Bands of Kaffir warriors
4. Ty Cobb
5. Dawn goddess
6. Cruising
7. Wails
8. Darken
9. South African province
10. Relent
11. Egyptian queen
12. "__ Were King"
13. Direction: Abbr.
18. Belles __
22. Mars: Prefix
24. Early Tuileries resident
27. Seventh Ave. figure
28. Unkempt
30. Barrel
33. Naval officers: Abbr.
34. Head bone
35. Height
36. U.S. Indian
38. Style of car
41. Greek letter
44. Clip
46. Ram's mate
49. Dome of note
53. Stalk
55. Congo sight
56. Actress Terry
57. Della or Peewee
59. Chinese dynasty
60. "I never take __ after dinner"
62. Doctrine
63. Inter-office machine: Abbr.
65. Before, poetically

ACROSS

1. Whale's captive
6. Disengaged: Abbr.
9. Order to a dog
14. Funeral oration
15. Agency of U.N.
16. Hodge's other half
17. Automotive disaster
18. Never, in Bonn
19. Mongol, for one
20. Flattening with a hammer
22. Tantrum throwers
24. Hold back
25. Rough
26. __ Paulo
27. Lamour wear
31. Guns or Scott
35. Moth family
38. Play
39. Canine sound
40. French eye
41. Braggart's quality
44. Stupid
45. Arctic ship
46. Farm sound
48. Roman poet
50. Woolly animal
54. Daydream
57. Obvious
59. Sweetheart: Sp.
60. Cuckoo
62. Pickling solution
63. Highest point
64. Remick
65. Gull
66. Dispatch
67. Sea call
68. Low-class Anglo-Saxons

DOWN

1. Vehicle
2. More mature
3. "Long time __"
4. Insurance man
5. Athenian judge
6. Belfry sounds
7. Eastern collegian
8. "__ is human . . ."
9. Berlin prison
10. Subsequent
11. Adams
12. Seaweed substance
13. Ranges of perception
21. New Deal initials
23. Neighbor of Hung.
28. Greek theaters
29. River nymph
30. Sets
31. Spanish painter
32. Erie Canal city
33. Austen heroine
34. Arguer for the defense
36. Scrap
37. Sore losers
42. Change course
43. Limerick land
44. Up to
47. __ to the good
49. Arrangements
51. Behind: Sp.
52. Stone marker
53. Oakley
54. Kind of worm
55. S.A. tree
56. Arteries: Abbr.
58. Scatters
61. Recent: Prefix

31

ACROSS

1. Elec. units
5. Tree with poisonous sap
9. James Truslow or John Couch
14. Flying turn
15. Hottentot tribesman
16. D.F.C., for one
17. French miss: Abbr.
18. "__ I didn't already know"
19. Previously, old style
20. Hit show
22. Stuck fast
24. Small: Suffix
25. Monster
27. Well-known Loch
28. Pierce
30. Certain bridge bids
32. Wild habitat
33. Bookkeeping abbr.
34. Belief in one God
38. Containing nitrogen: Prefix
39. Things to get hot under
41. Recent: Prefix
42. Size of type
44. Business: Suffix
45. Tunisian port
46. Corporal or sergeant
48. __ spade a spade
49. Place for a coin
52. Years and years
53. Wing
54. National concern
56. Deducted
60. Counterpart
61. Test
63. Flexible shoot
64. Has a good standing
65. Muscle twitches
66. Prospector's quest
67. Exercise vigorously
68. "Touché" weapon
69. Son of Seth

DOWN

1. Gifts for the poor
2. Taupe
3. National concern
4. Schoolbook
5. Two-toed sloth
6. Beethoven symphony
7. "What a good boy __"
8. Kenya outing
9. Eastern nurse
10. National concern
11. Love
12. Horses
13. Greenland vehicles
21. Poetic contraction
23. "__ Rides Again"
26. Old sailing ship
28. Biblical country
29. Axis follower
31. Querying sounds
33. Hat
35. National concern
36. Official stamp
37. Cauterizing material
39. Bill's partner
40. National concern
43. Whole number
45. Fit for marketing
47. Prairie wolf
48. Calloway
49. Pinnacle
50. Folklorist Alan
51. Egg-shaped
55. Part of R and R
57. Otherwise
58. Within: Prefix
59. Letters
62. Split

32

ACROSS

1. Pitcher part
6. Ad offering
10. Accessories
14. Anathema
15. Bible book: Abbr.
16. Nimbus
17. Forest of "As You Like It"
18. Arena
19. Believe, old style
20. Tear
21. Blues composer
22. Witty remarks
23. High note
24. Rib
25. Islands in North Atlantic
26. King of Morven
28. Meditative
30. Remove, in a way
31. Continent
32. Looked slyly
33. Historical records
38. Yorkshire river
41. Slag
42. Fairy-tale words
46. Average
47. Ranges
48. Radium discoverer
50. Supplement, with "out"
51. Join the poker game
52. Type of Greek column
53. U.S. Indians
54. Neighbor of Ky.
55. Of the ear
56. Assumed proposition
57. Old expletive
58. Sea eagle
59. Scarlett
60. Dunks
61. Droops
62. Lazy ___

DOWN

1. Alarming, old style
2. Descendants through a single strain
3. Military weapons
4. Secondhand
5. Decade
6. Marsh birds
7. From within: Lat.
8. Two-seated carriages
9. Irritable
10. Robin's friend
11. Dawn goddess
12. F.D.R.'s prep school
13. Notching instrument
21. Hibernated
24. Like cheese
25. Betrothed
27. Needlefish
29. Noxious
34. React to a dull speech
35. Short songs
36. Old name for Parnassus
37. "Death of a ___"
39. Island in Indian Ocean
40. Hardening
42. Harangues
43. Metaphysical word
44. Bit of shut-eye
45. Corrects
49. Prepares potatoes
52. Female animals
53. Hawaiian island
56. Two, in Spain

33

ACROSS

1. Stroll
6. Comedian Bert
10. Rascals
14. Marner
15. Understanding reply
16. __ contendere
17. River source
19. Yesterday: Fr.
20. Researcher's aid: Abbr.
21. In front
22. Unit of weight
23. Danny or Sammy
25. Gasoline Alley family
27. Pacific island
29. Leading
32. Exhausted
34. Indians
35. Possessive
38. Disinclined
39. Pharaoh, for one
40. Varnish ingredient
42. Kind of lot
43. Jockey Arcaro
45. Fives, nines or elevens
46. Owls
48. Aleutian island
49. Place of torment
52. Western hero
54. Type of race
55. Numbers
58. European fish
61. Mild oath
62. Shape of a chess piece
64. Verne character
65. Tops
66. City in Peru
67. Uniform
68. Mary and Catherine: Abbr.
69. Power source

DOWN

1. Tennis ace
2. Appearance
3. Blemish
4. Boy
5. Attempt
6. Money, in Milan
7. Sailing
8. Restaurant V.I.P.
9. Radiation unit
10. Divided
11. Fabric
12. Fold
13. Manners
18. Evergreen genus
22. Catchall home area
24. Relative
26. Drink
27. European capital
28. Like peas in __
30. All over
31. Ford
33. Speculation
35. Hat
36. Lazarus
37. Chance
41. Shakespearean character
44. Assume
46. Kind of collision
47. Withered
49. Dunne
50. Region of Israel
51. Sweetheart
53. Staff members: Abbr.
56. River of France
57. Functions
59. Famous U.S. editor
60. Kind of cheese
62. Possesses
63. Covering

34

ACROSS

1. Book reviewer, of a sort: Abbr.
5. Boatmen's river
10. Bator's partner
14. Specialty of Brockton, Mass.
16. Timber wolf
17. Native of the Volunteer State
18. Ages ago
19. Burr or brogue
20. ___ personae
22. Sewing and others
23. "The Joys of Yiddish" author
24. Theodore White subj.
25. Kind of bridge
26. Undermines
30. Poetic contraction
31. Wherewithal
33. Proceeding
34. Oil-well equipment
35. Without a mate
36. G.I.'s garb
38. Technical study: Abbr.
39. Part of a fishline
41. Bowler's despair
43. Longfellow's contemporary
44. Early ascetic
46. Swoboda
47. ___ ex machina
48. Quinnat and sockeye
50. Trite stuff
51. Journalist's milieu
54. Diet's cousin
56. Words of understanding
57. Boardwalk stroller
59. ___ out of it
60. Price fixers, of a sort
61. That girl's
62. Ebbets Field name
63. Existence, in philosophy

DOWN

1. Movie canine
2. Harness parts
3. Doorkeepers, in France
4. Beliefs
5. Very spacious
6. Endorsements
7. Sprawl
8. Growls
9. Consanguineous
10. Vladimir Ilyich ___ (Lenin)
11. Boodle
12. Hillside shelter
13. Certain votes
15. With 53 Down, clothing
21. Most paltry
23. Burma and others
24. Intrinsically
25. Held the reins
27. Posse's prey
28. Unexpected meetings
29. Hogs' housing
31. Hungarian playwright
32. Lawgiver
37. Sound of traffic
40. Suez Canal name
42. Do public relations work
45. Juliet, for one
47. Give
49. Code man
50. Meal for Caesar
51. Birthplace of Constantine
52. Old slave
53. See 15 Down
54. Dotted with stars, in heraldry
55. Gaelic
58. Prefix for deal or deed

35

ACROSS

1. Political group
5. Finns' neighbors
10. Tax
14. Mauna Loa coating
15. Frightening
16. Loyal
17. "__ There"
18. Figure of speech
19. Cinderella garb
20. Dovetailing piece
22. Lapse
24. Small insects
26. Kind of pudding
27. Wane
30. Henry VIII's sixth
31. Knack
32. Nullify
34. License-plate attachment
35. Thaws
39. Temporary
41. Hilltop fort
42. Assignment
43. Thing of beauty
44. Character in "Quo Vadis"
45. Running game
46. Welsh name
48. Plant
49. Customers
52. Implement for Rodin
54. Chokes
56. Thoreau outings
60. Theatrical award
61. Old district of Asia Minor
63. Not mad
64. Canal
65. Football kicks
66. Throw off
67. Musical instrument
68. Hide
69. Exclamation

DOWN

1. Design in Rorschach test
2. Bathe
3. Wall appliance
4. Pool shot
5. Tennis term
6. Radio message
7. Byword
8. Pan's creation
9. Prophet
10. Arrangement of parallel bands
11. Steep rocks
12. "You __ to be in pictures"
13. Snappish
21. Check sharply
23. Particle
25. Going out, in a way
27. Corrupt
28. Kind of china
29. Bridle parts
31. Moreover: Sp.
33. Leveled
36. Intimations
37. Spanish river
38. Arrange compactly
40. Cookout
41. Returns to the scene
43. Place of suffering
47. Fresh
49. Complete
50. Prop up
51. Man's nickname
52. Flat-headed nail
53. Beam
55. Upsets
57. Lhasa monk
58. Grow together
59. Matched groups
62. Certain Wednesday

36

ACROSS

1. Khan and others
5. Broadway flop
9. Fundamental
14. Busy one's self with
16. Pickling agent
17. Highly wrought
18. School course
19. Not sweet
20. Dance
22. Forward
23. Flocks of wildfowl
25. Brings into agreement
27. Norwegian poet
28. Asian country
30. Litigant
31. East or West __
32. Pronoun
35. Laugh, in a way
39. Representative: Abbr.
40. People apart
41. Bacteriologist's wire
42. Important range
43. "Come home; __ forgiven"
44. Reader of an almanac
47. Narrow headband
49. Fit to __
50. Suddenly
53. Kind of dance
55. Fruit parts
57. Chew on a sparerib
59. Take effect
60. Speech
61. Sight or touch
62. Crucifix
63. French river

DOWN

1. Festivals
2. Carl Sandburg's birthplace
3. Thing for timid people to take
4. Cry
5. Chemical element
6. Racetracks
7. Parcel out
8. __ Rabbit
9. Container: Abbr.
10. Asian peninsula
11. Squelch
12. Weak
13. Affords
15. __ Goodfellow
21. Propelled
24. Inspiring fear
26. Island in Aegean, to Italians
27. Russian hut
28. Dyeing vats
29. Harem rooms
31. Snow runner: Var.
32. Frameworks
33. Doubt
34. Regards
36. Ranger or wolf
37. Hindu god
38. Head, in England
42. Moslem princes
43. Church area
44. Watch parts
45. Make up for
46. Show again
47. Ipso __
48. Bothered
51. Incentive
52. European leader
54. Equal
56. Behold
58. Certain horse

37

ACROSS

1. Phone
5. Anita and Barbara
11. Erode
14. Busy as __
15. Waken
16. Asian deer
17. Dylan song
20. His: Fr
21. Ancient Asian
22. Rub out
23. Often-lent thing
24. Aide: Abbr.
25. Argot
28. Spring riser
30. Sea birds
34. Service charges
37. Kind of beer
38. Space
39. Red-yellow color
40. Dame Rumor
41. One opposed
42. Chorine's benefactor
44. Ship part
45. Weight
46. ". . . in someone __ arms"
47. Legal term
50. Chum
51. Light craft
53. Burn
55. Commercial degree
58. Gene Kelly film
61. Lodging place
62. "It's all the __ me"
63. Preposition
64. Cha
65. Escapes
66. Hammer part

DOWN

1. Hacks
2. Skilled
3. Certain people, zodiacally
4. Ayres of films
5. More stable
6. Dry
7. "__ but the brave . . ."
8. Word of contempt
9. Remains
10. Prognosticators
11. Greek goddess
12. Tops
13. Kennedy
18. Reflection
19. Victoria or Yosemite
23. Requiring
24. Tarzan
25. Former Belgian Premier
26. Actor Greene
27. Sharp ridge
28. Honor
29. Name for a discothèque
31. Anchorage areas
32. __ guerre
33. Props
35. Ethiopian title
36. Medit. island: Abbr.
43. "The Wreck of the Mary __"
48. Clamor
49. Of the kidneys
50. Hopi prayer sticks
51. Movies, in Roma
52. Held
53. Prune: Scot.
54. Feminine suffix
55. Thick hair
56. Mailman's hazard
57. In a while
58. Meet
59. Baking pit, in Hawaii
60. Irving character

38

ACROSS

1. City of Texas
5. U.S. research org.
8. Droplets
11. City of Spain
13. __ gras
14. Star in Cetus
15. Some platitudes
18. Title: Abbr.
19. Holly
20. Of yore
21. Negri of the silents
22. Livingstone's part of Africa
24. Constellation
27. Beldames
29. Musical instrument
30. Central state
31. Leg up
35. Within: Prefix
36. Principal force
37. Popular color
38. Famed couturier
39. Impersonates
40. Kind of practice
41. Set right
43. "Mack the Knife" creator
44. __ a sheet
47. Honor cards
49. Ancient Greek dialect
50. Found a line
51. Twice
54. Part of a "Keep Out" sign
58. Advantage
59. Pronoun
60. Smutch
61. Part of D.V.
62. Snoop
63. Latin "to be"

DOWN

1. Carry on
2. Class comprising the birds
3. French numeral
4. Corrida kudos
5. Nut: Fr.
6. Show __
7. Red or Black
8. Rectifier
9. Sea eagles
10. Common contraction
12. Musical direction
13. Sideshow attraction
14. Fountain items
16. The works
17. Sped
21. Disparaging
22. Below
23. Art course: Abbr.
24. Not up
25. Rajah's spouse
26. Preposition
28. One-sided wins
32. Prefix with valent
33. Quiet spell
34. Cloy
36. __ California
40. Cleans up
42. Numerical prefix
44. Toweled
45. Multitude
46. __ Jones, English architect
48. __ Magnon
50. Nimble
51. Arm, in France
52. "How sweet __!"
53. Auld lang __
55. Summit
56. Land mass: Abbr.
57. Juin, juillet et août

39

ACROSS

1. Adjective suffix
4. Immense
8. Location
12. Stake in a game
13. "__ by land . . ."
15. Asian range
16. __ on the map
17. Nellie Forbush's home
19. Comic strip character
20. Man's nickname
21. Integers: Abbr.
22. City on Rio Grande
27. Book of Bible: Abbr.
28. Boys
32. Terrapins' home
37. Cooker
38. Indian garment
39. Taxed
41. Dismounted
42. Substantiate
44. Superficial
46. Up in arms
47. Up: Prefix
48. Philadelphia attraction
55. Friend: Fr.
58. Forms in Greek philosophy
59. Calorie project
61. Home of Three Rivers Stadium
65. Doctrines
66. Space
67. Flower stalk
68. Hint
69. Grant's __
70. Genesis name
71. Region: Abbr.

DOWN

1. __ course
2. Kwajalein, e.g.
3. Abate
4. Book: Abbr.
5. Cuckoo
6. Attack
7. Sir, for example
8. California's Big __
9. Minnesota product
10. Mexican delicacy
11. Fraternal men
12. Indian mulberry
14. Bend
18. Tests
23. Some
24. Feature of Utah flats
25. Chicago airport
26. Underworld figure
29. "Whatever __ wants . . ."
30. Bad
31. Jet __
32. Trading center
33. In a line
34. Competitor
35. "Nothing doing!"
36. Coup __
38. Hot Springs, for one
40. Renounce
43. Indians
45. Commit a crime
49. Baby wear
50. Infer
51. Showed again
52. Decree
53. Thread
54. Nocturnal mammal
55. __ on the back
56. Spanish painter
57. Article
60. Part of Mao's name
62. Restaurant check
63. Mail center: Abbr.
64. "For __ a jolly good fellow"

40

ACROSS

1. Lend a hand
5. Hokum
9. About
14. Certain shape
15. Calhoun
16. Of a space
17. Western sight
18. Setting apart
20. Lures
22. Part of a golf club
23. Lose interest
24. Peer Gynt's mother
25. Drink
26. Serpent
29. Pinafore
31. German area
33. Prolong the coffee break
35. Pry
37. Newton
40. Accuse in a courtly way
42. Get feline revenge
44. Dress material
45. Cliff
47. Mother of Apollo
48. Kinds
50. Colors
52. Engage in seamy work
53. Iowa Indians
55. ___ rule
57. First ___
59. Noun form: Abbr.
60. Examines oneself
65. Clarify
67. Toward shelter
68. ". . . ___ horse to . . ."
69. Scent
70. Trick
71. Lapse
72. Confines
73. Defeats at bridge

DOWN

1. Direct to a target
2. On the level
3. Foot model
4. Without frills
5. Stable-owner's concern
6. Soil
7. Overdue debts
8. Church songs
9. Gas users
10. Annoy
11. Keeps on making a point
12. Hiawatha's craft
13. Writer of success stories
19. Sweetsop
21. Camper's gear
25. Kind of metabolism
26. Word of regret
27. Short-billed rail
28. Pernickety
30. Ages
32. Broadcast
34. Goes to the wall
36. Biblical brother
38. Deed, in France
39. Dog
41. Pen pal
43. Grooving tools
46. Parlor-game subject
49. Vanish: Scot.
51. Drink slowly
53. Heavy stake
54. Go, in France
56. Sharpen the razor
58. Darlings
60. River in Bavaria
61. Panay town
62. Hint
63. Tryout
64. Observes
66. Japanese herb

41

ACROSS

1. Barley beards
5. Word for some budgets
10. Clean the deck
14. Bar
15. Buffalo of India
16. Line-marking material
17. Acrobatic routine
19. Arthurian woman
20. Pad
21. Roman gods
23. Advice to Macduff
26. Appraise, with "up"
27. Rubbish
30. Free and clear
32. Certain compasses
35. Of the shoulder
36. Accompany
38. Shooter
39. Palm fiber
40. Tend, in a way
41. D.D.E.
42. Schubert's "__ könig"
43. Most wintry
44. Bowfin genus
45. Met again
47. Kind of cross
48. Scornful look
49. "Pardon me!"
51. Pay
53. Muckraking articles
56. Souls: Lat.
60. Sandarac tree
61. Recoil
64. Constituents of modern jam
65. Tea fare
66. Gardner
67. Mad, in Scotland
68. Audience reactions, sometimes
69. Beginning

DOWN

1. Helper: Abbr.
2. Stop!
3. Insensible
4. Brilliant
5. Savory
6. Dublin initials
7. Wildebeest
8. Word to a lifeguard
9. French heads
10. Flimsy
11. Season
12. Friend, in Lille
13. Garden areas
18. Sincere
22. Kind of light
24. "I'm not __ interested"
25. Time to start over
27. Horse opera
28. Warning device
29. Rivals the one-hoss shay
31. Thin paper
33. Former actor Jack
34. Promise
36. Cistern
37. Small bird
40. Stings
44. Resort near Nice
46. "Get __!"
48. Blab to the D.A.
50. In disarray
52. Horse features
53. "To __ his own"
54. Certain photo
55. Humane org.
57. Old gray one
58. Asian tree
59. Pieced out
62. Quarrel
63. Wayside, for one

42

ACROSS

1. Derrick part
5. Mild expletive
10. Mesozoic et al.
14. Stravinsky
15. Con __ (tenderly)
16. Honduran port
17. Isinglass
18. ID on stationery
20. Desk item of yore
22. Purse item
23. __ ease
24. Girl's name
25. Miami Beach features
27. Supports
31. __ nous
32. Disillusions
33. Mother's command
34. Site of Sugar Loaf
35. Husbands
36. Ripen
37. Cathedral: Ger.
38. British auto parts
39. Woman thief, in Rome
41. Shows contempt for
43. Summoned
44. Branch of medicine: Abbr.
45. Sans __
46. Musical direction
49. Rhythm
52. Comedian's forte
55. Brand
56. Restless desire
57. Kind of sale
58. First name in baseball lore
59. Sounds of discovery
60. Transfers
61. Anglo-Saxon slave

DOWN

1. Opera role
2. Once more, Western style
3. Saying popularized on TV
4. Vessel
5. Giant slain by Athena
6. Fish
7. Peppery
8. Craft
9. Early in the A.M.
10. Of a group
11. Emit vapor
12. Jai __
13. Marquis de __
19. Becomes angry
21. French pronoun
24. Adjusts
25. Flocks
26. Shish kebab ingredient
27. Desire wrongfully
28. Marquee names
29. Tidal flood
30. Stand in good __
32. Isaac's mother
35. Blood-pressure word
38. Nonsense
39. Honor
40. Gluck opera
42. Time periods
43. Moves on momentum
45. Location
46. Capital of Western Samoa
47. Famous Yankee
48. Early South American
50. Son of Adam
51. Gaelic
53. Chill
54. Reference work: Abbr.

43

ACROSS

1. Roentgen discovery
5. Coil: Prefix
10. Curves
14. Colleen's land
15. Morals man
16. Exchange fee
17. Harass
18. Thorny
20. French season
21. Life stories, for short
22. Missiles
23. Cheese bases
25. Cans
26. Measures: Abbr.
27. Like some birds
31. Proverb
34. Hamlet's objective
35. Eye part
36. Greek letters
37. School orgs.
38. Newspaper article
40. Mimics
41. Yankee Doodle took one
42. Anger
43. Intrigue
44. Oppressive
48. Breed of hog
50. Guthrie
51. Farm unit
52. Hatred of foreigners
54. Diminutive ending
55. Inner: Prefix
56. Jostle
57. Property claim
58. Shoal
59. O'Casey and others
60. Diet

DOWN

1. Medit. vessel
2. Lariat
3. Ram
4. In addition
5. Indian antelopes
6. Melons and squashes
7. Egyptian goddess
8. Nessen
9. Broadway events
10. Good-time Charlie
11. S-shaped curve
12. Gains
13. Drunkard
19. Burn
21. Plant stem
24. Describing some spirits
25. Not dissonant
27. Bristles
28. Heraldry word
29. Mark
30. Meeting: Abbr.
31. Syrian city, to French
32. Pedestal part
33. "It's __ to tell a lie"
34. Actor Conrad
36. Rolls
39. Deck
40. Mars: Prefix
42. Relatives
44. Constellation
45. Old port of Rome
46. Absolute
47. Ancient name for Aswan
48. Sand hill, in Britain
49. Wavy, in heraldry
50. Eban of Israel
52. Dry: Prefix
53. Bravo
54. Pixie

44

ACROSS

1. Gypsy
4. Roll logs
8. Father, in Spain
13. Nigerian people
14. Ancient theaters
15. Wartime menaces
17. Dogie phrase
19. Spreading out
20. Clermont
22. Celebrations
25. Passé
26. King, in drama
27. Former Chief Justice
30. Longing
34. Man's nickname
35. French waterway
36. New England city
37. Famed musicals
40. Having auricles
41. Idler
42. Poker word
43. Scanty
44. Plaintiffs
45. Breakwater
46. Space
47. Dice player
48. Alaska
55. Swapped
56. Le Roi Soleil
60. Horse
61. Moslem call to prayer
62. Ivy Leaguer
63. Dig
64. Gender: Abbr.
65. Small drink

DOWN

1. Outfit
2. Waistband
3. Quip
4. Soft mass
5. Lion
6. Let
7. Lake: It.
8. Go after
9. To the rear
10. Stupid one
11. Part of a fence
12. Latin abbr.
16. Cute
18. Distant
21. ___ news
22. Enamels
23. TV adjunct
24. Sidewise: Prefix
27. Who, in Italy
28. Bank capers
29. British victim in Revolution
30. Adjective ending
31. Surveyor's equipment
32. Louisianian
33. Miss Prynne
35. Postal initials
36. Grain: Fr.
38. Muffin
39. Dutch weight
44. Kind of shoe
45. Willie of baseball fame
46. Avidity
47. Lighter part
48. Aves
49. Son of Aphrodite
50. Twist
51. Spanish port
52. Pastry
53. Slime
54. Cookout on Oahu
57. Strange: Prefix
58. Sinkiang river
59. Big shot: Abbr.

45

ACROSS

1. Eastern-church title
5. Old Syrian fabric
9. Thing of value
14. Shades
15. Road, in Germany
16. Extreme
17. Former, old style
18. Height: Prefix
19. Kemal and others
20. Saver of a sort
23. Brit. fliers
24. Turkish weights
25. Home of el toro
28. Steelhead
30. Camp item
32. __ Nidre
33. Swan genus
35. French possessive
36. Tidal flood
37. Deck officer
39. Remove
41. Some mail addresses: Abbr.
42. Landon and others
43. Force, in old Rome
44. Austrian statesman
46. Labor org.
47. Hook
48. Banquet
51. Post-__
53. Burden
56. P.I. tree
57. Goatsuckers
60. Former Met pitcher Roger
62. Crooked
63. Music groups
64. Swiss city
65. Network
66. Peak
67. Man of many causes
68. Sandarac
69. Timetable, for short

DOWN

1. Have __
2. College figure
3. One way to stand
4. Wine city of Italy
5. Taken __
6. Hiding place
7. Poinsettia, for one
8. Soon
9. One seeking to escape reality
10. Electioneer
11. Uncomfortable time
12. One reaction to a mouse
13. Corp. officials
21. In __ (wholly)
22. Two fins
26. Gare du __
27. Pub drinks
29. Caucho trees
31. Dawn goddess
34. Make over
36. Scottish hill
37. Damage
38. Phone greeting, in Paris
40. Initials on a dismissal notice
45. "Win __, lose . . ."
47. __ counter
49. Famous dancer
50. Threw
52. Biblical possessive
54. Blood vessel
55. Beauty-parlor gear
58. S.A. rubber
59. Lupino and others
60. Firearm: Abbr.
61. Gov't. agency

46

ACROSS

1. African village
5. Pokes
9. Broadcast
14. Gully, in North Africa
15. Adjective ending
16. "__ là?" (Who goes there?)
17. W.W. II powers
18. Exactly right words
20. Reading aid
22. Lets up
23. Dear me!
24. Kittenish sound
25. Hussar's gear
28. Enraged
32. Residence
33. Sweetheart
34. Verb ending
35. Belgian city
36. Got along
37. __ au rhum
38. Sharp-cornered: Abbr.
39. Bombastic
40. Goof
41. Danger
43. Unseaworthy
44. Black
45. Pinza
47. Civvies
49. Sneaked away
53. Table wines
55. __ de Pinos
56. "Feed __, starve . . ."
57. Encourage
58. Winglike
59. Opens wide
60. Occupied
61. Taboo thing

DOWN

1. Exchange
2. Rainy-day cry
3. Tennis term
4. Certain bridge plays
5. Agra's river
6. African plants
7. Swiss coin
8. Older ones: Abbr.
9. Harsh
10. Struggle
11. Ceremonial
12. Nights before
13. Existed
19. Taunted
21. Robt. __
24. Colon and dinar
25. Hindu society
26. Have __ to pick
27. Small drum
28. Prolix
29. Moon goddess
30. Soviet republic
31. Arctic pioneer
33. Famed blues composer
36. Wooden cask
37. Crudely obtuse
39. Newspaper section
40. Radar reading
42. Trivial nonsense
45. Gardner et al.
46. Piquant
47. Transparent mineral
48. Running alone: Abbr.
49. Philippine port
50. Formerly Christiania
51. __ Bator
52. South Sea staple
53. Sharp turn
54. Small amount

47

ACROSS

1. Agreement
5. Billiard stroke
10. Prod
14. French composer
15. Mme. de __
16. Get under one's skin
17. Islands off Ireland
18. "__ Venice"
20. Desire eagerly
22. Inlet
23. Point in one's favor
24. Cuckoo
25. Rodents
28. Huntley and others
30. Egg: Prefix
31. Winter ailment
34. Certain neckline
36. Table syrups
38. Bikini, for one
39. Owns
40. Pronoun
41. Role in "Carmen"
43. Specialty for Schwarzkopf
44. "Ballad of the __ Cafe"
45. Fiber cluster
46. Poet Marianne
47. German composer
49. "Brother __"
52. Near
55. Indian weight
56. Musician Kaye
58. U.S. pianist of 1800s
61. Name in N.Y. theater
62. Math ratio words
63. Daises
64. It's often golden
65. Heyerdahl
66. Former Olympic star
67. Part of a Grieg title

DOWN

1. Old Spanish coin
2. Copland
3. Well-tempered item
4. A flat, for one
5. College degree
6. Sergeant __
7. Indian garments
8. Washington V.I.P.'s
9. Hebrew judge
10. Herbage
11. Artist's medium
12. Lily
13. Skillful
19. Some musical works
21. Gustav Holst symphonic work
26. Had a bite
27. Mother of mankind
29. Robust
31. Strauss opera
32. __ majesty
33. Addict
34. Containers
35. Portico, in Sparta
36. Partner of feather
37. Partner of Sonny
39. TV special for Bob
42. State: Abbr.
43. Chaney
46. Game fish
47. Instructor
48. Union general
50. Plentiful
51. Does an office job
52. Shake: Abbr.
53. Empty talk
54. Klemperer
57. Port on Guam
59. Navy man: Abbr.
60. Neighbor of Neb.

48

ACROSS

1. Turner
5. Candy
10. Circle of water
14. Animals
15. Banish
16. Time __ half
17. Linen fiber
18. Link
19. Designations for secret papers of 1790s
20. So-so
22. Gender
23. Makes friends
24. Audience
26. Slacken
28. Helped
32. __ yellow leaf (old age)
36. Crafty
37. Army V.I.P.
39. Doctor's instrument
40. Live
41. Ship wrecked off U.S. in 1928
43. Gardner
44. José's operatic victim
46. Ad __
47. Beaver skin
48. Lengths
50. Vexes
52. Mastodon features
54. Recent: Prefix
55. Historian's concerns
58. Querying words
60. Medit. ship
64. Resembling: Suffix
65. Seat
67. Defendant's plea
68. __-Coburg
69. Florida city
70. Corn lily
71. Tennyson lady
72. Garden flowers
73. Roman portico

DOWN

1. Attic
2. Shaft
3. Certain tide
4. Care
5. Commandment number
6. Cuts
7. Jack-of-all-trades
8. Melts
9. Kind of man
10. Brazilian dances
11. Cameo stone
12. Dressing tool
13. Russian agency
21. Grammar case: Abbr.
23. Queen of Scots et al.
25. Rulers
27. Wordbook
28. In front
29. Cleansing agent
30. Put into action
31. __ Plaines
33. Part of a Dickens title
34. Emphatic negation
35. Attracts
38. Indefinite degree
41. Planet
42. Plunder
45. Like household gas or water
47. Western capital
49. Draft
51. Lone Star nickname
53. Marine hazard
55. Eleanora of stage
56. King or Ladd
57. Urban vehicle
59. Kind of flight
61. Squarish
62. Yale men
63. Layer
65. Bribe
66. Negligent

49

ACROSS

1. Grizzly, for one
5. Uses the teeth
10. Tissue suspension
14. French pronoun
15. Have __ (watch out)
16. "I'm all __"
17. Parisian friends
18. Maugham novel
20. One on a fixed income
22. Morning event
23. Frightening
25. Large shark
26. "The Age of __"
28. River to Rio Grande
31. __-toe
34. Cry of disgust
36. Lizard
37. Two __ kind
38. Leave port
41. Bowling number
42. Kind of verb: Abbr.
44. Partner of dash
45. __ a bee
47. Lama land
49. Famous rider
51. "It's __ to tell a lie"
53. Tape again
57. Mishandled
60. Narrow
61. Redundant city
63. Hayworth
64. "__ Rhythm"
65. Bird sound
66. Steady
67. We: Fr.
68. Type of remark
69. Office item

DOWN

1. Scouts' founder
2. Gantry
3. Put in a row
4. Turn the key again
5. Type of lie
6. Mythological flier
7. Russian river
8. Asteroid
9. Antitoxin
10. Barrel of suds
11. Tourist mecca
12. Work units
13. Words of understanding
19. Bean or dragon
21. Concepts
24. Shift of a sort
27. Air group: Abbr.
29. Genus of trees
30. Without: Fr.
31. "Hop __!"
32. Moroccan area
33. Fonda film
35. One way to spend the winter
39. Craggy hill
40. Wigglers and spinners
43. End-of-game announcements
46. Fastened
48. River to the Danube
50. Type of threat
52. Salamanders
54. Drab color
55. Appraises
56. Bent the elbow
57. Victor's words
58. __ Maggiore
59. Day starter
62. Pacific neckpiece

50

ACROSS

1. Supervise
8. Buckingham and Crystal
15. Construction worker
16. Perk up
17. Air-signal devices
18. Non-blood relative
19. Noisy, in music
21. Source of formic acid
22. Gibbon
23. Stupefy
26. Aphrodite's prize
29. Pinnacle
30. Festivals
33. Cheers
34. Darling
36. Potato bud
37. Exclamation
38. "__ Sylphides"
39. Educ. group
40. Folk-lore heroine
43. Bare place on mountainside
44. Cathode's partner
45. Dotted cube
46. Keystone-cop event
47. Fortitude
49. Macaw
50. Anne or Marie: Abbr.
52. City near Albany
57. Crescent-shaped
60. Milk glass
61. Haliotis
62. Ancient district of Greece
63. Chopin composition
64. "Let's __" (child's favorite)

DOWN

1. Spheres
2. __ armis
3. Eternally
4. Abrogates
5. Asian plain
6. Weird
7. Formerly, of old
8. Footbridge
9. Bruckner or Chekhov
10. Position of golf ball
11. Current unit, for short
12. African port
13. Kind of jacket
14. Dispatched
20. Woodwind
24. Sounds of disgust
25. West
26. Palm
27. Deposit
28. Extraordinary
29. Well-known look-alike
31. Fields
32. Icy look
34. Lancelot or Galahad
35. Pekoe
37. Metrical units
41. Presidential initials
42. Property right
43. Small onion
46. Bring into existence
48. Drift
49. Turkish coin
50. Thick slice
51. Helicon
53. Castile
54. Wing: Fr.
55. Blue grape pigment
56. Perused
58. Wholly
59. __ man

Answers

1

```
S C U P S   T I A S   C O N S
H O R A E   O R L E   I M A M
I M A G E   P R O D   R A T E
M O L O K A I   E A T C R O W
    D O L C E   T A U
B E D A U B   S P E L L I N G
L A R   T U T T I   C A N O E
U T A H   M E R E S   R E V E
N E M O S   S E D E R   R E S
T R A V I A T A   N E S T L E
    E F T   T A S S E
W H A R T O N   R E T R A C E
H O N E   L E E R   I V I E D
O V E R   L A V A   V E R D E
M E W S   S T A Y   E S S E N
```

2

```
E Q U A B L E   B O A S T E R
G U N R O O M   U P B O R N E
R A C K S U P   S T U D I E S
E S O   S P E C I E S   B M I
S H U N   E R R E D   R U I N
S E T U P   O E R   P A N E S
  S H A R E R S   D U D E S
    N I L S   H A R I
  C O C O A   T A X I C A B
S A V E R   B A N   M A D A M
I R E S   L A R G O   L A R A
M A R   M I S S I V E   M B S
I M A G I N E   N E L L I E S
L E G U M E S   G R I S T L E
E L E M E N T   S T A T E L Y
```

3

```
W A S P   P A L O S   I R A N
E C H O   A G O R A   M I C A
E R O S   D O U B L E P L A Y
P E W T E R   S O V I E T S
    W A V E R S   N E O
A G I L E   E A R   R U S T S
B U N   N A P L E S   S T O W
A I D   T R E L L I S   A W E
S L O B   C L I E N T   G E E
H E W E R   S E N   A L E R T
    T I M   S T A T I C
O B L I G E D   S E T O F F
D R A M A T U R G Y   M A I L
D I M E   A N N I E   U C L A
S E E S   L E A S T   S H A G
```

4

```
  C A W   C O R E S   M I L O
B A R I   O P E R A   I N I T
A V E S   N A V A L   D E V I
N I C H E S   U T I L I Z E S
C L A Y P I G E O N S
    W I S E     E T H A N E
R H F A C T O R S   S A T O N
E E L S   S L U M S   N O R D
A M A H S   S E A L S K I N S
P O N Y U P   C I T Y
    B L A C K P E P P E R
F I R E S A L E   S P A R T A
A M I D   S L U S H   N U N S
T I M E   M A T E O   K N A P
S T A N   A Y A R D   Y E S
```

5

```
L I O N S   I T S A   H A H A
O N T O P   S A I L   O X E N
F R O T H   O K L A H O M A N
T E E   I S L E T   U R A R E
    O N E T O   B R A N D
M C M L X X   N E E D Y
O O I D   K A R E L   F E D
O N C E I N A L I F E T I M E
D Y E   M A L L S   A L M E
    M A G I C   B U R S A R
  S L O G S   O L E N T
S T O R E   U M I A K   D I A
C R O S S O V E R   I S I N G
O I S E   H E R A   N O R G E
T A E L   M A S S   D I K E S
```

6

```
NASA · SNAFU · ABCS
OWNS · TALON · GOOP
REAL · OTTER · ASTA
ASPIRATE · ESTHER
· KATY · TAPE ·
PREENS · DESISTED
LOPAT · PITON · ELI
APOS · QUEEN · SPUR
TEC · BURTS · CHIDE
ASHTREES · GOODER
· EASE · BLOC ·
EXTANT · SWANKIER
PROP · IOWAN · ECRU
IAGO · OLAND · ROIL
CYST · NEMAS · SNEE
```

7

```
· SARAH · TEENER
ALAMO · WANDERED
SHIVER · ABNEGATE
LABE · SULLA · ASIF
ARAL · ENTE · STUNT
TABS · SIE · SPIRAL
ENA · DEAR · LIVELY
· CANT · MICE ·
MOTORS · GAPE · DEM
EVINCE · RIP · PINA
NETTY · DAZE · AVIS
ARAR · BODED · TOSS
CANALIZE · OVERLY
ELICITED · FENCE
LATTER · FETED ·
```

8

```
SQUID · CHIMERA
TUNDRA · AERONAUT
RATION · BRINGSTO
AIROUT · BONA · POT
FLUTTERING · DUCT
EYESHADES · LITRE
· TVS · CAVIAR
AMPERES · FOMENTS
TERROR · POX ·
ANENT · TRACKSTAR
LESE · PROMONTORY
OLS · LAIT · MORBID
SAUTERNE · BLAISE
SURNAMES · SLIDER
· SETFAST · STENS
```

9

```
HORSE · SWEDE · ODA
AROOM · PALED · NAN
SCUBADIVING · ENG
PAT · NOTE · IMAGE
· LANE · PAEAN ·
RELATE · GEMSTONE
IRATE · BESET · TOP
VASE · SENOR · OHNO
EST · ELLIS · FREED
REIGNITE · HEARSE
· NEEDS · POLL ·
BELEM · POLO · PFC
ARI · INFLUENTIAL
LIN · EELER · RETIA
LEE · SOYAS · YEARN
```

10

```
ANC · TAMPA · HEP
LEAS · URALS · SAVE
SOPPINGWET · EVEN
ONTARIO · BEARERS
· INKS · ERIE ·
· BOIS · INSOMNIA
PLUS · PRO · ISDONE
GOSH · REBID · IDES
ABLATE · LDS · POLE
SYRETTES · LIME
· METE · PATE ·
SALADIN · COCOTTE
PROD · ENCLOSURES
ANNA · SISAL · SILT
DOE · TSADE · CEE
```

11

```
L U N A   H A S   N U B I A N
A P O T H E G M   A T A X I A
M O V E A B L E   B O R I N G
A N A   T R E E S   P E A T S
    W H E T   T A I L
N A R R O W   M A L A Y A N S
O S I E R   D I V A N   G O P
L I M N   V O T E R   C O M A
A D E   S E M E S   C A R A T
N E R V E G A S   P A R A D E
  A L A I   S A R D
S N A R K   N A I V E   B E A
C A N D I A   C R E E P E R S
A S T O R S   M E R R I M A C
T H A N K S   E S S   G A S H
```

12

```
M A S T S   S W A T   R E C D
A L O H A   T O B Y   O V E R
R O D I N   E R I C   B A D E
G U A R D S   L E O N I D A S
    S L O Y D   B O N E R S
P I S T O L E S   B U S
A R I   T O M E S   N O B E L
G O L F   S E R A C   N O S E
E N O L S   N I O R D   L A S
    A H A   E N O R M O U S
P O T T E R   S E P I A
S C U B A R I G   S E N O R S
A R R U   A G A R   S T R A W
L E N S   N O M E   U L T R A
M A S H   T R E T   P E H A N
```

13

```
M E T A   A G A T E   C A P A
A B E T   C U M I N   O V A L
C O N F E C T I O N   N E L L
E N T I R E   S O L A C E S
    R A D I I   B E N
R E A S S E S S   L A T E S T
O M I T   L O V E S   N C O
S I S   R E A L I S T   L O W
E L L   I R M A S   P A W N
S E E I N G   T O P S O I L S
    A G O   E R U P T
P R O M O T E   R A I D E R
A H A B   I R I D E S C E N T
P E R U   Z A N D E   H A T E
S A S S   E T T E S   E R O S
```

14

```
E G E S T   M T N S   A Q U A
L E F T A   O H I O   S U N G
S A F E T Y B E L T   P A T A
  R U N   O M E   L I C I T
  B L O C K A N D T A C K L E
B O G   R E N D E R S
O X E Y E   O V A   U S D C
C E N T E R O F I N E R T I A
E S T S   O R T   R O O S T
    S W A H I L I   N C O
H A R D L I N E B A C K E R
A L A R Y   L A N   A C E
S O J A   S H I N G U A R D S
T E A K   A O N E   A B O I L
A S H E   O Y E Z   R A P T O
```

15

```
L E I S   P A C E   C A R I A
A X L E   E R R S   O B O L S
G I L A   R E A S O N A B L E
S T E R L I N G   R I T E S
    C O L A   C A F E
A M A H S   C A T E R I N G
B A L E S   G O N E R   D I N
E N D S   B R E E D   S E T A
A N E   P R O D S   S T A R T
M A R P L O T S   O R L E S
    R A K E   S T O A
P E A C E   C H A N N E L S
M I S T E R C H A N   G R I T
I N N E R   H A R K   E S S E
D E E D S   A T E S   R E A R
```

16

S	C	R	I	M	P		S	U	N	S	E	T
F	O	R	E	V	E	R		T	R	A	P	P	E	R
E	M	U	L	A	T	E		I	G	R	A	I	N	E
R	E	S		N	E	S	T	L	E	D		T	A	P
R	O	A	M		R	I	O	T	S		B	O	C	A
E	N	D	O	W		D	A	S		T	A	M	E	S
T	E	E	T	E	R	E	D		L	A	T	E	S	T
			H	I	E	D		T	A	M	A
A	S	S	E	R	T		S	H	R	I	V	E	L	S
T	H	I	R	D		H	U	E		L	I	M	I	T
M	O	B	S		S	I	E	P	I		A	I	N	E
O	W	E		B	A	N	D	I	E	D		N	E	A
S	E	R	V	A	N	T		P	R	O	T	E	A	M
T	R	I	E	S	T	E		E	N	R	I	N	G	S
	Y	A	N	K	E	D		R	E	M	O	T	E

17

C	L	A	P		S	T	I	R	S		J	E	N	A
H	O	H	O		K	O	R	A	N		A	V	E	R
A	W	O	R	M	I	N	A	F	U	R	C	O	A	T
P	S	T		A	R	A	N		B	A	K	E	R	Y
			P	I	L	L		A	B	I	E
S	K	I	L	L	S		S	W	E	L	T	E	R
A	N	N	A	S		B	O	A	R	S		N	A	P
R	O	S	Y		B	E	A	K	S		M	D	I	I
A	W	E		D	R	A	K	E		H	O	U	S	E
	S	T	A	R	E	R	S		G	A	P	P	E	D
			B	O	A	S		L	A	N	E
U	N	M	A	S	K		E	E	R	O		I	C	C
S	C	I	S	S	O	R	S	G	R	I	N	D	E	R
I	O	N	E		F	U	S	E	E		O	L	L	A
A	S	K	S		F	E	A	S	T		G	E	L	T

18

D	O	M	A	I	N		A	T	R	O	P	A
E	V	I	L	L	Y		P	R	O	P	O	S	E
S	T	E	R	I	L	E		P	O	L	E	N	T	A
A	A	R	O	N		C	A	L	E	N	D	A	R
L	I	S		A	T	A	L	L		H	E	R	L
A	L	E	P		B	A	L	L		M	A	R	T	Y
D	E	E	R	P	A	R	K		B	A	N
	D	R	I	E	S	T		R	A	I	D	E	R
			N	E	H		M	A	L	D	E	M	E	R
C	R	O	C	K		S	I	N	K		D	I	V	E
H	A	R	E		H	A	N	K	Y		N	E	P
A	V	A	I	L	I	N	G		S	T	E	A	L
S	I	N	G	I	N	G		W	O	M	A	N	L	Y
E	N	G	O	R	G	E		A	T	O	N	C	E
E	E	R	I	E	R		R	A	G	G	E	D

19

C	A	M		M	O	T	E	L	S		P	S	I	S
U	D	I		I	M	A	R	E	T		R	U	L	E
P	O	L	Y	D	I	P	S	I	A		O	P	E	N
	R	I	A	N	T			A	G	R
P	A	T	R	I		S	O	U	R	C	R	E	A	M
O	R	I	N	G		P	A	N	O	R	A	M	A	S
L	E	A	S	H		A	T	R	O		M	E	R	S
			T	O	R	M	E	N	T
A	N	T	A		I	R	E	S		A	L	O	F	T
S	C	A	P	E	G	O	A	T		N	A	C	R	E
S	O	U	P	B	O	W	L	S		T	R	E	A	T
	R	E	B			P	A	G	A	N
E	M	I	T		C	O	R	P	U	L	E	N	C	E
R	A	N	I		O	R	M	O	L	U		I	E	S
D	I	E	T		T	R	A	I	L	S		A	S	P

20

S	A	L	P		R	A	P		P	I	C	K
A	D	A	R		E	R	A	S		A	D	A	N	A
G	I	V	E	S	B	A	C	K		R	O	D	I	N
	B	A	Y	O	U		K	E	G		L	I	F	T
	E	X	T	E	M	P	O	R	I	Z	E
F	O	L	D		T	A	E		P	A	Z
I	R	E		D	A	R	N	S		J	E	R	K
B	E	D	R	O	L	L		Q	U	A	S	H	E	S
	G	A	E	A		Y	O	U	T	H		U	N	A
	A	L	I		L	I	I		A	S	T	O
	B	U	L	L	F	I	D	D	L	E	R
L	O	K	I		E	T	H		I	R	E	N	E
A	M	A	Z	E		T	A	N	Z	A	N	I	A	N
I	B	S	E	N		O	N	C	E		O	R	S	O
S	E	S	S		D	O	S		T	A	T	S

21

```
JANE MASON DADS
IRON OSTEO ABIE
LORD ICOSI TORT
TOMORROW SLEUTH
    ROAN BIER
GRASPS PRESSING
RANEE CRASS LON
ABED SHUNT SIVA
IBA SPANS UPPER
LIRIPIPE TRIALS
    GALE CHAT
UNFURL GAROTTES
NORA ANODE IOTA
DION GOUGE NUNS
OLGA ESTES GRAS
```

22

```
POMP DIPS SEWED
ALEE IDEA TREVI
READ NELL UNTIE
COLDCOMFORT BLT
    LOS PETAL
SIDEWALK DETAIL
ARR SUERS RINSE
BEYS ROOTS SKEW
INGER SNAKE ERE
NEUTER AGITATES
    LADED LID
CIC WARMBLOODED
ACHOO EIRE POGO
SEENO SLOT TRAM
ADDED SOWS SALE
```

23

```
BALTI JAY ACTS
AGAIN OURS CLAP
RELET INSINCERE
REORIENT AERATE
    SMUT ALTERED
SIR ARSONISTS
CREATE CID ITAL
AMILE BTS MOOLA
RANT DEE CONRAD
    SERRATION YES
PATROON TRAM
ELANDS ACADEMIE
NOTASSUCH IDIOT
CHET YARE SIENA
EASE WED MANAS
```

24

```
FARGO UTAH REST
OPINE RELY ESPY
BIFURCATES CAIN
SSE SALE TRIUNE
    STRS BEEP
PATES AUROREAN
CASED LILI ONNO
RUHR SAMBA CATO
ALEE TIES PATEN
MINOTAUR CITES
    GILS DOTE
FURROW OILS ARE
AREA ASBESTOSIS
LISP RIOT ORION
ACTH TRES PEASE
```

25

```
TESLA SHAH EKED
ODEUM REDO XERO
GARLICSALT HAIL
AMBUSH PITTANCE
    SOW BEAU
TUSK IRA ABSORB
ANTE CASK ATSEA
XRAYTECHNICIANS
IRISH KEEN OGEE
SARTRE SAD NEWS
    OONA DIZ
GARNERED GESTIC
OBOE OREGONPINE
BLUR LIEU DATED
SEES LEMS AROSE
```

26

```
CAR   LTCOL  LEAD
LIEU  AROMA  ETTE
EDEN  VIRES  TUNA
FALSEIMPRESSION
  USETO   ROC
RAMIT  ORA  SALEM
EMOTES ALL  LEDA
CIGARETTEFILTER
ANUB  ARE  STIGMA
POLLS IFI  STOAT
   ETD  INDIA
JAPANESESANDMAN
ALEC  COLUM  AERO
DUET  ADDLE  YAMS
EMPS  LASTS   LYE
```

27

```
FAST  ADOPT  TANK
OMAR  SULLA  ALAI
GILA  ABEAR  NEIN
GRANT LONDONFOG
   SAKI  SYNE
CALAMINE  CRAWL
OTIC  LESLIE  VIA
DONT  TRAIN  SONS
ENE  ASSUME  EWES
SENSE  SARGASSO
   ARAS  BTUS
TOKYOROSE  TODAY
ISEE  GLEAN  NONE
ASER  OVINE  ETNA
SANS  TENSE  DEAR
```

28

```
ECCE  MOTA  HARSH
CHAT  AMOR  ORATE
LAMELLATE  LAMIA
AFIRE  RENAL  IRR
TENNER  MADAM
  OATER  ONEWAY
CARLSTADT  DRAMA
OLE  SPEWS  SIR
LEAST  TAILGATED
TELLER  NIOBE
  YAHOO  TREPAN
OFF  COPRA  ELATE
SILVA  EDGARAPOE
SNEAK  REED  REND
ADDLE  ARES  DREY
```

29

```
SRI  TEAKS  OMNIS
HEM  HOSEA  REEFS
APPLESEED  ALFIE
KLIEG  ANDANTE
OYSTER  SERG  RMS
  TOOK  NEE  TOE
CHERRIES  OFHIDE
MYLEG  GAR  RATED
DOESIT  CHEERILY
RIV  ART  OWED
SDA  PIES  ESTHER
  THEMATA  TOILE
ITISA  PINEAPPLE
STOIC  OPART  PES
MYNAH  TEPEE  ONE
```

30

```
JONAH  DET  SPEAK
ELOGE  ILO  PODGE
EDSEL  NIE  ASIAN
PEENING  RANTERS
  RETARD  RUDE
   SAO  SARONG
GREAT  NOCTUIDAE
ROMP  GRR  OEIL
IMMODESTY  CRASS
SEALER  BAA
  OVID  ALPACA
IMAGINE  BLATANT
NOVIA  ANI  BRINE
CREST  LEE  LARID
HASTE  SOS  ESNES
```

31

```
A M P S   U P A S   A D A M S
L O O P   N A M A   M E D A L
M L L E   A S I F   A F O R E
S E L L O U T   A D H E R E D
  U L E   O G R E   N E S S  
E N T E R   R A I S E S      
L A I R   B A L   T H E I S M
A Z O   C O L L A R S   N E O
M I N I O N   E R Y   S F A X
    N O N C O M   C A L L A  
S L O T   E O N S   A L A    
P O V E R T Y   R E B A T E D
I M A G E   O R A L   B I N E
R A T E S   T I C S   L O D E
E X E R T   E P E E   E N O S
```

32

```
S P O U T   S A L E   B A G S
C U R S E   O B A D   A U R A
A R D E N   R I N G   T R O W
R E N D   H A N D Y   M O T S
E L A   C O S T A   F A R O E
F I N G A L   R U M I N A N T
U N C A S E   A S I A        
L E E R E D   A N N A L S    
      O U S E   S C O R I A  
O N C E U P O N   M E D I A L
R O A M S   C U R I E   E K E
A N T E   D O R I C   O T O S
T E N N   O T I C   D A T U M
E G A D   E R N E   O H A R A
S O P S   S A G S   S U S A N
```

33

```
A M B L E   L A H R   I M P S
S I L A S   I S E E   N O L O
H E A D S T R E A M   H I E R
E N C   A H E A D   C A R A T
    K A Y E   W A L L E T S  
O A H U   A H E A D O F      
S P E N T   E R I E S   H E R
L O A T H   A N T   E L E M I
O D D   E D D I E   T E A M S
    H O O T E R S   A D A K  
I N F E R N O   E A R P      
R E L A Y   F O U R S   I D E
E G A D   H O R S E S H E A D
N E M O   A O N E   T A C N A
E V E N   S T E S   S T E A M
```

34

```
A C C T   V O L G A   U L A N
S H O E M A K I N G   L O B O
T E N N E S S E A N   Y O R E
A C C E N T   D R A M A T I S
  K I T S   R O S T E N      
P R E S   L O W   E R O D E S
E E R   M E A N S   E V E N T
R I G   O D D   O D S   S C I
S N E L L   S P L I T   P O E
E S S E N E   R O N   D E U S
    S A L M O N   C O R N    
N E W S R O O M   S E N A T E
I S E E   P R O M E N A D E R
S N A P   E S T I M A T O R S
H E R S   R E E S E   E S S E
```

35

```
B L O C   L A P P S   S C O T
L A V A   E E R I E   T R U E
O V E R   T R O P E   R A G S
T E N O N   O V E R S I G H T
    M I D G E S   H A S T Y  
E B B   P A R R   A R T      
V O I D   T A B   D E I C E S
I N T E R I M   R E D O U B T
L E S S O N   G E M   N E R O
    T A G   E V A N   S O W  
U S E R S   C H I S E L      
T H R O T T L E S   W A L K S
T O N Y   I O N I A   S A N E
E R I E   P U N T S   E M I T
R E E D   S T A S H   R A T S
```

36

```
AGAS BOMB BASAL
LABOROVER BRINE
ELABORATE LATIN
SEC BOLERO BOLD
 SKEINS ALINES
IBSEN KOREA
SUER SIDER SHE
BRAYLIKEADONKEY
AGT ONERS OESE
 ANDES ALLIS
FARMER FILLET
ATEE ASTART TAP
CORES PICKABONE
ENURE UTTERANCE
SENSE ROOD YSER
```

37

```
CALL SANTAS EAT
ABEE AROUSE ROE
BLOWININTHEWIND
SES MEDE ERASE
 EAR ASST
SLANG SAP ERNS
PORTERAGES ROOT
AREA ALOMA FAMA
ANTI SUGARDADDY
KEEL TON ELSES
 INRE PAL
CANOE SEAR MBA
SINGININTHERAIN
INN SAMETO INTO
TEA ELUDES PEEN
```

38

```
WACO NBS DEW
AVILA FOIE MIRA
GENERALIZATIONS
ESQ ILEX OLDEN
 POLA DARKEST
ARIES CRONES
BANJO IOWA HELP
ENTO BRUNT AQUA
DIOR ACTS SKULL
 ADJUST WEILL
WHITEAS ACES
IONIC SIRE BIS
PRIVATEPROPERTY
EDGE OURS STAIN
DEO PRY ESSE
```

39

```
 IAL VAST SITE
ANTE ONEIF URAL
ADOT LITTLEROCK
LULU ALEX NOS
 ELPASOTEXAS
 NAH MALES
 MARYLAND STOVE
SARI TRIED ALIT
PROVE EXTERNAL
ATWAR ANO
 LIBERTYBELL
AMI EIDE DIET
PITTSBURGH ISMS
AREA SCAPE CLUE
TOMB ENOS TER
```

40

```
HELP BLAH CIRCA
OVAL RORY AREAL
MESA EARMARKING
ENTICEMENTS TOE
 NOD ASE BEER
ASP TIER SAAR
LOAF NOSE ISAAC
ARRAIGN SCRATCH
SATIN SCAR LETO
 ILKS HUES SEW
SACS ASA AID
PLU INTROSPECTS
ILLUSTRATE ALEE
LEADA ODOR RUSE
ERROR PENS SETS
```

41

```
AWNS  TIGHT  SWAB
SHUT  ARNEE  LIME
SOMERSAULT  ENID
TABLET  PENATES
   LAYON  SIZE
OFFAL  NET  GYROS
ALAR  BEWITH  TAW
TAL  BABYSIT  IKE
ERL  ICIEST  AMIA
RESAT  TAU  SNEER
    AHEM  REMIT
EXPOSES  ANIMAE
ARAR  SPRINGBACK
CARS  SCONE  ERLE
HYTE  YAWNS  SEED
```

42

```
MAST  PSHAW  ERAS
IGOR  AMORE  TELA
MICA  LETTERHEAD
INKWELL  HANKIE
    ILLAT  TONI
HOTELS  CRUTCHES
ENTRE  SOURS  EAT
RIO  SAVES  AGE
DOM  TYRES  LADRA
SNEERSAT  CALLED
    PATH  SOUCI
ARIOSO  CADENCE
PUNCHLINES  SEAR
ITCH  ICENT  TRIS
AHAS  CEDES  ESNE
```

43

```
XRAY  SPIRO  BOWS
EIRE  AESOP  AGIO
BAIT  SPINESCENT
ETE  BIOS  NIKES
CASEINS  TINS
INS  SONGLESS
ADAGE  VENGEANCE
LASH  BETAS  PTAS
EDITORIAL  APERS
PONYRIDE  IRE
   PLOT  ONEROUS
DUROC  ARLO  STY
XENOPHOBIA  ETTE
ENDO  ELBOW  LIEN
REEF  SEANS  FARE
```

44

```
ROM  BIRL  PADRE
IBO  ODEA  UBOATS
GITALONG  RADIAL
   FULTONSFOLLY
GALAS  OUT
LEAR  CHASE  ITCH
ART  RHONE  BARRE
ZIEGFELDFOLLIES
EARED  DRONE  POT
SLIM  SUERS  MOLE
   GAP  FADER
SEWARDSFOLLY
TRADED  LOUISXIV
SORREL  AZAN  ELI
SPADE  NEUT  NIP
```

45

```
ABBA  ACCA  ASSET
HUES  BAHN  UTTER
ERST  ACRO  TURKS
ASTITCHINTIME
RAF  OKES  ESPANA
TROUT  TENT  KOL
OLOR  MON  BORE
MATE  ERASE  RFDS
ALFS  VIS  RAAB
ILO  GAFF  FEAST
MORTEM  LADE  DAO
WHIPPOORWILLS
CRAIG  AWRY  DUOS
BERNE  RETE  ACME
NADER  ARAR  SKED
```

46

```
STAD JABS STREW
WADI ULAR QUIVA
AXIS MOTSJUSTES
PINCENEZ EASES
   ALAS MEWL
SABRE WORKEDUP
ABODE HONEY IZE
MONS FARED BABA
ANG WINDY BONER
JEOPARDY LEAKY
   INKY EZIO
MUFTI CREPTOUT
ZINFANDELS ISLA
ACOLD ABET ALAR
GAPES BUSY NONO
```

47

```
PACT MASSE GOAD
LALO STAEL RILE
ARAN CARNIVALOF
COVET RIA ASSET
ANI HAMSTERS
  CHETS OVI FLU
VSHAPE TREACLES
ATOLL HAS THESE
TOREADOR LIEDER
SAD NEP MOORE
  TELEMANN RAT
ABOUT SER SAMMY
GOTTSCHALK PAPP
ISTO PODIA RULE
THOR OWENS ASES
```

48

```
LANA TAFFY MOAT
OXEN EXILE ANDA
FLAX NEXUS XYZS
TEPID SEX MIXES
   EAR RELAX
ABETTED SEREAND
FOXY GEN XYSTER
ARE VESTRIS AVA
CARMEN HOC PLEW
EXTENTS BOTHERS
   TUSKS NEO
DATES EHS XEBEC
ULAR STOOL NOLO
SAXE OCALA IXIA
ENID PHLOX XYST
```

49

```
BEAR BITES BREI
ELLE ACARE EARS
AMIS RAZORSEDGE
RENTIER SUNRISE
DREADFUL MAKO
  REASON PECOS
TICTAC BAH GILA
OFA SETSAIL TEN
INTR DOT BUSYAS
TIBET REVERE
  ASIN RERECORD
ILLUSED INSULAR
WALLAWALLA RITA
IGOT TWEET EVEN
NOUS SNIDE DESK
```

50

```
OVERSEE PALACES
RIVETER ANIMATE
BEEPERS STEPSON
STREPITOSO ANT
   APE BENUMB
APPLE TOR GALAS
RAHS SWEETHEART
EYE FIE LES NEA
CINDERELLA SCAR
ANODE DIE CHASE
  METTLE ARA
STE RENSSELAER
LUNATED OPALINE
ABALONE AETOLIA
BALLADE PRETEND
```